vintage
weddings

To Allan and Emily, with love.

THIS IS A CARLTON BOOK

Published in 2011 by Carlton Books Limited
20 Mortimer Street
London W1T 3JW

10 9 8 7 6 5 4 3 2 1

A CIP catalogue record for this book is available
from the British Library.

ISBN 978 1 84732 771 0

Printed and bound in China

Senior Executive Editor: Lisa Dyer
Managing Art Director: Lucy Coley
Design: Barbara Zuñiga
Illustrations: Adam Wright
Photography: Karl Adamson
Copy Editors: Nicky Gyopari and Jilly MacLeod
Picture Researcher: Jenny Meredith
Production: Kate Pimm

PREVIOUS PAGE A 1940s
wedding gown by Charles
James, circa 1948–9.

RIGHT Long 'Twinkle' gown
in silk by Alice Temperley,
scattered with hundreds
of three-dimensional silk
flowers and embellished
with sparkling lines of
Swarovski crystals.

PAGE 4 Embroidered and
beaded cream dress from
the early 1960s.

vintage weddings

one hundred years of
bridal fashion and style

Marnie Fogg

CARLTON
BOOKS

Contents

Foreword by Bruce Oldfield OBE

I follow the same process when designing a wedding dress as I do when designing my main couture line and ready-to-wear ranges – my aim was, and is, to flatter. It always has been. I became interested in fashion when I was a teenager, but trained to be a teacher in Sheffield. I realized that if I wanted to be a designer now was the time, and it was a case of do or die. I went to study fashion and textiles at Ravensbourne College before going on to St Martins School of Art, as it was then called. I was only there for ten months when, alongside Yves Saint Laurent and Bill Gibb, I was asked to put on a fashion show to promote a new scent that Revlon were producing, called Charlie. This was picked up by *Women's Wear Daily* and resulted in the New York store Henri Bendel offering me a job.

I have been designing bespoke wedding dresses since 1975, alongside the main couture line. In 2010 I realized that I need a dedicated bridal salon – bridal gowns take up a lot of space – and it was fortuitous that premises became available directly opposite my main shop on London's Beauchamp Place.

At my salon, the bride-to-be visits the showroom to view a small collection of couture dresses, for an initial consultation, and to examine a variety of fabrics and techniques. The collections just are a starting point. We can make minor adjustments to the custom-made line, but with a bespoke dress we factor in any ideas that the bride-to-be might have herself. We also discuss any themes for the party, the venue, the number of guests and religious or cultural requirements (e.g. covered shoulders). All of these practicalities are considered, together with an honest appraisal of her figure!

Some designers get cross when brides arrive with pictures torn from magazines, but I think its great – it gives the best indication of how that bride sees herself. The more elaborate the designs, the more time it takes, from designing and getting approval from the bride, mother of the bride and, somewhere down the line, Dad. Next come the toile fittings for the underpinnings of the dress through to the outer sections. These often have ornate embroidery on every piece of pattern, which I draw up myself before handing over to the embroiderers. Then the fittings in cloth take place, before the final assembly of the finished, embroidered dress. This can take between three and five months.

I like to start with unadorned, plain fabric. I then embellish it with hand-work, such as embroidery and beadwork, or with fabric manipulation, such as draping and ruching. All the garments and every process are worked at on site. I am very hands-on through the entire sequence of work; I oversee everything, even though it might not be possible for me to attend all the fittings.

My clothes are appealing because they have structure – they look soft on the outside, but have an infrastructure on the inside. It is very important to reflect the bride's personality with elegant, beautiful clothes that retain a gentle lightness and fluidity. A deceptively simple cut, sumptuous fabrics and intricate detailing and embellishments are all integral to the understated design, which mixes tradition and sophistication with a fresh, modern twist.

ABOVE AND RIGHT
Two designs from Bruce Oldfield's 2010 bridal collection, 'Grace' and 'Morgan'.

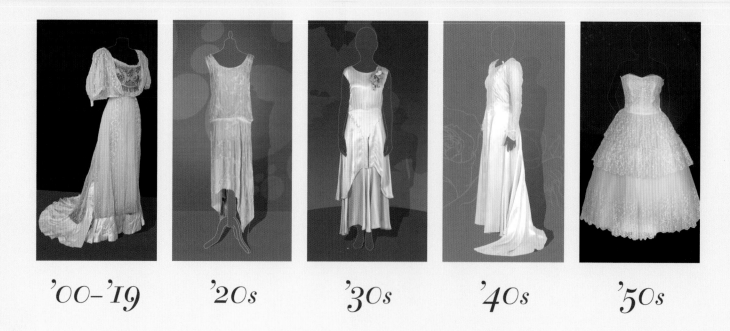

'00–'19   '20s   '30s   '40s   '50s

Introduction

The bridal gown is a dress that is potent with meaning. It is worn for what is still considered a significant rite of passage, an occasion steeped in ancient superstition and overlaid with religious significance and cultural expectations, and therefore not to be chosen lightly. At the beginning of the twentieth century, the wedding dress assumed its role as the most important garment a woman could ever wear – destined to be worn for just one day and possibly the most expensive dress she will ever buy. Faced with such a momentous decision, many prospective brides looks to all sources for inspiration, from contemporary bridal styles to historical themes.

This book places vintage wedding dresses within the context of the fashions of the time. It starts with the influence of the early couturiers, when wedding gowns were designed by the foremost court dressmakers of the day, such as Lucile and the couture House of Worth. As the twentieth century progressed, wedding dresses began to be designed and manufactured by specialist bridal firms, who were able to satisfy a growing market that appeared after the Second World War due to the burgeoning ready-to-wear. Labels such as Priscilla of Boston filled the gap between wedding dresses designed by influential couturiers, such as Pierre Balmain and Christian Dior, and mass-market dresses from department stores, or those made by a family seamstress. Later in the century, custom-made wedding gowns were also being offered by designers such as Bellville Sassoon, alongside their couture line.

The relationship between high fashion and wedding dress design has varied over the decades, sometimes reflecting current trends and at other times wildly diverging. Certain silhouettes have become wedding gown classics, whether they are 'in fashion' or not. Since its inception during the Victorian period, the full-skirted crinoline has remained a favourite with many brides. It was, however, only actually fashionable during

'60s   *'70s*   *'80s*   *'90s to Now*

the 1950s, an era that celebrated the hourglass figure, and in the 1980s when it was popularized by Lady Diana on her wedding to Prince Charles.

The clinging, bias-cut, silk-satin dress, made popular by the French designer Madeleine Vionnet in the 1930s, remains a perennial favourite, as does the use of lace to achieve full-on femininity. Certain elements of the bridal outfit remain relatively constant, such as the veil, train and headdress, but these are also subject to fashion trends as well as the overall style of the dress. All the elements of the 'bridal look' provide a plethora of collectable vintage items for the bride-to-be, who is looking to the past for inspiration.

Rather than buying into the formulaic froufrou of a commercially designed wedding dress, the contemporary bride can express her personal style far better by referencing styles of the past and sourcing original vintage pieces. The vintage-dressed bride knows that an original gown will usually be made of a finer fabric and will have more exquisite workmanship than can be found in many new dresses. A vintage piece may be constructed from materials such as duchesse satin or silk brocade, rather than polyester, and have hand-worked rather than machine-made beading and embroidery embellishment.

Most importantly of all, the vintage bridal gown is unique. When offered the best of bridal couture and bespoke from the world's leading designers, such as John Galliano and Alber Elbaz of Lanvin, Sarah Jessica Parker, as New York heroine and style icon Carrie Bradshaw in the film *Sex and the City* (2008), chose to wear a vintage cream, silk-satin, two-piece from the 1970s for her city hall wedding to Mr Big. Like Carrie, the contemporary bride has the freedom to take what she wants from the past – a fragile antique piece of point d'Angleterre lace, a slip of bias-cut satin or an original wasp-waisted crinoline from the 1950s – and put it together in her own inimitable way.

1900–19:
Frills, Flounces and Furbelows

The wedding customs and rituals that we now consider 'traditional' and are still observed today were firmly fixed in place by the beginning of the twentieth century. The floral bouquet, the array of bridesmaids, the bride's trousseau, the 'best man', the wedding cake and, above all, the white dress were all familiar aspects of the Edwardian wedding. As *Godey's Lady's Book*, an American periodical and influential arbiter of fashion and etiquette founded in 1830 in Philadelphia by Louis Antoine Godey, decreed in 1849: 'Custom has decided, from the earliest ages, that tint white is the most fitting hue, whatever may be the material. It is an emblem of the purity and innocence of girlhood, and the unsullied heart she now yields to the chosen one.'

Although the full-skirted crinoline of the nineteenth century gave way to gowns draped over the S-shaped corset, the wedding dress of the upper-class bride continued to retain the full-length train, an established element of court dress. In Great Britain it was the custom for the aristocratic bride and groom to be presented to the reigning monarch after the wedding ceremony, and for this the sleeves of the dress would be removed and the neckline lowered. Wedding dresses were often designed with this occasion in mind with a removable yoke, or chemisette, of lace or semi-transparent material inserted into the bodice of the dress.

The burgeoning popularity of the department store and the increase in mass production at the turn of the century meant that almost every woman could realize her dream of being married in a 'new' wedding dress. The style of the dress was much influenced by the society weddings reported in the women's pages of the new mass dailies and women's periodicals, such as *Ladies' Home Journal*.

The changing position and aspiration of women in society and the exigencies of the First World War rendered the lace frills and furbelows of the Edwardian era as dated and inappropriate. The wedding dress, however, continued to retain its role as the centrepiece of the all-important ceremony of marriage. Free from whalebone and corsetry, it became subject to the influence of the 'artistic' movements of the day, epitomized by the designs of the British court dressmaker, Lucile, and her compatriot and competitor, Ada Wolf.

The Edwardian Wedding

The 1840 wedding of the Queen Victoria to her cousin Albert of Saxe-Coburg, surprisingly a love match in an era of arranged marriages for royalty, proved enormously influential throughout the early Edwardian years. The Queen's ivory silk and Honiton lace dress started a tradition of white wedding dresses and, rather than the more formal tiara, the Monarch wore a wreath of orange blossom, a Mediterranean symbol of fertility, to hold her veil in place. It was a touching acknowledgement of the romance of the union, and one that was much-copied.

The romance and mystique of the Edwardian era is evoked by images of life in the country house, a place of peace, tradition and beauty, where afternoon tea is served under the shade of a spreading cedar tree, the pastoral landscape bathed in perpetual sunlight, and the air redolent with the smell of roses and cut grass. An age of ostentation and conspicuous consumption, women's dress reflected the leisured lives they led. Constrained by the S-shaped corset that thrust forward the breasts and flattened the stomach, covered from head to toe in layers of lace and silk, complete concealment of the female form was customary practice. From the high-boned collar to the ground-sweeping train, long gloves and veiled hat, no glimpse of flesh was to be seen until after dark, when necklines plunged extravagantly to reveal the voluptuous form of the archetypal female Edwardian beauty.

Customarily adorned in cascades of lace, lavish pin tucks and pleating in the softest of materials – muslin, crepe de chine, *mousseline de soie* (a crisp, lightweight silk muslin) and chiffon – in the sweet-pea colours of azure, mauve and palest pink, the wedding dress of the prospective bride differed only marginally from the fashionable dress of the era. Maria McBride Mellinger in her book *The Wedding Dress* quotes the American magazine, *The Ladies' Home Journal*, which adjured the bride-to-be, 'It should always be remembered that no matter how beautiful the neck and arms of a bride are, she is sinning against good form who does not have a high neck and long-sleeved bodice.' The high neckline

ABOVE RIGHT Queen Victoria in her ivory silk wedding dress on her marriage to Prince Albert in 1840. The Monarch established the paradigm for wedding gown finery for future generations of brides, consolidating white as a traditional colour for the bride's dress.

RIGHT A wedding wreath head-band of orange blossom dating from 1900. The orange plant blooms and bears fruit at the same time, signifying fecundity and fruitfulness. Most wreaths were replicas made in wax and passed down from mother to daughter.

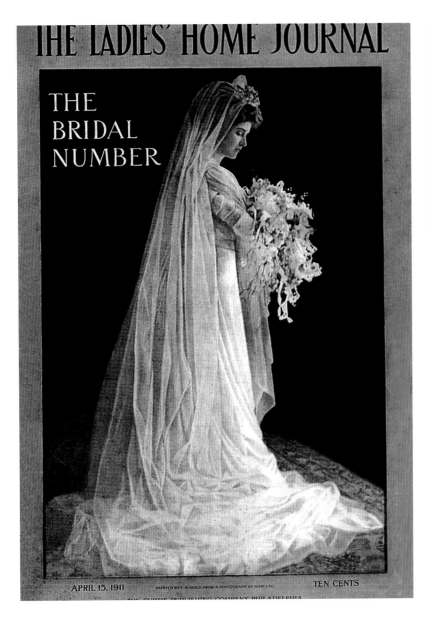

THE LADIES' HOME JOURNAL

THE BRIDAL NUMBER

APRIL 15, 1911   PAINTED BY F. X. GUILD, FROM A PHOTOGRAPH BY MARCEAU   TEN CENTS

MEN'S ATTIRE

In an era of such lavish embellishment men's wedding finery provided a sober contrast to their prospective wives. Deploying the traditional standards of elegance and cut typical of English tailoring, the groom was required to wear a black frock coat, the simplicity of which derived from the military greatcoat of the nineteenth century. This was partnered with narrow grey striped trousers and worn with a lighter-coloured waistcoat or vest. The shirt collar would be starched, mirroring the high-boned collar worn by the bride. A top hat completed his ensemble. By 1910 morning dress was more common, the jacket cut away in a curve over the hips and buttoning high on the chest. The tradition of the grooms' buttonhole, a flower picked from the bride's bouquet and inserted into the lapel of the jacket, recollects the era of medieval courtly love and the chivalric ideal when a young knight was allowed to display the 'favours' of his chosen lady.

was known as the 'wedding band collar'. Stiffened and often bejewelled, it ensured perfect posture and emphasized the complex swathes and elaborate curls of the Edwardian high-combed hair. To this structure would be attached the wedding veil. A symbol of modesty, representing Hymen, the goddess of marriage, the veil also purported to keep evil spirits at bay. Obscuring the face during the church ceremony, the veil is only lifted once the vows have been exchanged, symbolizing the breaking of the hymen on the wedding night.

Brides have not always worn white. Indeed 'white' is something of a misnomer; silk could not be bleached a bright white without damaging the structure of the thread, so 'white' dresses were generally cream or ivory in tone. During previous centuries, brides wore their 'Sunday best', whatever the colour. Even a bride who wore white would expect to wear her dress again, with train and flowers removed, particularly for the round of post-wedding visits the couple would be expected to make to various friends and family.

ABOVE In a cover from *The Ladies' Home Journal*, 1911, a model wears a cathedral veil as well as a full court train attached to the shoulders. Magazines were an increasing source of information on wedding etiquette and fashion.

RIGHT Although men wore the traditional frock coat with top hat for formal weddings, the fingertip-length veil of the bride, suspended from two clusters of orange blossom, and the size of the bouquet, indicates that the ceremony is a restrained one.

RIGHT An ingénue Edwardian wedding dress, the youthful silhouette emphasized by the 'something blue' sash and the high neckline bordered with a demure lace collar. The small *gigot* sleeves have deep buttoned cuffs. The fullness of the skirt falls from the hips, elongating the bodice to accommodate a band of embroidery.

FAR LEFT AND DETAIL ABOVE Worn over the inhibiting S-shaped corset, this wedding dress exemplifies the fashionable propensity in the belle époque for lavish decoration from lace insertions and white-on-white embroidery. The over-bodice displays the 'pouter-pigeon' silhouette formed by the corset, and the high waistline provides fullness without volume.

LEFT A wedding gown by Noelie & Cie, with a hint of a bustle in the draped skirt, probably designed to be worn beneath a jacket or cape, dating from around 1915. Bare arms were deemed unacceptable for an appearance in church until later in the century.

BELOW A delicately embroidered detail from the bodice of the Edwardian dress in sheer, lightweight batiste, pictured right.

The Ceremony

Not only was the marriage ceremony subject to scrutiny, every aspect of the wedding was recorded in the popular press, including the presents and the contents of the bride's trousseau. It was assumed that the upper-class home would already be well furnished with all the accoutrements necessary to run a household, including family silver and heirloom china, as well as a well-stocked linen cupboard. Instead, the bride would be given more personal presents, such as extravagant furs or jewellery. The tiara was a popular choice, as was a strand or two of pearls. Pearls symbolize purity, and were the attribute of the virgin martyr Saint Margaret of Antioch, the patron saint of childbirth. As symbols of fertility, pearls were worn by the founders of dynasties and royal houses, including the late Queen Elizabeth the Queen Mother, photographed with her famous triple row of pearls holding her firstborn child, the future Queen Elizabeth.

The wedding service could only take place between the hours of eight in the morning and midday before 1886, hence the need for a 'wedding breakfast' following the ceremony. Once the hours were increased to include the afternoon, lavish, many-coursed banquets were introduced. Transporting the 'society' bride between the locations of home, church and the banquet had to take into account the length of the train and the height of the hair. The Edwardian couple would probably use a

horse and carriage, available from Harrods in London's Knightsbridge, where the couple could order their wedding cake, shop for linen and hire 'First-class horses and carriages, including Coachman in Livery'.

At a time when wealth ceased to reside in the ownership of land and began to be replaced by the 'new' money made from trade, banking and industry, stylish and ostentatious weddings were no longer limited to the aristocratic upper classes. The advent of photography and the increasing popularity of society journalism, which recorded in minute detail the wedding finery of the upper classes, disseminated this information to their middle-class counterparts, very much as *Hello!* magazine does today. Court dressmakers such as Sarah Fullerton Monteith Young, renowned London

store Russell and Allen in Europe and Mrs Connolly in America would have their designs featured in society magazines such as *Queen*, as in the marriage of Miss Gordon to a Mr Lawson in 1898, for example: 'The bride looked lovely in her ivory satin gown, embroidered in pearls and diamonds with chemisette and sleeves of old duchesse point [lace] on body and train.' Although etiquette books of the period such as *How to Dress and What to Wear* (1903) lamented ostentation and warned against, 'the choice of white elephants which the white satin costumes of other years have so often proved', they were largely ignored. In America, too, weddings were seen as an opportunity to exhibit personal wealth and social standing, the bride dressed by the couturier of choice, Charles Frederick Worth.

LEFT An evening gown from the House of Worth dates from 1914. The silhouette is one of restrained elegance; a peplum of transparent tulle, caught and closed with a corsage at the centre front of the high waist, is grown to fall in a fringed and curved hem from hip level, descending to form a pooling train behind. The cap sleeves provide an element of modesty.

Charles Frederick Worth and the 'Dollar Duchesses'

British-born Worth established his first dressmaking business in the rue de la Paix in 1858, his commercial success rooted in the custom of the Empress Eugenie at the court of Napoleon III. He transformed dressmaking from a craft into a business. Rather than women dictating their requirements to the dressmaker in their own home, Worth demanded that clients travel to the couturier to choose from a series of designs which were then subsequently made to measure, requiring several fittings for a perfect fit. Haute couture (literally 'high-quality sewing') refers only to this bespoke process. Worth also displayed new lines on mannequins in a series of parties and events that were a precursor to the fashion show. Although the couturier died in 1895, the house lived on with Worth's sons Jean-Philippe and Gaston at the helm, influencing not only the fashion of the haute bourgeoisie of Europe but also serving the needs of the newly wealthy North Americans, who willingly undertook the long sea voyage to Paris and time-consuming fittings necessary for a bespoke wedding dress.

Worth was the couturier chosen to design the wedding dress of Consuelo Vanderbilt, one of the so-called American 'dollar duchesses' – rich American brides brought into Britain to rescue a fiscally ailing aristocracy. However, this process was not simply an exchange of title for money. Anglo-mania was rife on the continent. In his book *Them and Us*, Charles Jennings reports that even

The New York Times declared, 'Rich American men, more especially New York men, are essentially commercial. Their wives and daughters, on the other hand, are not, and the cultivated among them are apt to find a more sympathetic and congenial companion in a foreigner who has left college only to travel and cultivate his mind and body than in a young man who has stuck down to business at 16.'

It was a period of unprecedented American wealth and the match between one of the great heiresses of America, Consuelo Vanderbilt, and the Duke of Marlborough, the most eligible peer of Great Britain in 1895, set the paradigm for highly publicized lavish splendour. American heiresses were the celebrities of the day and crowds of more than 2,000 people thronged the streets around St Thomas Church in New York City where the ceremony was to be held. The wedding dress reputedly cost $6,720.35 and was made from cream-white satin with graduated flounces of point lace and trails of orange blossom. Its train was 4.5 metres (15 feet) long and embroidered with pearls and silver, falling in double pleats from the shoulder. *The New York World* newspaper provided the information that the bride-to-be had a waist size of 50 cm (20 inches), and the society magazine *Town Topics* even secured descriptions of the bridal underwear: 'It is delightful to know that the clasps of Miss Vanderbilt's stocking supporters are of gold, and that her corset-covers and chemises are embroidered with rosebuds in relief.'

BELOW LEFT A House of Worth wedding dress dating from 1896. An extreme example of the gigot or leg-of-mutton sleeves in fashion at the end of the nineteenth century, the pearl embroidered silk gown is moulded to the statuesque form, with fishtail sleeves split to extend over the hand.

BELOW RIGHT A 1912 wedding gown by the label Shogren. The label, headed by two sisters, was based in Portland, Oregon. In white silk and silver lamé, the dress has a cross-over bodice and low, square neck. American wedding dresses rarely had need to deploy the chemisette, as brides were not presented at court.

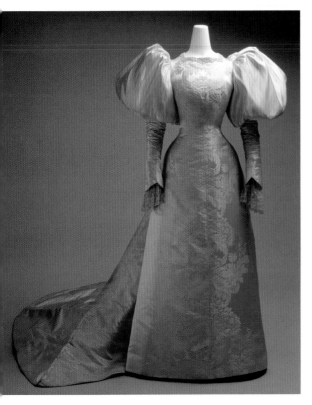

The Medieval Mode

When every morning brought a noble chance,
And every chance brought out a noble knight.
   Idylls of the King, Alfred, Lord Tennyson

Avant-garde was a term first used in 1880 to describe the work of modern French painters and writers; by the turn of the century it was a description that could be applied to fashion, particularly the Bohemian taste, which now became marketable through shops such as London's Liberty & Co. of Regent Street, founded by Arthur Lasenby Liberty in 1875. Originally known as the Oriental Emporium, the store sold furniture, textiles and dresses inspired by the Aesthetic Movement, a reaction against the mass-production of the Industrial Revolution. Architect and designer E W Godwin was asked by Arthur Liberty to start up the dress department and foremost designers of the day, including Charles Rennie Mackintosh and C F A Voysey, all designed textile patterns. The emporium included an Artistic Costume Studio, from which avant-garde figures such as the actresses Ellen Terry and Isadora Duncan purchased gowns in the 'aesthetic' mode, a look that reflected the movement's desire to bring art into life. These loose and flowing garments, reminiscent of medieval gowns and the era of courtly love, eschewed the restrictive corset and high collars typical of the Edwardian era and were inspired by the images seen in art galleries and the lines of the Symbolist poets. These 'artistic' gowns, often in linen or cotton rather than silk, were hand-painted with Art Nouveau imagery: scrolls of elongated sinuous natural forms and flora in muted and subtle colours such as yellow and green were a result of a collaboration with dyer and printer Thomas Wardle, who produced a range of silk dyes for the company marketed as Liberty Art Colours. Liberty's wedding dresses appealed to the artistic minority, attracted by the Bohemian reputation of the company for 'alternative' dress.

Mariano Fortuny's Delphos robes, simple columns of pleated silk, reminiscent of medieval dress, represented freedom from the conventions of the traditional wedding dress. The dress first appeared around 1907 and was very simply cut to hang loose from the shoulders, with a wide bateau neckline and caught at the waist with a decorative belt. The borders of the dress, sides and cuffs were usually finished with a series of small Venetian beads in different colours, which were both ornamental and functional, in that they weighed down the dress. The model originally described in Fortuny's patent was a Delphos with batwing sleeves, but numerous variations were subsequently produced, some with short sleeves, some with long, wide sleeves tied at the wrist; others were sleeveless. The silk was dipped in dye several times, producing the signature lustre of the garments.

English dressmakers Lucile (Lady Duff-Gordon), and her contemporary and competitor, Ada Wolf, were both exponents of this romantic, alternative way of dressing the bride. As the decade progressed, the medieval influence extended to mainstream fashion. The S-shaped silhouette was replaced by a high-waisted tubular line, with a beaded, braided sash slung low on the hips and trailing sleeves. The complex structures of hair padded out with artificial pieces called 'transformations' of the earlier Edwardian period were replaced by almost nun-like veiling, worn low on the forehead and caught with a band.

LEFT A wedding gown by Liberty & Co., dating from 1906. The London store specialized in 'alternative' dress for the Bohemian customer. Its low-cut, swagged bodice opposes the prevailing trend for the high wedding-band collar. The skirt and train are in cream satin with collar and sleeves of machine-made lace. An embroidered train is decorated with pearls.

ABOVE Promotional illustrations of wedding dresses from the archives of Liberty & Co. Marketing material was distributed to publicize their products.

LEFT Dating from 1905 this dress has all the hallmarks of the Edwardian wedding gown: the high-boned collar, the lace chemisette, here with matching lace sleeves, and grown-in sash, embroidered and fringed and falling to the hem of the dress from a high, pointed waistband.

Out of the Boudoir

The Edwardian trousseau provided the prospective bride with all the accoutrements of seduction. Cascading petticoats were known as 'froufrou', a word that described the rustle of taffeta when rubbed against the coarser material of the skirt. Lavishly embroidered stockings were held up by beribboned garters, often the 'something blue' from the adage, 'something borrowed, something blue, something old, and something new'. The exoticism that was a feature of fashion following the success of the Ballets Russes production of *Scheherazade* in 1910 represented a different, headier version of femininity. The impact of non-Western aesthetics on clothing construction provided couturiers such as Paul Poiret and Madeleine Vionnet with a new design vocabulary, one that included antique textiles lush with embroidery in a saturated colour palette for garments designed to be worn without corsets. These included the ornate and luxurious tea-gown. Previously restricted to personal use in private areas, the tea-gown now became acceptable wear in public. One of its first exponents was the American couturier, Jessie Franklin Turner. An advertisement appearing in American *Vogue* from the era writes of her work, 'For hours of ease, a New York designer adds inspiration to the beauty of rare fabrics and harmonizing colours'.

Other new items of underwear were appearing as lingerie cast off its utilitarian aspect and designers devised diaphanous delights such as the *robe d'interior*, the *peignoir* and the *robe de chambre* in silk, chiffon and lace. Caroline Cox describes in her book *Seduction* the luscious lingerie of court dressmaker Lucile (Lady Duff Gordon) who wrote in her memoirs, *Discretions and Indiscretions,* in 1932:

> *I hate the thought of my creations being worn over the ugly nun's veiling or linen-cum Swiss embroidery, which was all that the really virtuous woman… permitted herself. I vowed to change all that, and made plans for the day of chiffons and laces, of boudoir caps and transparent nightdresses… so I started making underclothes as delicate as cobwebs, and half of the women of London flocked to see them. Those saucy velvet bows on the shoulder might surely be the weapons of the woman 'who was not quite nice?' but slowly one by one they slunk into the shop in a rather shame-faced way and departed carrying an inconspicuous parcel which contained a crepe de chine or chiffon petticoat.*

The Bystander, June 15, 1904

Sport, Travel & Fiction

The BYSTANDER.

Art Literature & the Drama.

No. 28.—Vol. III. [Registered at the G.P.O. as a Newspaper.] Wednesday, June 15, 1904 [With Supplement, 6d. By Post. 6½d.]

Photo by

Johnston and Hoffmann

Lady Duff - Gordon

As "Madame Lucile" Lady Duff-Gordon has achieved a position among the leading modistes of the day. Her younger sister is Mrs Clayton Glyn, the well-known author of "The Visits of Elizabeth"

ABOVE Foremost English dressmaker Lucy Christiana, Lady Duff Gordon, known as Lucile, is here featured on the cover of the 1904 edition of the *Bystander*. Initially a designer of lingerie, she applied her ultra-feminine aesthetic to outerwear. Her first wedding dress was for her sister, the romantic novelist Elinor Glyn.

THE RING

This ring is round, and hath no end, So is my love unto my friend.
Inscription on a sixteenth-century posy ring

The ring, more than any other item of jewellery, is imbued with a powerful significance. Even in these post-feminist times, an engagement ring is much anticipated and much flaunted to an interested audience. With every gesture of the hands, the ring is evidence that the wearer has been claimed and is a willing participant in a romantic rite of passage. A closed circle, the ring is endless, symbolizing the enduring nature of the love between two people. Though subject to the vagaries of fashion, the essential meaning of the ring has remained constant. It is an external symbol of a sacred or secular union between lovers or a husband and wife. Etruscan, Greek and Roman cultures all have records of ring wearing, but the ring has its mythical origins in the story of Prometheus, as recounted by Pliny in his natural history. Bound to the Caucasian Rock for stealing the fire of the gods, Prometheus is finally released by Jupiter on the condition that he always wears an iron link from his chains, with a piece of rock mounted on the ring. Thus he remained symbolically and permanently bound to his rock, just as the wedding ring purports to bind together husband and wife.

The tradition of placing the engagement and wedding rings on the fourth finger of the left hand has its origins in history. Classical authors such as Macrobius proposed that there was a vein from that finger which ran directly to the heart. By the sixteenth century the English *Book of Common Prayer* explicitly pronounced the fourth finger of the left hand to be the site of the wedding ring, which is generally never used for any rings other than those worn to commemorate a wedding or an engagement.

The wedding ring is not merely a component of the legally binding contract between husband and wife; it is instilled with a mystical and superstitious significance. It has been a vital element of betrothal for more than a thousand years, and in the Middle Ages the exchange of rings was more legally binding than the wedding ceremony itself and of lasting symbolic value, even if only made of a humble twist of rushes. Marriage then was less a romantic union than the formation of a new household, a transition that was significant for the whole community as it represented an affiliation between families and the ownership of land.

Even though marriage has arguably become less significant in contemporary society, the ring still has a special place in jewellery's lexicon as representing ownership, as well as status. From a male perspective, at a time when objects were routinely invested with certain powers a ring could be seen as a talisman to keep his wife in check. Modern marriage ceremonies customarily see the exchange of rings between men and women, but this was only approved by the Roman Catholic Church in 1956, when, under pressure from the American jewellery industry, the Congregation of Sacred Rites permitted the double ring ceremony.

Gold is traditionally the material used for wedding rings, a substance that has always incontrovertibly signified wealth due to its malleability, imperishability, lustre and its relative rarity. By association with the sun and light and therefore divine power, gold implies incorruptibility, again a paradigm for the union between partners. During the 1920s and 30s, however, in an attempt to exploit the market and increase profits, American jewellers marketed platinum over gold and began introducing matching engagement and wedding rings, often sold boxed together. There was even an unsuccessful attempt in 1926 to market an engagement ring for men. The trend for simplicity and the plain gold band is a contemporary phenomenon, usually worn with a simple diamond engagement ring, diamonds representing faithfulness.

VERLAG DER BAZAR-ACTIEN-GESELLSCHAFT, BERLIN

▲ High-waisted dresses

The high waist and shorter skirts of the post-war silhouette are evident in this fashion plate of a '*Fête Parisienne*' wedding party in New York, illustrating designs by Premet, Jenny, Worth and Paquin, and dating from 1916. The central wedding gown by Lanvin references her celebrated *robe de style*.

Key looks of the decade
1900–19

Gigot sleeves

Also called leg-of-mutton and popular at the end of the nineteenth-century, the wide puffy sleeveheads tapered to a narrow forearm. This style reinforced the hourglass 'S' silhouette with wide shoulders, a tiny waist and wide hips.

▲ Edwardian silhouette

A prospective bride admires a typical wedding gown of the Edwardian era. The dress is draped around the S-shaped corset, which pushes forward the 'mono'-bosom and draws in the stomach, an effect emphasized by the deep frill of the bodice.

◀ White lace

Lavish application of lace was a feature of the Edwardian period. Hand-made lace would be handed down from bride to bride, incorporated into the dress or worn as a veil. Machine-made lace was an increasingly popular substitute.

High hair styles and veils

Elaborately structured hair styles were topped with voluminous veils during the early years of the nineteenth century, but gave way to simple nun-like coverings worn low on the forehead by the end of the era.

Wedding band collars

The high-neck stiffened collar, made of a band of lace, adorned most Edwardian wedding gowns. It was paired with the lace chemisette that modestly filled in the bodice front and neckline.

◀ Flowing and unstructured
Dating from 1918 this coat
and dress represents a less
formal approach to the wedding
ceremony, particularly when
partnered with a large picture hat.
The high-waisted gown finishes
just above the ankles, with the
longer coat forming a train.

Bohemian swagged bodices
An alternative to the Edwardian
band, the low-draping neckline
was a feature of the unstructured
style of dress as represented by
the tea-gown, with trailing, wide
sleeves and feminine detailing.

▶ Orange blossom
Orange blossom, a symbol of
fertility, and myrtle, sacred to
the goddess of love, Venus, are
combined in this bouquet dating
from 1900. Wax replicas were
used to replace the natural
flowers and blossoms.

1920s:
All That Jazz

OPPOSITE A silver silk brocade bridal gown designed by the House of Callot Soeurs for Edna Johnson, dating from 1926 and photographed by Edward Steichen. The semi-transparent tunic is worn over a mid-calf dress. The tulle veil is caught each side of the head with a cluster of orange blossom, confirming the adage, 'the shorter the dress, the longer the veil'.

The carnage of the First World War and the resulting 'lost generation' of men of a marriageable age meant that not all women could expect marriage to be their destiny during the 1920s. The weddings that did occur were considered celebratory, particularly ceremonies that involved the royal family, which were seen as an excuse for national rejoicing.

At the beginning of the decade brides wore versions of the Medieval style previously made popular by Lucile. Increasingly, the dominating silhouette became tubular; a line emphasized by the addition of a transparent embroidered and beaded overdress, shorter than the silk-satin gown beneath. This allowed for the gradual shortening of the skirt, which never, however, reached the unprecedented heights of daywear, remaining mid-calf to just below the knee.

New methods of advertising, such as movies and the radio, allied to mass production increasingly commoditised the wedding ceremony during the 1920s. The growing consumer culture resulted in the white wedding dress becoming the norm for all levels of society and the focal point of the marriage ritual. The rise of specialist bridal salons within the department store and the burgeoning women's ready-to-wear industry replaced the personal service of the dressmaker who had previously visited the home of the middle-class client. The aristocratic bride-to-be engaged the services of a court dressmaker such as Madame Handley Seymour or, if a moneyed American, travelled to Paris to attend the House of Worth for dress fittings.

Toward the end of the 1920s embellishment gave way to the importance of line and cut, and hair and hemlines lengthened to create a more womanly silhouette. Throughout the following decades fashion continued to influence the style of the wedding dress, but it was during this period that key elements such as the veil, the bouquet and the use of white became a permanent fixture in the visual vocabulary of the wedding.

Royal Weddings

Press coverage of royal weddings in previous decades sustained the mystique of the institution by allowing the public a small but rigidly controlled glimpse into the lives of the aristocracy. The wedding of Henry, Viscount Lascelles, to Princess Mary (daughter of George V) in 1922 led to an unprecedented amount of media coverage that nevertheless promoted a flattering public image. Unusually, sketches and descriptions of the gown, made by the House of Reville, were released to the public. A well-known fashion house, Reville was started in 1906 by William Reville and Miss Rossiter. By 1901, Reville had become the court dressmaker and they designed the coronation robe for Queen Mary in 1911. Princess Mary followed fashion by choosing a medieval-style low-waisted gown girdled with a double row of pearls, finished with a silver rose and tied in a lovers' knot. The court train of duchesse satin was shot with silver with a deep border of lace at the sides and embroidered with emblems of the British Empire: rose, shamrock and thistle, the lotus of India, the wattle of Australia, the maple leaf of Canada, and the tree fern of New Zealand. The

groom wore the full dress of the Grenadier Guards, a scarlet tunic with blue collar and cuffs, and a bearskin headdress with a white goat's hair plume.

The nuptials of Prince Albert, Duke of York to the Lady Elizabeth Bowes-Lyon in 1923 also took place in the public domain. Royal wedding ceremonies were usually held in a royal chapel such as the one at Windsor, but when King George V announced the engagement he broke with tradition by declaring that the wedding would be held at Westminster Abbey; the last time a king's son had been married there was Edmund, Earl of Lancaster (son of Henry III) in 1269. This was to satisfy public interest in the wedding as a means of upholding morale, understandably deflated after the ravages of the First World War. The Duke became the first royal to wear the uniform of the newest branch of the forces, the RAF, for a wedding. The bridal gown, designed by Madame Handley Seymour, had two trains: one the traditional full-length court train from the shoulders and the other attached to the hips. The bride's headdress was worn low over the brow, clasping the veil to the bride's head. The traditional bouquet does not appear in her official photographs as she laid it at the tomb of the Unknown Warrior on her way out of the abbey, in memory of her brothers and others killed in the war. Other brides wearing the medieval-style gown carried sheaves of white lilies, deemed to represent purity in the era of courtly love. These would be carried over one arm, rather than holding the bridal bouquet in the centre of the body.

ABOVE Royal weddings influenced popular taste. Here, an exact replica of Princess Mary's wedding gown is worn by Hollywood actress Marion Davies in 1922. Made by Reville, it was imported by Franklin Simon & Co., New York.

LEFT Lady Elizabeth Bowes-Lyon, the future Queen Mother, on her way to her wedding to the Duke of York. The gown was designed by Madame Hanley-Seymour in the medieval style with a square neck and dropped waist.

OPPOSITE The marriage of Princess Victoria Alexandra Alice Mary to Henry Charles George, Viscount Lascelles, later the Earl of Harewood, in 1922. The loose medieval-style gown is caught in at the waist with a girdle tied in a lovers' knot.

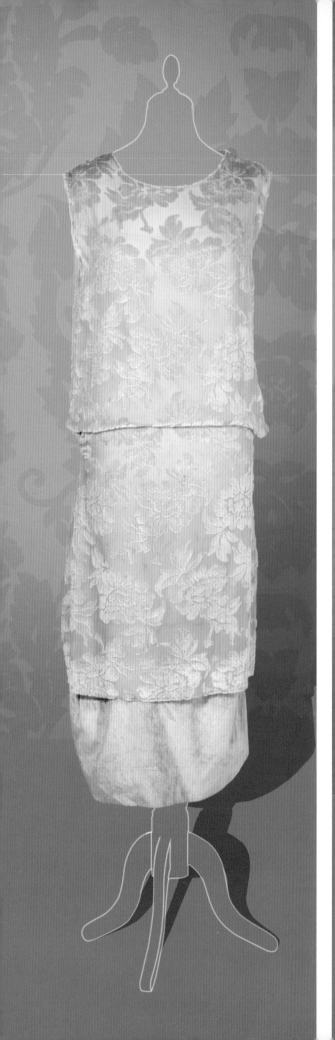

LEFT AND BACK VIEW ABOVE
A silk velvet flapper dress dating from the late 1920s, beaded and embroidered with stylized Art Deco floral patterning. The handkerchief-point hem marks a compromise in the transition from the shorter styles at the beginning of the decade to the calf-length of the 1930s. A subtle train is gathered into the waistline at the back.

FAR LEFT A 1920s flapper dress in devoré velvet, a laborious and expensive printing technique which renders fabrics thinner in specific areas by chemically removing component fibres from the fabric. The printed imagery is derived from traditional floral brocades.

The Flapper Bride

As the decade wore on the medieval style fell out of favour. Jazzy, febrile, fast and furious, the spirit of the age presaged a new aesthetic, modern and streamlined, rendering the 1920s bride unrecognizable to the previous generation. The new woman was captured by illustrators such as Benito, George Barbier and Lepape, and the photographer Adolph de Meyer in fashion magazines such as *Harper's Bazaar* and *Vogue*. Influential Parisian designer Coco Chanel was redefining the female wardrobe with clothes that reflected the active, purposeful lives of women newly engaged with physical fitness and sporting activities. Liberated from the confines of the Edwardian corset and the high-boned collar, women of the Jazz Age relished the freedom of the flapper look and dropped their waistlines and necklines accordingly. It was the fashion for college girls to wear untied galoshes, which flapped as they walked, hence the name 'flapper'.

The embodiment of a brave new world, these 'bright young things' flew in the face of convention to smoke, drink cocktails, and rouge their earlobes and newly exposed knees. As hemlines for daywear rose from the ankle to well above the knee, and skirts grew ever more abbreviated, the length of the wedding dress followed suit. Chanel, with her pared-down aesthetic of relaxed simplicity, was the first designer to introduce the shorter style. Aristocratic ritual was still observed, however, with the long court train attached to the shoulders. In 1926, *Vogue* described trains that were 'transparent from the shoulders down to the part below the waist, most subtle curtained little windows through which the audience can glimpse the figure of the bride as she advances up the aisle.'

As the couturiers' collections in Paris celebrated the look known as the *garçonne*, the 1920s bride followed suit and favoured shimmering little shifts by Lucien Lelong and Jean Patou worn over a 'flattener' to decrease the size of the breasts. This dropped-waist chemise dress was simple in cut and construction, making it easy for the dressmaker to copy or produce by means of mass manufacturing. The cheaper versions were made from 'artificial' silk, marketed as rayon. The tubular silhouette was occasionally softened by the insertion of triangular pieces of cloth, or 'godets', into the skirt from the dropped waistline, leaving the handkerchief points swirling around mid-calf to show a glimpse of silk stocking. As hemlines hovered, a transparent overdress with a scalloped or decorated edge was deployed for more modest brides, decorated in winter with fur or feathers. The button boots of the Edwardian era gave way to beaded, embroidered or hand-painted silk 'Mary Janes', shoes with a single strap or T-bar fastened with a button at the side and with a low Cuban heel. These were eminently suitable for energetic dancing to the ragtime and blues music of the King Oliver Creole Band or swaying to the seductive rhythms of Broadway composer George Gershwin.

ABOVE At this informal wedding of 1929, the bridegroom wears a lounge suit and spats, and the bride's mid-calf lace 'flapper' dress is accessorized with a wide-brimmed cloche hat.

LEFT The influence of Hollywood glamour can be seen in this bridal gown cut on the bias in ivory silk-satin dating from 1929. Only the long train differentiates this dress – with its asymmetrical sleeves and frilled detailing – from the eveningwear then in fashion.

Hats, Veils, Trains and Bouquets

The *garçonne* look also applied to hair. A rite of passage for the modern woman was to have her long, luxurious locks shorn, which significantly changed the style of the wedding headdress. The narrower silhouette demanded a small, sculpted head to balance the line of the clothes. This was also an era when personal servants were no longer available, having left service to join the ranks of working women outside the home. With no ladies' maids to undertake the daily dressing of the hair, a weekly visit to the hair-dressing salon became the customary experience of the modern woman, a ritual considered all the more important before the occasion of a wedding, the hairdresser now becoming a valuable adjunct to the prospective bride's entourage. Hair was first cropped in a straight line to chin level in a bob. As the decade progressed, styles became increasingly shorter, and by 1926 hair was shingled into the back of the neck in a style called an Eton crop. Shorn of their complicated chignons and curls, newly bobbed brides secured a 'Juliet' cap low on the forehead to attach the veil or wore a head-hugging cloche hat, with a small upturned brim, an opportunity to tuck in a spray of flowers, real or artificial. An alternative bridal headdress was a type of mob cap, with a high, shirred front that rested low on the forehead with a fanned piecrust of tulle at the back, referencing the popular Art Deco motif. Veils were also worn, often held in place with a circlet of flowers or low embroidered bandeaux.

The veil has become a vital accessory to the wedding dress, significant for its symbolic role. Often worn in lieu of the train, the veil sweeps to the ground, the general rule being that the shorter the dress, the longer the veil. At the beginning of the decade, lace was

TYPES OF VEIL	
Ballet/Waltz:	Falls to just above the floor.
Birdcage:	Covers the face and falls to just above the shoulders.
Cathedral:	The most formal of trains and falls for three and a half yards from the headdress.
Chapel:	A formal veil, which falls 2.3 metres (90 inches) from the headdress.
Fingertip:	Reaches to the mid-thigh and is suitable for all gowns.
Flyaway:	Multiple layers that just brush the shoulders.

most commonly used for veils, particularly heirloom lace belonging to the bride's family. Over time, however, fine silk tulle was preferred, for lightness and body.

Trains date from the Middle Ages, when the height of the headdress and the length of the train indicated the wearer's wealth and status, fabric being an expensive commodity. The train is a length of fabric that sweeps the floor, and the more formal the wedding, the longer the train and the more bridal attendants will be required to arrange it. A long train is particularly effective viewed from the back, if the venue is large enough for it to be spread flat on the ground. It is not appropriate for a ceremony in a small country church or a registry office.

As the bride's silhouette became more streamlined, the bouquet, conversely, increased in size. The popular 'shower' bouquet, Art Deco in style, was a cluster of blooms to which long ribbon streamers, tied in lovers' knots, cascaded to the hem of the gown. The tradition of throwing the bridal bouquet to unmarried female guests at the wedding probably originates with the fourteenth-century European custom of taking a piece of the bridal gown for luck. Over time, rather than tear apart the dress, an alternative was to throw a personal item of clothing, most particularly the bride's garter (then a silk sash worn below the knee). This custom evolved into throwing the bouquet of flowers, one that is now frequently discarded as being insensitive to the unmarried guests.

OPPOSITE An American bride, Ivy Sawyer, in a picturesque dress of pleated and frilled tulle. The 'shower' bouquet is typical of the period: long ribbons tied in lovers' knots extend to the hem of the dress from the central posy of flowers.

RIGHT A still from the 1924 film *Her Love Story*, featuring Hollywood silent screen star Gloria Swanson as Princess Marie wearing an excessively long train adorned with ermine, normally the prerogative of royalty.

TYPES OF TRAIN

Cathedral:	Longer than one yard, and usually several yards, worn at the most formal weddings.
Chapel:	For formal weddings, extends for one yard.
Court:	Consists of a separate piece of fabric attached to the shoulders. In the late nineteenth century the bride would be presented to court after her marriage and would wear the bridal gown adapted for the occasion, but with the train in place.
Detachable:	Normally attached at the waist, but may attach to the shoulders.
Sweep:	The train just brushes the floor.
Watteau:	Cascades from the shoulders, named after the Rococo painter Antoine Watteau, whose early seventeenth-century portraits portrayed fashionable women.

Decorative Effects and Deco Designers

The influence of Art Deco could be seen in all aspects of design. Originating in Paris with the International Exposition of Modern Industrial and Decorative Arts in 1925, the Art Deco movement came to dominate decorative design over the next two decades. It peaked in popularity in Europe during the 1920s, but continued in the United States throughout the 1930s. It was inspired by modern movements in art including Constructivism, Cubism, Futurism and the 'primitive' arts of other cultures, resulting in a highly distinctive pattern of geometric, angular shapes and forms.

The simple shape of the dress was a perfect base for elaborate embellishment and Cubist inspired non-figurative crystal beadwork and appliqué embroidery that reflected and caught the light. It added to the impression of movement and replaced the heavy *passementerie*, a woven constructed braid used as

an edging, of the Edwardian era. Parisian couturier Jeanne Lanvin was renowned for the intricate beadwork of her gowns, embroidered by the workers in the Lesage atelier, the 125-year-old establishment originally purchased from Charles Worth, the founder of haute couture, by the current owner's father. The *petites mains* ('tiny hands') could be numbered in their thousands in the 1920s, servicing the great couture houses of the era, which included Jean Patou, the Callot Soeurs and Edward Molyneux.

Callot Soeurs

Exponents of applied ornament, Callot Soeurs used heavy bead *passementerie* and hand-applied sequins of various weights and types on their boudoir-inspired tea-gowns, eveningwear and wedding dresses. These would be punched into filigree pinwheels or hammered

Tres Creaciones de Brandt

Traje para ceremonia de laminado beige y plata guarnecido con pieles.

Traje para señorita de honor de laminado de plata A. G. B.

Vestido para novia de brocado blanco, forrado de laminado de plata A. G. B.; velo de encaje antiguo.

MENSWEAR

London's Savile Row remained the style source for menswear. Morning dress continued to be considered appropriate for bridegrooms, accompanied by a top hat. It was the norm for the working- and middle-class groom to hire his wedding clothes; the morning suit had changed very little in style since its inception in the nineteenth century. However, for less formal weddings the lounge suit, based on the 'sack' suit, a daytime wardrobe essential, in navy or black, became acceptable wear. It was purchased from one of the increasingly popular mass-market men's outfitters such as Burton's, bought 'off-the-peg' but with the customer choosing the cloth, and with minor alternations made to sleeve and hem length. Suit jackets buttoned high on the chest and indented slightly above the natural waistline. Shirts had easily laundered and starched detachable collars and cuffs. Jackets were cut narrow to balance the increasing width of the trousers. In 1925 Oxford bags, first worn by that university's undergraduates, became popular, later to be introduced to the American public by the John Wanamaker department store. The Jay Gatsby look of a light-coloured flannel or linen suit became associated with upper-class American style, revisited in contemporary fashion by the designer Ralph Lauren.

A look favoured by men was the slicked-back hair worn by Hollywood heartthrob Rudolph Valentino in *The Sheik* (1921). Traditionally crafted shoes, always in black, were worn with the lounge suit.

flat, or applied in a fish-scale pattern to catch the light, raising the surface of the gown in a complex layering of decoration in diverse materials such as embroidered satin and various types of lace. The Callot Soeurs fashion design house opened in Paris 1895 and was operated by the four Callot sisters: Marthe Callot Bertrand, Regina Callot Tennyson-Chantrell, Joséphine Callot Crimon and the eldest, Marie Callot Gerber, who was in charge of design. Initially embellishing blouses and lingerie with antique lace and ribbons – their mother was a lacemaker – the company expanded to become one of the leading fashion houses of Paris in the 1920s, selling to an exclusive clientele in Europe and the United States.

ABOVE An illustration from *Art Goût Beauté* magazine from 1923 featuring a stylized rendition of a medieval-influenced bridal gown and bridesmaids' dresses, designed by Jean Patou.

OPPOSITE An illustration epitomizing Art Deco style, dating from 1924, features three designs by Brandt. The white brocade and satin bridal gown on the right combines a bateau neckline with a dropped waistline, referencing the geometric forms intrinsic to the design movement.

Cortège de mariée et petites robes d'enfants.
Création Jeanne Lanvin

Jeanne Lanvin

'Modern clothes need a certain romantic feel,' Lanvin declared, emphasizing that couturiers 'should take care not to become too everyday and practical'. The many wedding dresses she designed were clearly created in this spirit. Jeanne Lanvin had a deep attachment to the romantic and her designs were inspired by her daughter, Marguerite-Marie-Blanche, with youthfulness an enduring emphasis for both children and women.

Known for her exquisite *robes de style*, featuring an adaptation of the eighteenth-century pannier, Jeanne Lanvin (1867–1946) established France's oldest continuing couture house in 1889 when she was just 22 years old. In 1895, Lanvin married her first husband, Count Emilio di Pietro, an Italian nobleman, and two years later gave birth to a daughter, Marguerite, who invariably wore her mother's clothes. Lanvin initially opened a boutique on the rue du Faubourg Saint Honoré in Paris, followed by an induction into the country's Syndicat de la Couture in 1909. She studied Far Eastern and Middle Eastern dress and textiles, incorporating oriental influences with western decorative techniques to produce an array of floating feminine dresses in shades of pale pink, mauve, pistachio green and coral. The characteristic Lanvin broad-skirted silhouette, the result of ribbons and ruffles positioned at the side of the hips, was introduced in the 1920s and over the following two decades it was repeated in a variety of fabrics such as silk taffeta, velvet, metallic lace, organdy and chiffon. The pastel-coloured gowns were embellished with appliqué, beadwork and embroidery in one of the three ateliers owned by the house. Lanvin had her own dye works, where the designer developed her hallmark colour, Lanvin Blue, inspired by stained glass. The signature scent, Arpège, in a bottle featuring Paul Iribe's image of Lanvin and her daughter Marguerite was introduced in 1927 and continues to be a bestseller.

OPPOSITE An Art Deco rendering of an illustration for a wedding ensemble by Parisian couturier Jeanne Lanvin. The artless simplicity of the bridesmaids' dresses with their posies of flowers is offset by the Brancusi-esque features of the bride and the billowing folds of the patterned train, the tulle veil and the stylized shower bouquet.

LEFT Actress Joan Clement wearing a crepe de chine bridal dress embroidered with crystal bugles designed by Lanvin and photographed by Edward Steichen in 1926. The broad Bertha yoke collar extends to the ground, forming the train. Her veiled tiara is made of silver cloth and mother-of-pearl beads.

BELOW The etiolate silhouette and long lines of this ethereal columnar wedding dress designed by Lanvin are in contrast to the designer's more typical silhouette of the colourful *robe de style* worn by the adult bridesmaid.

Jeanne LANVIN

◀ Juliet headdress
So-called because of its similarity
to the Renaissance headdress of
Shakespeare's doomed lover in
Romeo and Juliet, the bejewelled
veil is worn here by the Duchess
Anna of France in 1927.

Key looks
of the decade

1920s

**Short and assymetrical
hemlines**
The flapper-style wedding dress
with a hemline rising to just below
the knee was typically shorter in
the back with a longer train. In a
departure from tradition, bridal
attire followed the fashions of
the day.

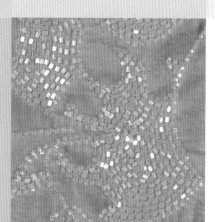

◀ Ornate beading
The simple silhouette of the
era was animated by lavish
embellishment such as beading
and embroidery by leading
exponents of the technique,
including Jeanne Lanvin and the
House of Callot Soeurs.

◄ Cloche hat and veil
Edwina Ashley wore a millinery-inspired cloche headdress combined with the cathedral train on her marriage to Lord Louis Mountbatten in 1922.

Shower bouquet
The elaborate shower bouquet, with its trailing ribbons tied in lovers' knots, superseded the Victorian hand-tied wedding posy. Some versions were so large as to overpower the bridal fashion, with sprays and buds inserted in the knots along the lengths of the ribbon streamers.

▲ Dropped waistlines
An image from *Le Petit Echo de le Mode*, 1923, France, features the dropped waistline of the 1920s silhouette, with further emphasis on the hips supplied by a knotted sash and the positioning of a corsage.

▲ Cathedral train
Charlotte Babcock Brown on her marriage in 1929 to Charles Coudert Nash poses in a classic bridal style, the ornate beadwork of the train displayed by swirling around the body to create a fishtail shape, which allowed her to descend a flight of steps.

1930s:
The Boudoir Bride

By the 1930s the boyish, short-skirted bride was replaced by one draped in bias-cut satins, prompting *Vogue* to report that, 'the bride appears at her loveliest in the new fitted and moulded gowns with long, sweeping lines'. The embellishment, ornament and medieval pastiche of the previous decade gave way to the sensuous uncluttered silhouette of the designs of Madeleine Vionnet of Paris, in which the natural curves of the woman were emphasized and highlighted by a sliver of white silk satin. Vionnet's dresses were widely copied, though not in such luxurious materials as the originals.

The newly invented fabric rayon, which had similar properties to silk, was an adequate substitute and was more affordable for those affected by the Wall Street Crash of 1929 and the subsequent global economic depression. During this period of economic hardship many couples deferred their wedding and the marriage rate dropped dramatically during the early years of the decade. Less affluent brides made do with their 'Sunday best' frock, a floral-patterned calf-length tea-dress, or chose a style that could be dyed a practical colour and worn again afterward.

The first magazine entirely devoted to brides and bridal fashion was the quarterly *So You're Going to Be Married*, later renamed *The Bride's Magazine* in 1936, and then shortened to simply *Brides*, which is still in existence today. This publication played a major role in the development of the bridal industry – advertising and merchandising wedding-related products. The magazine also reported on the Hollywood nuptials of the day, including those of the actress Merle Oberon to film director Alexander Korda, and popular comedienne Carole Lombard to Hollywood heartthrob Clark Gable. It was not only the weddings of the stars themselves that proved influential on popular taste – the white organdy party dress with oversized ruffled sleeves designed by costumier Adrian for Joan Crawford's title role in the film *Letty Lynton* (1932) was widely copied as a wedding dress and established Hollywood as an important fashion influence.

The Classical Bride

The statuesque silhouette of the classical bride of this period was influenced by the designs of Adrian in Hollywood and Madeleine Vionnet in Paris. Vionnet rejected the traditional dressmaking practice of fitting together numerous body-shaped pattern pieces. Instead she manipulated geometric forms such as squares and quadrants so that they draped around the body. Generally acknowledged to be the inventor of the 'bias cut', whereby fabric is cut across the grain rather than along it, Vionnet's process was more complex than this simple procedure. The couturier frequently cut the fabric, usually silk crepe, on the straight of the grain, then turned the pattern pieces so that they draped on the bias. The fabric would then be weighted at the edges and hung in the atelier, or workshop, for several weeks before being sewn together to alleviate any unevenness of the hemline. The flexibility of these processes resulted in the sinuous and body-conscious silhouette of the 1930s, and provided a simplicity of line and cut that was particularly suitable for brides. Underwear now included the new rubberized cotton yarn, Lastex, which further smoothed the silhouette.

LEFT AND OPPOSITE
A 1930s body-skimming bias-cut dress in silk satin with a matching cape. The neckline of the dress incorporates the trompe l'oeil effect of a beaded and embroidered bow, a device repeated on the back of the short cape and made popular by Elsa Schiaparelli.

While Vionnet pioneered the bias cut, Hollywood costumier Gilbert Adrian popularized it to a wider audience, the cinema-goers of the day. The white heavy silk-satin dress worn by screen siren Jean Harlow was featured in the proliferation of movie magazines that fed the fantasies of the bride-to-be, as did the public wedding of Princess Marina of Greece to the Duke of Kent at Westminster Abbey in 1934. Much admired for her fashionable style, the future Duchess chose British-born Edward Molyneux to design her wedding dress, rather than the Parisian couturiers she had previously favoured. British *Vogue* devoted an entire issue to the upcoming nuptials, delaying the day of publication until the day of the wedding itself. The issue included a sketch of the bridal gown, drawn at one of fittings at the Molyneux salon, a breach of protocol to which Buckingham Palace took exception. Renowned for his understated design style, Molyneux embraced modernism and banned all superfluous decoration. The long white and silver brocade gown complete with a motif of English roses was to become one of the most copied dresses of the twentieth century. A close-fitting sheath dress with long loose sleeves, the neckline was a discreet high 'V' shape. The court train hung from the shoulders, and her veil of family lace was lightened with metres of added tulle, achieving a width of 3 metres (10 feet) at the base, and fixed with a diamond tiara, immediately supplanting the orange blossom wreaths worn during the previous decades.

FAR LEFT A bias-cut dress with gored, fluted skirt by Parisian couturier Madeleine Vionnet dating from 1935. The knee-length white mink mantle adds a level of Hollywood glamour to the simple lines of the dress.

RIGHT A hand-sewn silk-satin dress with a softly gathered bodice attached to a V-shaped stomacher, which incorporates a fluted overskirt, dating from the early 1930s. One shoulder is adorned by a textile corsage.

Tulle was beginning to replace lace for the wedding veil. Norman Hartnell writes in his autobiography *Silver and Gold* (1955) of his delight that the wedding veil of Lady Alice, worn to her wedding in 1935 to the Duke of Gloucester, was to be tulle.

The ladies of the Buccleuch family were opposed to lace for Lady Alice's wedding veil. This pleased me for an antique bridal lace veil, extracted once a year from a grandmother's treasure chest and quickly replaced amidst sachets of lavender, rarely enhances the appearance of any bride. Lace, hanging lank and discoloured with age on each side of the face, resembles some attenuated judge's wig, contrasting ill with the young girl's beauty. A drifting cloud of crisp modern tulle is much more becoming, falling from a circle of blossom or from a sparkling tiara.

The court train was no longer a prerequisite of the aristocratic bride. Edward VIII, during the brief time that he was King of England, had no use for pageantry and abandoned the formal presentation of both debutantes and newly married women to the court. Both in white satin, the debutante would wear three white plumes in her hair, the emblem of the Prince of Wales, while the married woman would wear a tiara.

Royal Designers

Captain Molyneux's military self-presentation and English background made him the ideal candidate for aristocratic brides or those about to be married into the royal family. As Edward Molyneux of Paris, he had a London showroom, a direct competitor to Norman Hartnell, although his style was far less elaborate. A self-confessed 'designer for debutantes', Hartnell was a natural choice for a young girl dressed by him for her 'coming out ball' and presentation at court to call on when she required a wedding gown. Debutante Margaret Whigham, later the Duchess of Argyll, was dressed by Hartnell for her wedding to Charles Sweeney in 1931. The ivory satin wedding dress, with appliquéd orange blossom cut out of lace and embroidered with seed pearls and tiny glass silver bugle beads, had been worked on for six weeks by 200 seamstresses. The white tulle angel sleeves matched the tulle border of the cathedral train, 11.5 metres (38 feet) long and 2.5 metres (9 feet) wide, designed especially for the aisle of the leading Catholic church, the Brompton Oratory.

The bride received 3,000 wedding presents, including a collection of fur coats from her parents for her trousseau: a mink, two silver foxes, a six-skin sable stole and an ermine coat. Press attention and public interest in the wedding ceremony far exceeded that of contemporary royal weddings. According to the Duchess, 'Traffic in the Brompton Road and up as far as Hyde Park was brought to a standstill… Two thousand guests had been invited. A thousand more managed to gate crash their way in. There was not an inch of space in the church, and I was told afterward that people were standing on pews and clinging to the top of the pillars they had climbed.' With supreme narcissism, the Duchess adds, 'It was obvious that the people all round us were extremely happy. It was the darkest moment of the Depression, with millions of unemployed, but I think they felt our wedding had brought a flash of colour into a grey world. I hope it did.'

Hartnell's reputation for upper-class finery was consolidated with the commission to design the wedding dress for the Duchess of Gloucester in 1935, with bridesmaids' dresses for the Princesses Elizabeth and Margaret, the first step to being invited to design the wedding dress of the future monarch Elizabeth II in 1947.

ABOVE AND ABOVE LEFT
Exemplifying modern simplicity, and renowned for her personal style, Princess Marina of Greece wears a gown by Molyneux on her marriage to George, the Duke of Kent on 29 November 1934. Sketches for the bride's trousseau by Molyneux are above left.

OPPOSITE A sketch of Norman Hartnell's wedding-gown design for Lady Alice's marriage in 1935.

OPPOSITE Designed by British court dressmaker Norman Hartnell for the celebrated beauty, Margaret, Duchess of Argyll, on her marriage in 1933. The Princess-line gown with fluted sleeves utilizes all the skills of his atelier, with lavish use of appliqué, cut lace and beadwork.

RIGHT Norman Hartnell fits actress Florence Desmond for a wedding gown at his Mayfair, London salon in 1936. The design prefigures several of the design features pertinent to the coming decade: the ruched midriff, ballooned, cuffed sleeves and picture hat.

The New Informality

The aristocratic upper classes still favoured the country church wedding, and regarded the 'town' wedding with patronizing disdain. Nancy Mitford recounts in *The Pursuit of Love* Uncle Matthew's horror at the prospect of his daughter marrying in London.

> *Tony and his parents wanted a London wedding, Uncle Matthew said he had never hard of anything so common and vulgar in his life… he thought fashionable weddings were the height of degradation, and refused to lead his daughters up the aisle of St Margaret's through a crowd of gaping strangers. All these arguments were lost on Linda. Since the days when she was planning to marry the Prince of Wales she had had a mental picture of what it would be like… in a large church, with photographer's, arum lilies, tulle, bridesmaids and an enormous choir.*

For those who were not members of the aristocracy, the cost of the wedding ceremony could be adjusted, if necessary, to the financial exigencies caused by the Depression. The church ceremony began to be secularized during the 1930s, and many vows were now exchanged in a registry office or town hall, resulting in a greater informality in wedding-dress styles. In 1934 the permitted time to hold the ceremony was extended until six o'clock in the evening, which resulted in a rise in the popularity of exclusive hotels, such as the Ritz or Claridges in London or the Waldorf-Astoria in New York, being used as a venue for the reception; it could also take place in the bride's home for those in straitened circumstances. Wedding dresses did not diversify a great deal from the style of eveningwear, apart from the accoutrements of veil, bouquet and headgear. The long slim columns of bias-cut silk remained the same, the major difference being the new focus of erotic interest: the bare back, for evening.

For the less-formal wedding, printed flowered silk crepe or chiffon tea-dresses were worn, in the style of prevailing daytime fashion. The waist returned to its natural position, and although the skirt remained more or less perpendicular, it was shaped around the hips and fell to mid-calf during the day and ankle length for evening. An exaggerated shoulder line started to appear, and designs such as the 'butterfly' sleeve, a double layer of frilled chiffon, emphasized the silhouette of an upturned triangle. Hats replaced the traditional wedding veil; although the cloche hat was no longer worn, heads were still small in proportion to the body. The shingle was grown out and hair was worn with a small curl or chignon at the back of the neck, allowing for a dainty hat to be perched over one eye, or to accommodate a wide-brimmed straw for a summer wedding.

OPPOSITE Garlanded in pink paillette flowers, like Botticelli's *Primavera*, this ultra-romantic *Directoire*-style gauzy dress by Parisian couture house Lucien Lelong in 1938 is constructed from layers of pale blue silk chiffon, lightly gathered from a ruched bodice.

BELOW Dancer Jean Barry wears a white crepe roma tea-gown embroidered at the waist with grapes and leaves, by the American exponent of the tea-gown, designer Jessie Franklin Turner. Photographed by Edward Steichen in 1931.

Picturesque Style

The modern silhouette of the era, where cut and line predominated over embellishment, was punctuated by aberrations such as the dress worn by Joan Crawford in the film *Letty Lynton* in 1932. A fashion phenomenon, being at odds with the understated simplicity of the prevailing style, the long white evening dress in *mousseline de soi* influenced not only American but also European style. Charles Ekhart quotes an account in London's *Saturday Evening Post* (1935) in his essay *Fabrications* of the impact of the dress on an American fashion buyer:

> A certain gown worn by Crawford in a picture the latter part of 1932. You will recall it, I am sure, because it is still with us and promises to be a perennial – the one with the big stiff ruffles outlining the shoulders… The robe swept Paris not only after it had appeared in the film, but after it had been shown in the New York shops.

The 'picturesque' wedding gown became more prevalent toward the end of the decade. Also inspired by Hollywood, the elaborate, hooped crinoline shape emerged as a fashion front-runner for the prospective bride, as worn by Vivien Leigh as the heroine Scarlett O'Hara in the big block-buster movie *Gone With the Wind* (1939). The feisty and ravishing Scarlett twirled and stamped her way through the epic in gowns designed by Hollywood costumier Walter Plunkett, sparking a revival of the crinoline, which featured petticoats draped over 'cages' with side panniers. The gown worn by Scarlett for her first marriage, to Charles Hamilton, was widely copied by the ready-to-wear industry. It was a white satin dress made of 'Flirtation' brand rayon satin decorated with appliquéd fabric leaves; *Brides* magazine featured a ready-made copy of the gown which could be bought from Best & Company in New York for $85.

The state visit by the King and Queen of Great Britain to France in the early summer of 1938 was also instrumental in reintroducing the crinoline to the fashion silhouette. At the request of the King, Norman Hartnell designed a collection of dresses inspired by Franz Xavier Winterhalter's painting of Empress Elizabeth of Austria and her spangled tulle crinoline dress. The death of the Queen's mother, three weeks before the visit, resulted in all the gowns being remade in white, a royal prerogative for mourning. The all-white dresses composed of Valenciennes lace, silk, satin, velvet, taffeta, tulle and chiffon provided plenty of inspiration for the prospective bride-to-be. Other late nineteenth- and early twentieth-century references appearing in wedding gowns included huge gigot, or 'leg-of-mutton', sleeves and lavishly embellished skirts applied with garlands of embroidered flowers and swags of chiffon. These

inspired the theatrical bustled gowns by designers such as Balenciaga, Lelong and Jacques Heim. This nostalgic look at the crinolined form prefigured the New Look by a decade and changed the face of wedding fashion.

RIGHT American costumier Gilbert Adrian (1903–59), born Adrian Adolph Greenberg, was chief designer at Metro-Goldwyn-Mayer from 1927 to 1942. He left the film studios to launch his eponymous label selling bespoke clothing and a ready-to-wear line.

OPPOSITE Hollywood movie star Joan Crawford in the title role of Clarence Brown's feature film *Letty Lynton* (1932) wears a widely adopted gown by renowned Hollywood costumier Gilbert Adrian, which caused a sensation. The many layered sleeves are edged in sun-ray pleats, formed into a corsage at the waist.

BELOW A picturesque gown – incorporating 44 metres (48 yards) of satin and 18 metres (20 yards) of tulle – and reflecting the influence of the romantic epic *Gone With the Wind* (1939). The crinoline made a brief appearance on the fashionable bride until the onset of the Second World War and the introduction of rationing.

Second- and Third-Time Around Brides

The Queen of screwball comedy, Carole Lombard epitomized sartorial savoir-faire when she married much-loved Hollywood heartthrob Clark Gable in 1939. Formerly married to actor William Powell, Lombard first starred with Gable in 1932, in *No Man of Her Own*, but it was some time later before they fell in love. Gable was then filming *Gone With the Wind*, and on his first day free from the set he and Lombard travelled to Kingman, Arizona. Arriving late in the afternoon, they went straight to the courthouse for their licence and then on to the church for the ceremony. Gable wore a navy single-breasted suit, a white shirt and a patterned tie. Lombard looked elegant, understated and appropriate in a two-piece skirt suit with a single-breasted jacket and a knee-length A-line skirt designed by Irene, the leading costume designer at MGM. Worn with a simple polka-dot patterned blouse with a high fastening collar, Lombard kept it simple, she carried no flowers and wore no jewellery. In the later publicity shots she held a single red rose.

Hollywood costumier Gilbert Adrian designed the silk organdy wedding dress worn by the popular film actress Katharine Hepburn in her role as spoilt socialite Tracy Lord in the romantic comedy *The Philadelphia Story* (1940). Acknowledged to be one of the best of its kind, the film is based on a popular theme from the 1930s and '40s, in which a couple of divorcees, here played by Hepburn and Cary Grant as C K Dexter Haven, flirt with others and then remarry. Elements of Adrian's signature tailoring skills are evident in the slim silhouette and the triple lapels of the collar, which are turned back from a high neckline, with the edges rolled by hand. The ankle-length gown has long, cuffed sleeves edged in circular frills. The veil is replaced by a large-brimmed straw hat with long, broad ribbon ties left undone, worn on the back of the head, with a narrow band of artificial orange blossom tucked under the edge of the crown. The bouquet is a frilled circle of stiffened tulle.

On her wedding to the former Edward VIII, twice-married Wallis Warfield Simpson (later to become the Duchess of Windsor) set the paradigm for third-time-around style. Renowned for her hard-edged chic, unchanging raven's wing hairstyle and the soubriquet, 'It's impossible to be too rich or too thin,' Simpson chose for the design of her wedding outfit American-born couturier Mainbocher (who had changed his name from Main Rousseau Bocher when he opened his dressmaking establishment on the Avenue George V in Paris). Specializing in simple, conservative, elegant and extremely expensive fashions, Mainbocher designed a long column of a dress with a skirt cut on the bias, emphasizing the slender form of the future duchess, with a waist-length matching jacket. He usually incorporated labour-intensive details; here the midriff section of the jacket has a vertical row of covered buttons leading to the gathered bodice decorated with tiny rouleau

loops. The small, neat collar is brought together with a brooch. Edna Woolman Chase, then editor of American *Vogue*, did not approve. In her autobiography, *Always in Vogue* (1954), she wrote:

> The Duchess has many exquisite gowns in her wardrobe, but, candidly, for such an occasion as her wedding to a former English king, I think she and Mainbocher might have done better than they did. The gown is a perfectly straight, full-length, skimpy affair of pale grey-blue crepe… with a tight little uneventful jacket, and dull it is to look at.

Barbara Toner, the former editor-in-chief of *Bride's* magazine, thought otherwise: 'Americans were smitten with royalty and the royal wedding news was a sensation.

Wallis' trousseau of eight dresses and forty hats made fascination copy; her pale blue floor-length wedding ensemble by Mainbocher with a small matching hat inspired hundreds of copies.'

Wallis Simpson was a passionate collector of jewellery; on her wedding day she wore a diamond charm bracelet with nine crosses, each with an inscription of a significant event in the couple's lives. The Duchess, who always disliked the appearance of her hands, thinking them too large for her tiny frame, had matching gloves especially made to accommodate the wedding ring.

BELOW RIGHT A formal wedding still required the bridegroom to don the morning suit; a black tailcoat with grey-striped trousers worn with a high collared shirt, top hat and gloves.

MEN'S FASHIONS

Menswear began to take up the inverted triangle of the classic male silhouette, with broad padded shoulders and a draped double-breasted jacket, narrow at the waist and on the hips. Trousers had front double pleats and were pegged to the hem, with a severe pressed front crease. The waistcoat was discarded for informal daywear; with the invention of the wristwatch it was no longer required to incorporate the fob watch and chain. The Duke of Windsor was an enormous influence on the menswear of the day. A clothes fetishist, he popularized the Fair Isle sweater, plus fours and the Windsor knot – a method of knotting a tie – as well as making the soft shirt acceptable for eveningwear. Hair was kept short, smoothly brushed to one side from a parting, and usually treated with oil. Moustaches, as seen on most of the Hollywood leading men of the era, were popular.

The Tiara

Often known as the family fender in aristocratic circles, the tiara has been a popular feature of wedding attire since Princess Marina of Greece in 1934 replaced the then fashionable circle of orange blossom with the Russian fringe tiara, or *tiare russe*: an upstanding fringe of brilliant diamonds mounted in gold and set in silver. Hers was a gift from the city of London and dated from 1890. This type of tiara, popular in England at the time, could be converted into a necklace, and was made in many thousands during the end of the nineteenth and the beginning of the twentieth century.

The tiara represents the natural proclivity of all cultures to adorn the head – both to signify status, with a crown or tiara, to acknowledge the winner with the victor's laurel wreath, or simply to decorate. The word 'tiara' is Persian in origin, denoting the headdresses of the Persian kings, which were then encircled by diadems to hold the tiara in place. The Greek word diadem, which means to 'bind around', would originally have been constructed of natural flowers and foliage, and Greek craftsmen transformed these into garlands of the precious metal. Though less expert metal workers than the Greeks, the Romans added precious stones such as emeralds, sapphires and pearls to the design.

Subsequently neglected for many centuries, the tiara underwent a dramatic revival during the latter part of the eighteenth century. The rise of neoclassicism, the admiration for all things Greek, prompted by the arrival of the Elgin marbles in 1804, transformed fashionable dress throughout the continent. Worn with columns of high-waisted white neoclassical robes, the tiara became a fashionable accessory (though one worn only by married women), appropriate for all social occasions. The bridal tiara, whether inherited or purchased from one of the renowned jewellery houses that flourished during the accelerated consumption of the nineteenth century (such as Bulgari, Boucheron, Tiffany, Van Cleef & Arpels and Cartier) was a way of confirming the social wealth and status of the bride's family, to be worn not only at the wedding, but at her obligatory court appearance later. Nancy Mitford writes in her novel *Love in a Cold Climate* (1949) about the sad lack of such as gift for the prospective bride:

> Did you see what mingy little things they gave poor Linda? A cheque – yes, that's all very well but for how much I wonder? Cultured pearls, at least I imagine so or they would have been worth quite £10,000, and a hideous little bracelet. No tiara, no necklace, what will the poor girl wear at Court?

The crowning of the bride, whether with a garland of flowers or a bejewelled tiara, is a rite of passage, signifying the bride's change of status from single to married woman. Expensive tiaras are set with gems, the choice of stone dependant on the ancient lore of lapidary. In conjunction with the language of flowers, where every bloom has a specific meaning, the tiara then carries a potent visual message. Invested with meaning, jewels purport to be the bridge between the human and the divine; rubies banish sadness, the emerald expels evil spirits, the sapphire placates the wrath of God. Sentiment, symbolism and superstition are all implicated in the mystique of jewellery. Tiaras set with rubies and diamonds evoke passion, while a wreath of oak set with turquoise stands for the invincibility of true love. When Queen Elizabeth the Queen Mother (then Lady Elizabeth Bowes-Lyon) married in 1923, her father gave her a tiara in the form of a garland of wild roses, representing the pains as well as the pleasures of love, and set with rose-cut diamonds for eternity. Geoffrey Munn lists in his book, *Tiaras, Past and Present* (2002), the associations between flowers, stones and meaning.

The style of the tiara kept pace with the changing fashions of the twentieth century. The simple, elegant silhouette of the 1920s and 1930s and the shorter,

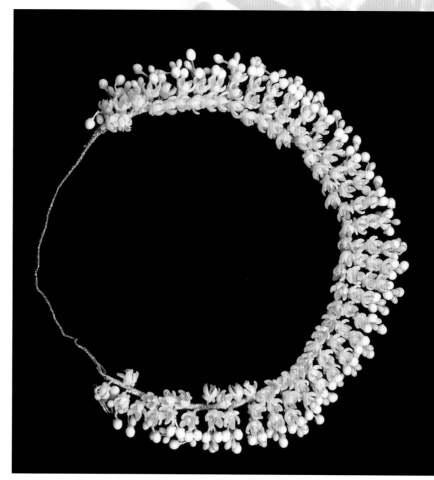

BELOW A wreath or headband worn to secure the veil, composed of racemes of yellow and white wax flowers, fixed onto wire, dating from the 1930s from Liberty & Co., London.

cropped hairstyles demanded a more modern tiara, often achieved by the breaking up of earlier pieces and resetting in the current Art Deco style. The Wall Street crash and subsequent economic depression meant that precious gemstones were replaced with the semi-precious aquamarines instead of sapphires, and citrine in place of topaz. Coco Chanel showed a range of diadems at her hotel in 1932 that defied the recession – mannequins adorned with diadems in the form of comets and stars, their foreheads hung with articulated diamond-set fringes.

THE LANGUAGE OF FLOWERS

Acorn:	Fecundity
Daisy:	Innocence
Ears of wheat:	Fertility and Wealth
Forget-me-not:	True love
Ivy:	Marriage
Laurel:	Triumph of love
Mistletoe:	A kiss
Oak:	Invincibility and Strength
Pansy:	Think of the giver
Rose:	Every aspect of love
Thistle flower:	The pleasure and pain of love

THE MEANING OF STONES

Amethyst:	Devotion
Diamond:	Forever
Emerald:	Hope
Moonstone:	Innocence
Pearl:	Love
Ruby:	Passion
Turquoise:	Remembrance and True Love

RIGHT The wedding of John Hare, Viscount Blakenham, and Nancy Pearson in 1934. The simplicity of the bride's unadorned wedding gown, incorporating a draped cowl neckline, allows for the display of an important heirloom necklace.

So You're Going to Be Married

An article on bridalwear in *Fortune* magazine in 1933 spurred *American House & Garden* advertising manager Wells Drorbaugh to launch a bridal publication in 1934. Initially called *So You're Going to Be Married: A Magazine for Brides*, the content included etiquette, beauty, the trousseau, gift giving and receiving, housewares, entertaining and bridal fashions, and enabled the prospective bride to source her chosen gown. Alexandra Potts, head of merchandising at *Bride's* from the late 1930s, developed a series of bridal clinics for suppliers and mass retailers and department stores to come together to see how they might best exploit the growing consumerism of the wedding process. Hosted by New York hotels such as the Waldorf-Astoria and the Ritz-Carlton, the clinics showcased the latest styles in gowns, flowers and other accoutrements of the white wedding.

The magazine is credited with the instigation of the bridal shop, a specialist retailer who offered a complete service from making the wedding gown to dressing the bridesmaids and the mother of the bride. The wedding bureaux or bridal salon in the increasingly popular department stores was also an option for the 1930s bride. Carson, Pirie, Scott & Company of Chicago claim to be one of the first in 1935, alongside Best & Co., as well as New York's Lord & Taylor. Previously the bride would have had to call on a number of individual retailers to fulfil all her needs, including the jeweller, milliner, stationer and caterer. Now she could do a one-stop shop under one roof. The gift registry run by such stores was an additional boon, whereby in-house purchases could be ticked off the list as they were bought for the bridal couple. Bridal fashion shows held by the stores also promoted trousseau items as well as consumer goods that the prospective housewife would need to set up a future home.

The rise of the ready-to-wear clothing industry and subsequent specialist retail outlets transformed the process of purchasing the wedding gown. A shift from custom-made to ready-made clothing resulted in less expense and more choice for the bride-to-be; commercial ranges tended to be more fashion led and responsive to current trends than those offered by a private dressmaker. As manufacturers of ready-to-wear bridal apparel expanded, branded wedding dresses began to be the norm for the middle-class bride.

It's a "Tested-Quality" Fabric

Courtaulds
RAYON

A Marriage has been Arranged

... and her bridal dress is of "Tested-Quality" Moiré Poult made with Courtaulds Rayon .. Price 7½ Guineas from the model gown department of **MARSHALL & SNELGROVE** Oxford Street, London, W.1

OPPOSITE A crepe wedding gown with a high neckline, train and headdress from 1934. The bouquet of calla lilies and lilacs are by New York florist Max Schling.

ABOVE The introduction of man-made fibres such as rayon infiltrated wedding dress design, here featured in this 1930s advertisement by London department store Marshall & Snelgrove. The wedding gown is a combination of fashionable trends of the past – the gigot sleeves – with modern fabric, Courtauld's rayon.

◀ Tea-dresses

An informal alternative to the traditional white wedding gown was the tea-dress in floral printed crepe de chine or rayon. This one, dating from 1930 and illustrated in *Vogue* magazine, is accessorized with a cloche hat worn low on the brow and a simple bouquet of marguerites.

◀ Picturesque style

A pre-war flirtation with the crinoline and the belle époque gigot sleeve by British designer Victor Stiebel (1907–76) for a wedding dress dating from 1938–39 in oyster slipper satin with a lace-edged overskirt. Elements of modernity come from the lace hat with the short, frilled veil and the tiny posy-style bouquet.

Key looks of the decade

1930s

Tiaras

With tulle replacing lace as the preferred veil material, the headdress needed the ability both to anchor and balance the volume of the veil, which the tiara provided. Modern Art Deco diadems set with semi-precious stones could substitute for traditional heirloom tiaras.

◀ Bias-cut silk dresses

Invented by Madeleine Vionnet, the bias-cut dress skimmed the body in a sliver of silk satin and ended in a fluted fishtail. The silhouette is balanced by the small, sculpted head with the veil drawn back and caught with a cluster of orange-blossom.

▼ Art Deco detailing
Typical Art Deco motifs, such as chevrons, geometrics and stripes, found their way into bridal designs, as well as daywear. This detail from a 1930s bias-cut, silk wedding gown displays a geometric styling in the bodice shaping and button and belt.

Artificial silk and diamanté
Fluid, body-clinging designs in rayon (called 'artificial silk') often featured draping and ruching – which worked well with the manmade fabric. Although little embellishment was required, diamanté had become popular and sparkling dress clips or jewellery lent Hollywood glamour to those unable to afford diamonds and real silk.

▲ Shoulder-hanging trains
A wedding dress of white and pale blue satin by Callot Soeurs, dating from 1931, with a tulle veil suspended from the shoulders. The overskirt of embroidered tulle is gathered up at the front into a large knot and allowed to fall to the ground.

▶ Ready-to-wear bridal
A wedding dress designed by fashion house Reville in dawn pink satin, dating from 1931. The pearl-embroidered scrollwork of the Vandyke points of the skirt are reproduced in the small, triangular godets in the sleeves, with matching embroidery on the edge of the pale pink tulle veil and low, square neckline.

Butterfly sleeves
Cap sleeves, usually in a lightweight fabric such as chiffon, were layered and split to fall each side of the arm, creating the effect of a butterfly's wings.

1940s:
Something Borrowed

OPPOSITE 'Babe' Paley, renowned for her personal style, on her marriage as Barbara Cushing to Stanley Grafton Mortimer Jr, wears a wedding dress designed by Mabel McIlvain Downs dating from 1940. The vertical ruched draping of the bodice continues down the outer seam of the sleeves in direct contrast to the horizontal ruching of the bodice.

With the onset of the Second World War, wedding practices and customs were inevitably subject to change. Long engagements culminating in lavish ceremonies were out of the question for most brides. Wedding dresses, if worn at all, were borrowed from an older sister or family friend and reflected the fashions of the previous decade with a long, narrow skirt, cut on the bias and long, narrow sleeves. More usually, the wartime bride went to the altar or registry office wearing a 'costume': a tailored suit cut on the lines of the military uniform with a celebratory corsage fixed to the lapel. Even Hollywood stars, with all the skills and resources of the Hollywood costumiers such as Adrian and Irene at their disposal, dressed down for their wedding day. Barbara Hutton, the Woolworth heiress, chose a blue silk costume with matching veiled hat for her wedding to Cary Grant in 1942, and Bette Davis, on her marriage to William Grant Sherry, also wore a broad-shouldered and slim-hipped suit.

The majority of women of marriageable age were conscripted into the services or engaged with war work on the land or in the munitions factories. Paris fashion lay dormant during the war years, although Lucien Lelong remained as president of the Chambre Syndicale de la Couture Pariesienne from 1937 to 1946. Some couturiers remained, but their influence was lost amid other, more important considerations. In the US, the separation from Europe encouraged a thriving ready-to-wear fashion industry with a unique perspective, resulting in practical, easy fashion that instigated the American sportswear aesthetic.

The end of the war did not mean the end of austerity. Clothing was still rationed, but there was also an eagerness to return to past traditions, including the white wedding. The post-war emphasis on the importance of the family and the return of women to running the home, the lavish excesses of Dior's New Look after years of austerity and the global interest in the marriage of the young Princess Elizabeth of Great Britain to Prince Philip of Greece and Denmark all contributed to the importance placed on the wedding ceremony toward the end of the decade.

The Wartime Wedding

A regular wartime column entitled 'Marrying in Haste, Accelerated Wedding Plans' in American *Vogue* recorded that:

> *Weddings nowadays hang not on the bride's whim, but on the decision of the groom's commanding officer. He names the day when he grants that unexpected furlough…The 1942 schedule may run something like this: engagement announced on Monday, invitations sent out by Telegraph on Wednesday, the last handful of rice and rose petals flung on Saturday.*

Of course, in food-rationed Britain no one would have dreamt of throwing an edible commodity such as rice. The wartime wedding was a utilitarian affair, bereft of most of the accoutrements that defined the ceremony. No church bells were allowed (they could be rung only as a warning of enemy invasion), a small cake made from powdered egg was hidden inside a white cardboard box to make it look bigger, flower gardens were given up to grow vegetables and the manufacture of luxury fabrics was redirected to the war effort.

The dominant daytime silhouette was one that reflected the practical needs of the wartime woman. Skirts short enough to ride a bicycle, jackets buttoned high to the neck for warmth, lacy sweaters to make the wool (unpicked from previous garments) go further, sturdy shoes and a shoulder bag. The British Board of Trade had rules and regulations under the 'Utility Scheme' that prescribed the amount of fabric used for each garment, resulting in unadorned suits with narrow reveres and flaps, rather than patch pockets and straight skirts. Designed by several prominent names including Hardy Amies and Norman Hartnell, the Queen's own dressmaker, these official Utility clothes were distinguished by the CC41 label.

Silk was needed to make parachutes and there was a ban on its use for both clothing and hosiery, one of the reasons why women started to wear slacks and trousers.

RIGHT Picking up her skirt to avoid the rubble of bomb damage in a war-torn Britain, Ena Squire-Brown, an international dancer famed for her Dove Dance, leaves her home for St George's Church in Forest Hill to marry her Royal Air Force sweetheart.

Wool was blended with less scarce fibres or recycled. Those women who possessed a pair of the new nylon stockings usually had some contact with America, where such things were available; most wore lisle stockings of knitted cotton and, when these ran out, nothing at all, staining the legs with various homemade mixtures such as gravy browning powder and drawing a line up the back of the leg to imitate the seaming of fully-fashioned stockings. As austerity increased so too did ingenuity. Designers responded to the challenge by reworking mundane and lowly materials to produce high fashion. The Italian shoe designer Salvatore Ferragamo utilized plaited raffia, straw and cork from which he constructed platform and wedge heels with the newly fashionable open-toe, although workers were banned from wearing these on the factory floor.

RIGHT One of the renowned Mitford sisters, Deborah Mitford, on her marriage to Andrew Cavendish in 1941. At the height of austerity, the bride wore a traditional dress by Victor Stiebel.

BELOW A heavy silk moiré wedding dress by Molyneux from 1948. Restrained in cut, the smooth bodice, off-the-shoulder décolletage and stately sweep of skirt are typical of the couturier's signature style.

MENSWEAR IN WARTIME

During wartime, men wore their service uniform for the wedding ceremony. At the end of the war the British Government Issue 'demob' suit was given to all men on leaving the services, usually ill-fitting and associated with the working class, who could not afford to visit a tailor. The style of suits had changed little since pre-war days: jackets were elongated with padded shoulders, wide lapels and narrow hips, and trousers had pleated fronts. David Kynaston records in his book, *Austerity Britain 1945–51*, civil servant Anthony Heap's experience of shopping for a suit:

Hopefully hied up to Burton's branch at The Angel, to order one of the fifteen "made to measure" suits that comprise their weekly "quota". Wanted a grey tweed, but as luck would have it, they hadn't any in this week's "allocation" of patterns-only blue worsteds. They would, however, try and get me a length next week. In which case, the suit would be ready in about nine month's time!

The severity of the tailored silhouette was offset by the wearing of elaborate hats, often extreme and idiosyncratic in design, constructed from spotted net, veiling and feathers, the detailing perched at the front of the head and with a snood attached to the back for the hair. *Mrs Miniver* (1942), a favourite wartime film of Winston Churchill, begins with the lead character purchasing a hat, delaying a London omnibus so that she can return to the shop and complete her purchase. A strange concoction of three flattened wings, the hat represents the importance of the frivolous details of life, even when threatened by encroaching war.

The wartime wedding was reduced to the oft-used phrase, 'make do and mend'. At the beginning of the war, each adult in Britain was allowed 66 clothing coupons, by the end this number had dropped to 36. Using furnishing fabrics for the dress (shades of Scarlett O'Hara in *Gone With the Wind*, who took down the green velvet curtains to make a dress in which to seduce Rhett Butler), net lace curtains for the veil, paper flowers for the bouquet, ingenuity and homemade fashions thrived. Those women who did manage to find a bale of cloth – whether silk or rayon, the dominant fabric of the decade – had it made up in the prevailing style of 1940s eveningwear, with a long, narrow silhouette, fitted bodice and a gathered sleeve head with a small amount of padding to reflect the squarer shoulder line. Labour-intensive dressmaking details such as rouleau loops over homemade buttons, and shirring and draping over the midriff, softened the silhouette and added an element of luxury. These were worn beneath a short bolero jacket or cape. For the first time there was no shame in women hiring a wedding dress. Firms such as Moss Bros, which had been hiring out men's wedding clothes since the 1890s, now began to offer a bridal service.

The aristocracy, however, defied the stringent wartime restrictions. In her book, *The Mitfords* (2007), the future Duchess of Devonshire, Deborah Mitford, writes of her coming nuptials to her sister Diana in 1941:

*Nancy is going to ask Cecil Beaton where to
have my dress made by a theatrical person
because it wouldn't be so expensive as
a proper shop. [It was made by London
dressmaker Victor Stiebel]. It's going to be
masses & masses of white tulle, tight bodice
and sleeves, a skirt such has never been
seen before for size. I don't mind if that is the
fashion or not, it's what suits me. And the train
will come out of the skirt & be enormous with
great ruches of tulle all down, otherwise the
skirt will be quite plain. What to wear on my
head I don't know & I know Mrs Stevens will
wreck my hair but I couldn't go to anyone else.
Then if the actual wedding doesn't cost too
much we could go a bit of a bust on the going
away one, have it from Worth or Molyneux*

*or somewhere… I'm going to begin on my
underclothes next week… If you are really
going to get me something, I would adore a
little jewel. Only you're not to spend too much
because it's the war & all.*

British couturier Edward Molyneux had moved his house to London for the duration of the war, and did not return to Paris until 1946. While in Britain he designed a collection of sculptural couture evening gowns with draped bustles in opulent fabrics which were solely for export to the American market. At the same time, he was one of the chief protagonists of a smart London style to which the fashionable upper classes still aspired, even in times of austerity.

BELOW This dress by Molyneux, dating from 1946, is demure and dignified. The neat Peter-Pan collar, full sleeves and short train are demonstrably a concession to daywear, as is the row of buttons and buttonholes, rather than the more frequently used rouleau loops.

THIS PAGE A wedding dress designed by Parisian couturier Lucien Lelong dating from 1946. The lightly padded shoulders and high-fastening neckline reflect wartime fashions of the day, off-set by layers of vertical frills that form a square yoke with the sleeves.

OPPOSITE PAGE An American pre-war excursion into the picturesque, influenced by romantic epics such as *Gone With the Wind* (1939), complete with face-framing bonnet and chintz-banded billowing crinoline skirt, photographed by Horst P Horst in 1940.

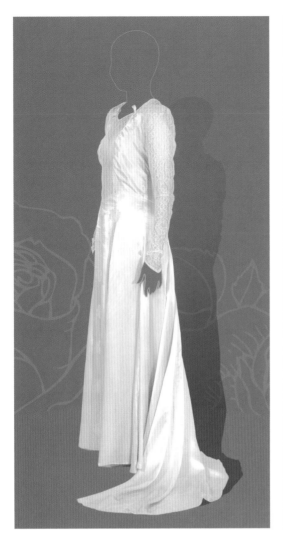

FAR LEFT AND ABOVE DETAILS
Dating from the early 1940s, this off-white satin dress with V-shaped bodice is overlaid with machine-made lace. The width of the skirt at the hemline is the result of 'fit and flare' seaming, which also incorporates a short train.

ABOVE LEFT An all-over machine-made lace 1940s wedding dress with cross-over seams on the bodice to provide shaping has a simple keyhole opening at the back, as zips were in short supply. The gown was designed to be worn over a sleeveless opaque white under-dress or petticoat.

BEST FACE FORWARD

During this period hair was worn shoulder-length and piled high on top. Perms were out of the question owing to restrictions on the manufacture of chemicals, so old-time methods were reintroduced to the boudoir, such as torn rags twisted around the hair and left in overnight, and a mix of a sugar and water to take the place of setting lotion. Women rarely had their hair done professionally during the war and the peek-a-boo fringe inspired by Veronica Lake was frowned upon in Britain, where hair was confined under a hairnet to prevent it being caught in machinery. The fashion was for rolls of curls in decreasing sizes from a centre parting, with the back hair pinned up or left to turn under in a pageboy style.

Femininity was represented by the burgeoning use of cosmetics. Increasingly considered important for morale during the war, it was considered a woman's duty to 'Put her best face forward'. American cosmetics company Revlon, founded by Charles Revson and his brother Joseph in 1932, along with a chemist, Charles Lachman (who contributed the 'L' in the Revlon name), started with a single product – a new type of nail enamel developed through a unique manufacturing process that used pigments instead of dyes. By 1940, Revlon offered an entire manicure line and added lipstick to the collection. The company began coast-to-coast advertising in the 1940s, using full-colour photographic advertisements for their matching nail polish and lipsticks with exotic and unique names, such as 'Paint the Town Pink', 'Bachelor's Carnation' and 'Sweet Talk'.

The Trousseau

During the war years the trousseau was also subject to wartime restrictions, and underwear was strictly 'underwear', rather than the more romantic lingerie. Nancy Mitford in *Love in a Cold Climate* recounts Lady Montdore's advice for the trousseau:

> The important thing, dear… is to have a really good fur coat, I mean a proper, dark one… Not only will it make the rest of your clothes look better than they are, but you really needn't bother much about anything else as you need never take it off. Above all, don't go wasting money on underclothes, there is nothing simpler – I always borrow Montdore's myself. Now for evening, a diamond brooch is a great help, so long as it has good big stones.

For those women who didn't like the idea of wearing their husband's pyjamas and underwear, artificial silk (or rayon, also known as 'art' silk) replaced real silk for lingerie and nightwear, and was often trimmed with hand embroidery and lace, or even, as a last resort, with net normally used for curtains. Novelist Elizabeth Jane Howard recalls in her biography, *Slipstream* (2002), buying the trousseau for her wedding in 1942: 'My mother concerned herself with my clothes and took me to Curzon Street, where Chris Ampthill designed and made my wedding dress of off-ration white lace, a soft turquoise dress and short-sleeved jacket to match, and two pinafore dresses, one of blue linen and the other of a pretty flecked tweed. Underclothes had to be made out of parachute silk and curtain netting.'

Advertisements for 'girdles' began to appear in magazines as Lastex – a rubberized yarn developed by the Dunlop Rubber company – was introduced into the manufacture of corsets; with the capacity for two-way stretch, girdles were often called 'pull-ons'. Corsets had very little to do with body weight. Young girls were routinely measured for their corset as a rite of passage, no matter what their size.

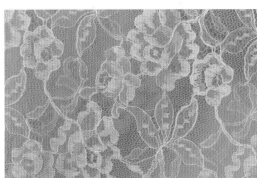

BELOW A late 1940s wedding dress with a ballerina-length hem and elbow-length sleeves, details that would become more popular in the next decade. The pleated skirt is overlaid with lace that is cut away at the side.

The American Bride

Bridal magazines continued to promote the formal white wedding ceremony. As Vicki Howard points out in her book, *Brides, Inc.: American Weddings and the Business of Tradition* (2006), 'weddings and marriage were seen as suitable symbols of the wartime aim of preserving the American way of life… wedding industries benefited ideologically from the war as the bride and patriotism went hand in hand to the altar'.

Bridal dress suppliers fought the restrictions placed on manufacturers during the war, claiming that long white gowns were vital to uphold morale, which resulted in an exemption from the War Production Board restrictions. The jewellery industry linked romantic love with the American way of life that the soldiers were fighting to protect and popularized the double-ring ceremony as a way of visually connecting the couple during the separations of wartime.

In America restrictions on dress were less severe. Although the government order L85 issued in 1943 regulated various aspects of clothing manufacture, these were not as stringent nor so rigidly adhered to as in Britain. Hollywood costumier Gilbert Adrian influenced the design of the Victory suit, the American version of Britain's Utility suit. Designers such as Claire Potter, Jo Copeland and Claire McCardell produced clothes independently of any Parisian influence, that were appropriate to the lives of modern women increasingly preoccupied with work as well as running the home. Problem solving was the defining characteristic of McCardell's ethos. One of the most influential American designers of the twentieth century, proponent of practical separates and instigator of the 'mix 'n' match wardrobe', when asked by American *Vogue* to design a wedding dress she created a soft-shouldered woollen dress with her signature dirndl skirt.

With the coming of peace, the formal white wedding once again became desirable. An entire industry gathered momentum to accommodate the post-war rush to the altar. Wedding specialists, department store consultants and entrepreneurs such as Priscilla Comins Kidder founded businesses predicated on the prospective bride's pursuit of perfection. A more tempered approach was recommended in *Vogue's Book of Etiquette* (1948), as quoted by Vicki Howard:

> *A real wedding required certain essentials,*
> *1. a religious ceremony; 2.a father, brother,*
> *uncle, cousin or other male relative, to give the*
> *bride away; 3. a best man for the groom; 4. at*
> *least one attendant for the bride; 5. a bouquet for*
> *the bride; 6. a ring for the bride. And, if possible,*
> *7. a reception, no matter how small, which need*
> *only entail a wedding cake and a drink in which*
> *to toast the bride.*

LEFT Post-war austerity is relinquished by Mrs William Talbert wearing a wedding gown designed by Ceil Chapman, in a 1948 photograph by John Rawlings. The duchesse satin gown is split to reveal a lace under-dress before extending into a short train. The décolletage of the horseshoe-shaped neckline marks a transition from the high necklines at the beginning of the decade to the more revealing later styles.

RIGHT Exponent of engineered couture, this Charles James wedding dress dating from 1948–49 has all the qualities associated with the designer's main line: the use of a weighty fabric, complex draping on the skirt and a sculpted silhouette, constructed here in shell-pink.

Priscilla of Boston

The rise of mass-production in post-war America and the upsurge in the number of weddings as men returned from the conflict resulted in a burgeoning market for the ready-to-wear wedding dress. It was now the case that every bride desired a white wedding gown, to be worn once on her special day. Wedding dress manufacturers such as Priscilla of Boston and the Alfred Angelo Company, founded in 1940 in Philadelphia by Alfred Angelo and his wife, Edythe Piccione, offered wedding gowns, bridesmaid, mother-of-the-bride and prom dresses. These companies did not carry full lines of stock for customers and so required appointments, ordering and fittings.

Priscilla of Boston was one of the first wedding-gown designers to promote own-brand name status, going from a small, family-owned business to one of national reputation. Known as 'Queen of the Aisle', Priscilla Kidder actively participated in every aspect of the wedding industry for almost 50 years and became a nationally known figure who journalists often referred to as the 'Dior' of bridal design. Born Priscilla Comins in Quincy, Massachusetts in 1918, she opened a small yarn shop in the community after finishing high school. Then, having completed her education in retail design at the New England School of Design, she took a job at RH White department store in Boston, Massachusetts, where she worked her way up from model to sales associate to assistant buyer in the bridal department. She married James Norton Kidder in 1940 and, with his help as financial consultant, left White's in 1945 and opened Bride's Shop on Boston's exclusive Newbury Street. The store grossed $10,000 in its first week of business.

In 1949 she moved into wholesale production, with stores and factories in Massachusetts and New York. The post-war demand for wedding gowns, combined with Kidder's understanding of the American market, ensured a flourishing business. She also designed dresses for bridesmaids, mothers of the bride and debutantes. Many prestigious commissions followed and in 1956 Kidder designed the bridesmaids' gowns for actress Grace Kelly's wedding to Prince Rainier. The extensive news coverage of the wedding added to Mrs. Kidder's celebrity. She was the first of a few wedding-gown designers to hand cut and appliqué French and Belgian laces as a design element, positioning the pieces apart rather than using the lace as a whole. Over the years the usage of imported cut lace over English net became her signature and was an enormous influence on other wedding-dress designers.

Priscilla of Boston consisted of numerous bridal lines, including the 'Priscilla', the 'Betsy', named for Priscilla Kidder's daughter and created in 1960 for the woman who wanted an inexpensive dress and the 'Teeny' line,

later renamed the 'Petite' line, designed for the smaller woman. The company eventually manufactured more than 2,000 dresses a month and, while Kidder continued to oversee the creative process, she also employed a small team of designers, including John Burbidge with whom she had been at college.

Priscilla was also directly involved with the stores that marketed her gowns. She travelled throughout the United States to hold fashion shows or visit showrooms. On these trips she advised brides on how to make their wedding the most special day of their lives. She kept a high profile in the media and created a distinctive image for herself that helped sell her products. Priscilla Kidder retired in 1993.

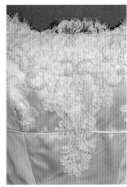

The Marriage of the Future Monarch

The wedding of Princess Elizabeth to Prince Philip in 1947 validated the nation's desire for luxury and ceremony following the privations of the Second World War. People camped out on the streets of London to capture a glimpse of the Irish State Coach carrying the young bride and her father to Westminster Abbey. A newspaper recorded,'Trafalgar Square was so crowded that not a pigeon could find a foothold'. Rationing was still in force and, although clothing coupons poured into Buckingham Palace from loyal citizens, there was some incipient resentment from others, as David Kynaston records in his book, *Austerity Britain 1945–51* (2007): 'The Camden Town branch of the Amalgamated Society of Woodworkers warned the King, "Any banqueting and display at your daughter's wedding will be an insult to the British people at the present time... and we would consider that you would be well advised to order a very quiet wedding in keeping with the times"'.

Royal dressmaker Norman Hartnell was commissioned to design the wedding dress and the eight bridesmaids' dresses, including the gown for the Queen's sister, Princess Margaret. Hartnell writes at length of the tension and speculation inherent in the task in his book, *Silver and Gold* (1955). Inspiration was culled from a painting by Botticelli, *Primavera*, in which the central figure is portrayed in 'clinging ivory silk, trailed with jasmine, smilax, syringa and small rose-like blossoms.' Ten thousand pearls were purchased from America and it was ascertained that the silk worms used for the satin dress were not Italian or Japanese, recent enemies of the country, but Chinese. The satin for the train was made at Lullingstone Castle, and Hartnell describes the process of designing the embroidered detail:

I laid out fifteen yards of tracing paper flat on the linoleum workroom floor… Graphite pencil in hand, I first marked out a long line from shoulder almost to the hem of the main backbone, a central line for the graduated satin syringa and orange blossoms. Similar pearl embroideries were to mark the border edges of the train.

Sitting cross-legged and suffering from a severe cold in the head, I marked in circles the rich white roses of York to be carried out in white satin, and centred by raised strands of pearls threaded on silver wire and raised up in relief. All these motifs had to be assembled in a design proportioned like a florist's bouquet. Wherever there was space or weakness of design I drew more wheat, more leaves, more blossom of orange, syringa or jasmine.

As with the later royal wedding of Lady Diana Spencer to Prince Charles, the design was kept secret until the day. The windows of the workroom were white-washed and curtained with thick white muslin to deter prying eyes (no telephoto lenses in those days). Fashion historian James Laver eulogized, 'In his design [for the wedding dress] based on Botticelli curves, he has scattered over the ivory satin garlands of white York roses carried out in crystal... the result is a colour scheme – yes! A colour scheme-surprising in its range, for a whole gamut of shades and contrast can be held within the span of colour which is itself no colour'.

The Queen's wedding breakfast in 1947 was subject to strict food regulations of the time and centred on game, which was not a rationed food. The simple menu, headed with the King's Crown over the joint initials GRE, was dated Buckingham Palace, Thursday 20 November 1947, and included Filet de Sole Mountbatten, Perdreau en Casserole, Salade Royale and Bombe Glacée Princess Elizabeth.

Flower arrangements were by Constance Spry, who numbered among her clients the Duke and Duchess of Kent and, somewhat controversially in view of the abdication crisis, the former King Edward VIII (as the

OPPOSITE Princess Elizabeth, later Queen Elizabeth II, with her husband Philip, Duke of Edinburgh, wearing a wedding gown designed by court dressmaker Norman Hartnell in 1947. The dress is partnered with a Russian fringe tiara, also worn by Princess Marina on her wedding day in 1934.

BELOW A fabric swatch showing a sample of Princess Elizabeth's wedding gown, embroidered in the Hartnell atelier on rich lustrous satin woven by the Scottish firm of Winterthur.

LEFT A sketch by the court dressmaker of Princess Elizabeth's wedding dress in white pastel on a black background, showing the ears of corn, Tudor roses and orange-blossom motifs that were embroidered onto the train.

OPPOSITE Mrs William F Talbert (formerly Nancy Pike) wearing her wedding gown by Ceil Chapman. Born in Staten Island, New York, Chapman started a company, Her Ladyship Gowns, with Gloria Vanderbilt before launching her own business in 1940. A fashion designer for the movies and television, she specialized in cocktail and formal eveningwear, often embellished with beads and lace.

Duke of Windsor) and Mrs Simpson. Spry was at the peak of her career when she organized the flowers for the Windsors' wedding in 1937, filling the house with pale pink peonies, lilies, lilac and trailing roses. For Princess Elizabeth's marriage Spry was confined to pink and white, but the floral artist was renowned for her informal approach to flower arranging, which she liberated from the constraints of conventional, stiff bunches of hot-house flowers to lush, deceptively artless arrangements which often included wild flowers and 'weeds' – when Jo and Laura Grimond married at the smart city church of St Margaret's in Westminster, Spry filled it with nothing but enormous arrangements of cow parsley.

The glorious execution of Princess Elizabeth's wedding gown and that of the bride's attendants provided fuel for the romantic fantasies of the post-war bride, still suffering the austerity of continued rationing. The fashionable extravagances of unashamedly sentimental films featuring wedding dresses such as the one worn by British actress Anna Neagle in *Maytime in Mayfair* (1949) also applied fuel to the fantasy. With screen costumes designed by Elizabeth Haffenden for Gainsborough studios in London, and Cecil Beaton in Hollywood, the wedding gown exemplified the newly romantic aesthetic. With the implementation of Dior's New Look and the Sweetheart line in America, conspicuous consumption was beginning to replace the 'make do and mend' ethos.

The New Look

Dior's New Look paved the way for wedding fashion to coincide with high fashion. The full skirts, supported by layers of petticoats and falling to below mid-calf, soft, the rounded shoulders and cinched-in waist, all represented full-on femininity that epitomized an end to austerity and a return to home and hearth for women. It was rapturously received by the fashion press. Edna Woolman Chase of American *Vogue* wrote, 'In the Spring collections of 1947, for the first time, his name [Dior], one of the brightest of the French couture, blazed into prominence.' There was also disapproval for such lavish use of material at a time when clothes were still rationed. David Kynaston records in his book, *Austerity Britain 1945–51,* the denunciation of the New Look in the *Reynolds News* newspaper by Mabel Ridealgh, a Member of Parliament, as an 'utterly ridiculous, stupidly exaggerated waste of material and manpower foisted on the average woman to the detriment of other, more normal clothing… Women today are taking a larger part in the happenings of the world and the New Look is too reminiscent of a caged bird's attitude. I hope our fashion dictators will realize the new outlook of women will give the death blow to any attempt at curtailing women's freedom'. On the contrary, however, women embraced the new feminine fashion. London department store Marshall & Snelgrove reported, 'We are selling nothing but New Look clothes, with nipped-in waists and rounded shoulder lines.' Princess Margaret, a subject of interest to her eager fans, had been given a private showing by Dior and wore the New Look to the celebrations for her parents' silver wedding anniversary.

Following the turmoil and sacrifices of the war, when concern with the frivolities of fashion had been unimaginable, the New Look affirmed optimism for the future and, although the profligate use of material proved impractical in daily life, it was a style that the bride-to-be embraced with enthusiasm. Although the daytime silhouette quickly segued into the more accommodating A-line and sheath dress, the wedding dress was the one gown for which a woman was prepared to suffer discomfort, generally preceded by a 'reducing' diet. The rounded shoulders, corseted waist and padded hips of the full skirts of the New Look became the paradigm of wedding-dress fashion. In an era when women were encouraged to leave their wartime jobs and return to homemaking and child bearing, the 'hourglass' figure – the all important ratio of waist size to breasts and hips – became representative of fecund femininity.

▶ Draped jersey
Densely pleated draped silk
jersey wedding gown in rose-
beige, dating from 1940. The
pompadour *chou* (a rosette)
holding the tulle veil in place is
influenced by the contemporary
high-fronted hairstyles.

Key looks
of the decade

1940s

Narrow silhouettes
With clothes rationing in full
force, the silhouette was naturally
narrow to conserve the costs
of fabric. The big-shouldered,
narrow-hipped shape also
reflected military styles.

V-shaped necklines
Wedding dresses were often
simple and practical, either
designed to double up as
daywear or homemade.
However, the slender satin
dress with a V-shaped
neckline covered with lace
or net became popular in the
later years of the decade.

▶ Wedding fashion shows
The increasing expansion of
the wedding industry included
the 'specialist wedding salon'
integrated into department
stores, with catwalk presentations
of the latest styles paraded to
prospective customers during
lunch or afternoon tea.

◀ Day dresses

Civil ceremonies became more acceptable during wartime and formal gowns were rarely worn or available. A day dress or two-piece 'costume' would be enlivened with a floral corsage, as worn for this wedding at London's Caxton Hall Registry Office in 1940.

Small bouquets

Due to the shortage of fresh flowers, bridal bouquets often took the form of small, round arrangements (also called 'ballerina' bouquets) composed of a central posy of a few fresh flowers encircled with tulle or net.

Bridal magazines

As post-war weddings began, once again, to be reported as important social events, society magazines such as *The Queen* increasingly featured the ceremonies and fashions of the era.

Veils and headpieces

The fashion was to wear the veil at the back of the head, either secured with an elaborate headdress and worn with an updo hairstyle, or as a short veil attached to a hat to complement a more austere wedding suit.

▲ Gathered sleeveheads

The squared-off shoulder – a gathered sleevehead formed over light padding – referenced the military uniform worn by women in the armed services.

1950s:
Silk, Satin and High Society

OPPOSITE *Vogue* customarily featured wedding fashions in the May and June editions of the magazine. This ivory satin wedding dress by British company Mercia, which cost just £29 at the time, has sleeves that can be removed to make a halterneck ball gown; the pageboy wears a hired Grenadier Guards uniform. Photograph by Norman Parkinson, 1952.

Following the exigencies of the Second World War, increasing prosperity throughout the 1950s made it possible for the 'dream' wedding to become a reality for nearly every woman. Prospective brides were inspired by the celebrity weddings of Hollywood royalty such as Elizabeth Taylor and Grace Kelly, whose dresses were designed by Hollywood costumier Helen Rose, purveyor of the 'Sweetheart' line.

As the decade progressed, wedding-dress design, though still rooted in tradition and retaining the vital components of train, veil and bouquet, began to acknowledge influences from high fashion. Modern brides were experimenting with different necklines, including the bateau, cut with a shallow curve across the collarbone to the same depth front and back, and shortening the skirt to ballerina length. Expensive dresses deployed the use of luxurious fabrics such as duchesse satin and lace, but with the development of synthetic fibres such as nylon, the ornate wedding dress became available to all and the first manufactured ready-to-wear dresses began rolling off the production line. In America, bridal fashion shows were immensely popular. These events, set up by department stores, featured a runway show, gift registry, men's department and houseware ideas to facilitate the bride on her way to the altar and beyond.

The Hourglass Silhouette

The heart-shaped bodice, corseted waist and full skirt of the Sweetheart line became a fashion staple for every-one, not just brides, during the 1950s. It formed the basic silhouette of the dress worn on the all-important American prom night, with cotton versions appearing as daywear in the form of the popular shirtwaist dress. This romantic look dominated the design of the wedding dress, and was underpinned by rigid corsetry, bras that moulded the breasts into points and layers of stiffened petticoats. It was in contrast to the increasing elegance of daywear, summed up by *Vogue* in the first month of the decade: 'Elegance postulates a rightness… a certain fastidious formality. It aspires toward the classic rather than the romantic. It is manifest in the line of the body, in the repose of the face.' The magazine went on to describe the 1950 body line: 'You see an unexaggerated bosom, a concave middle, a close hipline and a seemingly long leg.'

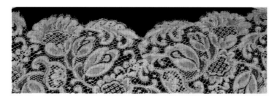

The era's cult of femininity required groomed glamour, which was expressed in waspie girdles, perfectly coiffed hair and a flawless maquillage. Various regulations on the etiquette of dress were touted by publications, and strict rules were put in place with regard to the choice of accessories. No woman went out without a hat and gloves, and shoes had to match the handbag. Although the look was ladylike, the hourglass figure could be exaggerated to stunning effect. Marilyn Monroe and Jane Russell sashayed their way to the altar in *Gentlemen Prefer Blondes* (1953), ending up in matching white-lace wedding gowns contoured to their spectacular figures.

During the years following the New Look, until his death a decade later, Christian Dior repeatedly changed the fashion silhouette, from the first revolutionary wasp-waisted collection in 1947 to the more wearable A-line of 1955, all of which were translated into wedding finery.

He recorded the rapid changes of the silhouette in his autobiography, *Dior by Dior* (1957):

In Spring 1948 came the 'Zig-zag' line, which gave the figure the animated look of a drawing. With winter, this tendency was confirmed by the 'Winged' line… The 'Midcentury' collection was very expert, and the collection of spring 1950 saw the triumph of the vertical line. Busts were narrowly moulded, waists well nipped-in and colours were clear like daylight.

Together with Hubert de Givenchy, Pierre Balmain and Cristobal Balenciaga, Dior was responsible for the flourishing post-war couture industry, supplying wedding gowns for the moneyed few and at the same time influencing the swiftly expanding ready-to-wear market.

OPPOSITE TOP LEFT A sample of guipure lace, a heavy, raised lace with an open background usually in large floral leaf patterns. The heavy stitching is embroidered onto paper (aetx cloth) that is then dissolved leaving the motifs to stand alone.

OPPOSITE, BELOW LEFT The bateau neckline became an increasingly popular alternative to the Sweetheart line. Here, it is formed by cutting into the guipure corded French lace of the bodice to form a scalloped edge. The skirt is of satin and ties in a bow at the back.

OPPOSITE RIGHT A fine example of the Sweetheart line, a heart-shaped form-fitting bodice combined with a full skirt. The decorous 1950s demanded that shoulders be covered; this net strapless dress with an embroidered front panel was designed to be worn with a cape, bolero or short jacket.

LEFT The padded hips of the New Look are combined with a small wing collar to provide the moulded bodice favoured by the contemporary bride, as is the newly bouffant veil. Photographed by Norman Parkinson for *Vogue* magazine in 1952.

Hollywood and Helen Rose

Hollywood costumier to the stars, Helen Rose, designer for more than 200 films for Metro-Goldwyn-Mayer and winner of two Oscars, made Dior's New Look her own when she introduced the Sweetheart line. It was first seen in a dress with a heart-shaped bodice with nipped-in waist and billowing skirt on Elizabeth Taylor in the film *Father of the Bride* (1950). The opening of the movie was released to coincide with Taylor's real-life wedding to hotel heir Conrad Hilton in 1950, a much publicized ceremony that was to be paid for by the MGM studio to whom Taylor was under contract, and for which Rose also designed the dress. Fifteen seamstresses took two months to complete the bridal gown, at a cost of $3,500. (According to Kitty Kelley in her biography, *Elizabeth Taylor: The Last Star* (1981), after the wedding MGM regretted their generosity and demanded the return of the dress and those of the bridesmaids.)

Consisting of 23 metres (25 yards) of shell-white satin embroidered with bugle beads and seed pearls, the dress had a 4.5 metre (15 foot) train of satin chiffon. Regardless of Taylor's desire for a plunging décolletage, Rose insisted that the heart-shaped bodice be covered with transparent lace up to the small, neat collar at the neck. Two double pleats of silk satin emphasized the famed embonpoint of the actress, forming a 'V' to match the V-shaped bodice. The veil, comprising 9 metres (10 yards) of silk illusion net, was secured with a Juliet cap covered in seed pearls. Followed up the yellow-carpeted aisle by six bridesmaids in daffodil-yellow chiffon, carrying huge bouquets of yellow tulips and daffodils, the double ring ceremony lasted 20 minutes and was followed by a lavish reception at the Bel-Air Country Club, with an elaborate five-tier wedding cake and a 120-cm (4-ft) ice sculpture of kissing doves.

BELOW Actress Elizabeth Taylor and her groom, Conrad 'Nicky' Hilton Jr, in the limousine that would take them to their wedding reception at the Bel-Air Country Club, following their marriage at the Church of the Good Shepherd in Beverly Hills, 1950.

Grace Kelly and Prince Rainier

Not only was she Hollywood royalty, when Grace Kelly married Rainier, Crown Prince of Monaco, in 1955, she became a real-life princess. Helen Rose was once again chosen to design the dress for a ceremony that combined a fairytale with Hollywood romance. The silhouette of the gown was suitably austere and, although the dress followed the Sweetheart line, the arch of the bodice beneath the lace is barely perceptible, and no flounces or ruffles marred the severity of the cut. The lavishness lay in the various textures of the luxurious fabrics. The subtle lustre of the skirt came from 23 metres (25 yards) of *eau de soie*, or 'skin of silk', a heavyweight smooth satin woven with an extremely fine ribbing. Ninety metres (98 yards) of tulle, 23 metres (25 yards) of silk taffeta and 275 metres (300 yards) of Valenciennes lace were also employed. The tightly fitting bodice of richly encrusted guipure lace was fastened with a row of tiny buttons from the pleated cummerbund at the waist to the stand-up collar. Together with the long, tight sleeves, the gown radiated an air of restrained yet regal glamour.

ABOVE Grace Kelly, pictured on her marriage to Prince Rainier of Monaco, wearing a dress designed by Hollywood costumier Helen Rose. A combination of luxurious textures, guipure and Valenciennes lace, heavyweight satin and tulle, the gown represented full-on 1950s glamour.

LEFT Prince Rainier III in full military finery and his bride, Princess Grace, on their wedding day in Monaco on 20 April 20, 1956.

Jacqueline Bouvier and John Fitzgerald Kennedy

As one of America's foremost and charismatic politicians, when John F Kennedy married Jacqueline Bouvier in 1953 the event was inevitably surrounded by intense publicity. The bride and her family wanted a sedate, quiet wedding but the groom's father, Joseph Kennedy, alert to the potential media coverage, intervened and 750 guests filed into the church for the nuptial mass, with 1,200 invited to the outdoor reception.

First introduced at a Georgetown dinner party in 1951, John F Kennedy and Jacqueline Bouvier saw each other frequently over the next two years. In June 1953, upon her return from Europe where she covered the Coronation of Queen Elizabeth for the *Washington Times-Herald*, Jacqueline accepted John F Kennedy's proposal of marriage. Jackie reputedly wanted an haute couture gown (her sister-in-law had married in Dior the previous year) but she was prevailed upon by her prospective husband to choose a more traditional dress. The gown required 45 m (50 yd) of ivory silk taffeta and took more than two months to make. It was the creation of Ann Lowe, an African-American dressmaker born in Grayton, Alabama, who had designed gowns for the matrons of a number of high-society families, including the du Pont, Lodge and Auchincloss families. Ms Lowe was 54 when she designed the Bouvier wedding dress, which featured a portrait neckline and bouffant skirt decorated with interwoven bands of tucking and tiny wax flowers.

THE ATTENDANTS

During the 1950s formal weddings required pageboys dressed in a kilt or a sailor suit, or even a miniature uniform such as that of a period Grenadier Guard, depending on the family tradition. Bridesmaids would be in ankle-length dresses, with small posies of flowers. For informal occasions and older attendants, short dresses that could be worn again were preferred. *Vogue* suggested various ideas for bridesmaids:

…several bridesmaids in white organdy with satin pumps dyed each in a different sugared-almond colour with matching satin sashes; different pastel-coloured tulle dresses, muted, unified by a top layer of grey chiffon. For a flock of white bridesmaids at an all-white wedding – caps of real ivy leaves, a trailing spray to carry, dark green strap sandals.

She also created the pink faille silk gowns and matching Tudor caps worn by the bridal attendants. According to her biographer, Kitty Kelley, Jackie later confided in her friend, the designer Carolina Herrera, that she hated the dress: 'the tight banding of the bodice emphasized her flat chest, and the circles of tucked taffeta on the skirt looked clumsy.'

The bride wore her grandmother's heirloom rose-point lace veil, attached to her hair with a small tiara of lace and traditional orange blossoms. She also wore a single strand of family pearls, a diamond leaf pin, which was a wedding present from Ambassador and Mrs Joseph P Kennedy, and a diamond bracelet that the groom had presented her with on the evening before the wedding. She carried a bouquet of white and pink spray orchids and gardenias. The engagement ring was from Van Cleef & Arpels and consisted of one 2.88 carat diamond mounted next to a 2.84 carat emerald with tapered baguettes. In 1962, the ring was reset to include round diamonds totalling .66 carats and marquise diamonds totalling 1.46 carats.

Following the 40-minute ceremony, at which a papal blessing was read, the new couple emerged into a throng of 3,000 wellwishers as they made their way by motorcycle escort to Hammersmith Farm, the Auchincloss estate overlooking Narragansett Bay. After two hours of greeting family and friends in a receiving line, the bridal couple joined the 1,200 invited guests for champagne and dancing to the music of Meyer Davis and his orchestra. For the first dance, the Kennedys chose 'I Married an Angel'. The couple cut a five-tier wedding cake, and then a luncheon of fruit cup, creamed chicken and ice cream sculpted to resemble roses was served.

RIGHT From her position on the stairs at Hammersmith Farm, Newport Rhode Island, where the reception was held, Jacqueline Bouvier Kennedy is captured by the photographer about to throw her bouquet of orchids and gardenias to the waiting guests.

OPPOSITE A bridal portrait of Jacqueline Bouvier (1929–94), the future First Lady, wearing a gown by American designer Ann Lowe for her wedding to John F Kennedy in 1953.

Modern Style

As the decade progressed, the Sweetheart line underwent subtle changes. The bridal gown was now frequently designed to be worn alone after the wedding as a strapless evening gown, with a cropped bolero-type jacket with three-quarter-length sleeves worn over the top for the ceremony itself. London court dressmaker Hardy Amies designed a wedding dress which was advertised as being dual purpose in 1950. 'Hope' had a strapless bodice, with lace bands appliquéd on the full organdy skirt, accessorized with a white lace jacket. *Vogue* reported in 1952 that 'it's a dying tradition, alas, that the bride wears her dress but once and puts it away for her daughter to wear,' and showed as an example a gown with detachable sleeves, the horseshoe collar forming the bodice of the ball gown.

The 1950s was an era in love with the hat and, as a result, the tiara became much less popular. Small saucer-shaped hats decorated with beading or flowers and worn low on the forehead, or a shaped band curving over the crown of the head from to ear to ear replaced it, although small bridal crowns were briefly fashionable following Queen Elizabeth's coronation in 1953. Veils were short and to the shoulder, described by *Vogue* as 'an abbreviated flare of white tulle'. A short-sleeved

gown would be accessorized with white doe-skin gloves extended over the elbow and crushed into pleats over the wrist. It was now customary to buy the engagement ring and the wedding ring together, an indissoluble pair. Constance Spry was still the society choice for flowers, with simple bouquets of lily of the valley and fern, or a single stem of Longi lily tied with white satin.

MENSWEAR

For formal weddings the morning suit was still *de rigueur*. The lounge suit was increasingly the favoured option, traditional in style and crafted by a personal tailor on Savile Row or bought from one of the multiple stores. Gregory Peck in the film *The Man in the Gray Flannel Suit* (1956) summed up the 1950s conformity in menswear design. For younger men, a new silhouette emerged in the middle of the decade influenced by Italian designers such as the Brioni brothers, who introduced a shorter, single-breasted jacket with a natural shoulder line worn with narrow, tapered trousers. The traditional wide tie was replaced with a narrow knitted one, often with horizontal stripes, and worn with a soft collared shirt. In the US, the 'Ivy league', with its roots in the collegiate system, also offered a slim silhouette, as seen in the two-button Brooks Brothers suit worn by a youthful President Kennedy as well as Frank Sinatra, Dean Martin and Peter Lawford, otherwise known as the infamous 'Rat Pack'.

BELOW A dual-purpose silk-satin halterneck wedding gown and ball gown designed by British dressmaker Hardy Amies. For the ceremony the arms would be covered by a matching bolero with three-quarter-length sleeves.

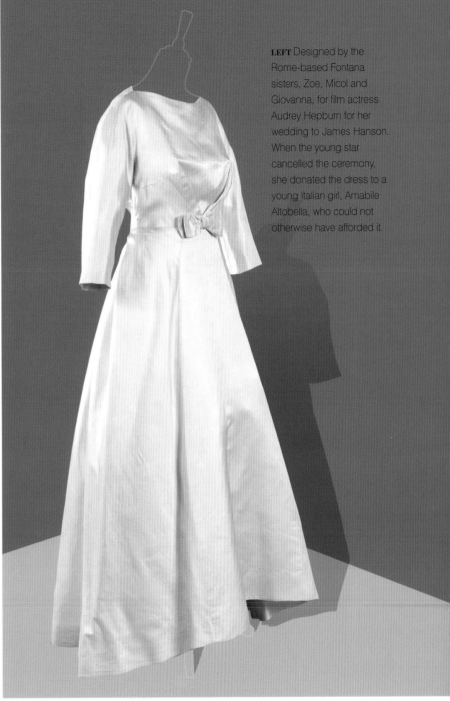

LEFT Designed by the Rome-based Fontana sisters, Zoe, Micol and Giovanna, for film actress Audrey Hepburn for her wedding to James Hanson. When the young star cancelled the ceremony, she donated the dress to a young Italian girl, Amabile Altobella, who could not otherwise have afforded it.

The silhouette of the wedding gown became less rigidly structured over the next few years, responding to changes in mainstream fashion. Although still tight on the bodice, the waistline dropped slightly, and the full skirts tended to be made from softer materials, tulle and chiffon replacing the ribbed silks and duchesse satin more commonly used during the earlier 1950s.

In 1954, Dior introduced a newly flattened bosom with the introduction of the 'Degas' line, which was cut to lie straight across the top of the breasts like a ballet tutu, and the 'Tudor' bodice, where the breasts swelled discreetly above it, both styles being influential on the design of wedding dresses. Skirts finished at mid-calf, or just below, in a swirl of chiffon, displaying Cuban- or kitten-heeled shoes with a rounded toe in a style popularized by shoe designer Roger Vivier. Actress Audrey Hepburn epitomized the ballerina-style dress in the film *Funny Face* (1957), wearing it on a modelling shoot, dancing in the grounds of a church as she waits for her prospective beau, played by Fred Astaire. The 'bateau' neckline worn by the waif-like Hollywood star was designed by her favourite couturier Hubert de Givenchy (although Edith Head was given screen credit for the clothes) to hide the hollowness of her collar-bones. The dress was simple and modern, unlike the one Hepburn had worn previously for her own wedding to fellow actor Mel Ferrer in 1954. Designed by French couturier Pierre Balmain, the gown had a high stand-up collar and billowing sleeves gathered into the elbow that swamped her tiny figure. It came to mid-calf and was fitted in the bodice with a wide sash and a centre-front fastening of tiny buttons. On Hepburn's gamine hairstyle was perched a coronet of real roses.

The popularity of the daytime cocktail dress, less formal than a dinner dress, and worn in response to the burgeoning popularity of the cocktail party, influenced the style of wedding gowns. Short sleeves were just becoming acceptable, although it wasn't until the next decade that entirely sleeveless gowns were deemed appropriate. Couturiers such as Balenciaga introduced tunic tops over long, straight skirts and popularized the three-quarter-length sleeve, eventually introducing the 'chemise', or sack dress, in 1957. The Empire line, in which the waistline is elevated to just below the breast, was introduced in 1958, providing a youthful, *ingénue* silhouette that would become the dominant shape of the 1960s and pave the way for a complete change in wedding style.

ABOVE LEFT Audrey Hepburn (1929–93) on her marriage to Mel Ferrer in 1954, wearing a gown designed by Parisian couturier Pierre Balmain.

ABOVE AND RIGHT Hardy Amies uses an all-over lace with a raised metallic gold thread for a wedding gown that features long, fitted sleeves fastened with rouleau loops on the wrist. The skirt is cut in panels from the waist seam, resulting in a smooth line over the hips and fullness at the hem.

OPPOSITE, TOP RIGHT AND DETAIL
A classic 1950s silk dress with a wide, shallow neckline and darted waistline, embroidered with a leaf and flower design in pearls, seed pearls and gold sequins on a cream background.

TYPES OF NECKLINE

Bateau: Worn by Audrey Hepburn in *Funny Face* (1957), the bateau neckline is cut straight across the collarbone to the same depth at the front and back of the dress and opens one inch in from each shoulder.

Fichu: Constructed from a frilled fichu, which is then gathered into a point at the top of the breasts. This neckline was a feature of the wedding dress worn by Lady Diana Spencer on her wedding to Prince Charles in 1981.

Halterneck: This wedding-gown neckline features straps that wrap around the back of the neck, leaving the shoulders and arms bare.

Horseshoe: A U-shaped wide band that forms a halterneck and meets under the bust, enclosing a low-cut bodice of lace or other material.

Jewel: A plain, round neckline, the jewel collar is used as a base to showcase some exceptional jewellery.

Off the shoulder: This falls below the shoulders with a small sleeve on the arm. The bodice needs to be self-supporting with this style, which often includes a gusset under the arms to hold the sleeves in place.

One shoulder/Asymmetric: Popular in the twenty-first century, this is a gown with a single strap or an asymmetric neckline.

Portrait: A collar that frames the bride's neck and shoulders, as seen in Jacqueline Bouvier's dress on her wedding to John F Kennedy in 1953.

Queen Anne: This features a high collar at the back and sides of the neck, slowly curving down into a low, open heart-shaped neckline.

Scoop neck: Features a low, U-shaped neckline.

Square neck: A neckline shaped like a half square.

Strapless Simply a bodice, self-supporting and heavily boned, this style leaves the neck and shoulders entirely bare. It is often worn beneath a small bolero or short jacket for the ceremony.

Sweetheart: Popularized by Hollywood costumier Helen Rose in the 1950s, this neckline follows the line of the top of the breasts, above a tight bodice. Universally flattering, it has become a classic. It can be partnered with an Illusion neckline, as was the case with Elizabeth Taylor's wedding dress in 1950, when a transparent lace, chiffon or net fills the gap between the bodice and the neck.

V-neck: Can be wide or narrow, and can apply to the front and the back of the dress. The line of the 'V' can also be extended to the waistline, making the waist look narrower.

Wedding band collar: Popular in the 1890s when the high fitted collar would be boned to keep upright. It was a shape also popular in the 1970s with the revival in Victorian-style wedding dresses.

RIGHT AND ABOVE DETAILS
An all-over lace wedding gown with pointed bodice, echoing the V-shaped neckline and worn over a silk-satin underskirt. The lace is scalloped at the neck and hem, while the sleeves are to angle over the hand.

TOP LEFT AND RIGHT
A romantic, medieval-style dress and train by Parisian couturier Balmain from 1954, appropriately modelled on the bank of the river across from Notre Dame Cathedral. The unusual oval-shaped train is bordered with a frill and attached to the peplum at the back of the skirt. A flowing train from the high headpiece emphasizes the gown's medieval quality.

FAR LEFT Designed by Balmain in 1950, this gown features a gathered tulle collar brought together with a textile rose.

LEFT Dramatic folds of heavy silk satin are gathered each side of the skirt and secured with a flat bow in this 1951 Balmain dress. The grown-on collar and semi set-in sleeves create a moulded bodice.

PIERRE BALMAIN
COUTURE

LEFT Another ingénue style from Balmain dating from 1956. The bodice is gathered into the high waist of the dress and around the neckline to form puff sleeves, with the train attached to the shoulders of the gown.

TOP LEFT Creating volume at the back of the dress for dramatic effect up the aisle, the fullness of this skirt forms a tie at the back, which then extends into a train. Designed by Balmain in 1952, the V-shaped bodice is accentuated by the high, turn-back collar.

ABOVE A softer and more youthful silhouette from Balmain in this wedding gown dating from spring 1955, with the crinoline skirt banded with a deep, fine-pleated frill, edged with small textile flowers. The bodice is informal with short, set-in sleeves and a round neck, decorated with the same flowers as the hem.

LEFT A duchesse satin bridal gown by Norman Hartnell dating from 1950 marks the beginning of a decade in which the bridal gown plays centre stage and the wedding ceremony achieves a new importance. The silk tulle overdress is appliquéd with satin flowers around the neck and skirt.

RIGHT A duchesse satin wedding gown by Norman Hartnell dating from 1957, with curved, piped inserts of beaded and sequinned embroidery extending to form the collar of the dress and appearing to create a large bow with the ends emerging from a satin insert on the bodice.

The Trousseau

The trousseau was still a requisite of the bride-to-be, but by the 1950s it was neither as extensive nor as all encompassing as it had been in the past, as confirmed by _Vogue_ in 1951:

> _A trousseau for today can no longer boast a "dozen of everything"… Seal of success: a few good accessories in black and white are all you need, plus a single topcoat. Pack your matching luggage, durable and light, for a porter-scarce Europe, and you're off – the world at your feet._

It was the era of many underpinnings. Bras were rigid in construction, circular cups had rows of stitching to reinforce the cone-shape and there were no deviations such as half-cups or balconettes. The new satinized Lastex – 'a fitting yarn for the finest foundations' – was now dyed to make corsets in both pastels and strong, bright colours such as yellow, jade and crimson, but they were still substantial garments. There was a clear differentiation between underwear and lingerie. Petticoats were simple and plain to keep a smooth line under clothes, the more expensive ones in crepe de chine. A more sensual experience was offered by Frederick's of Hollywood, established in 1946 by ex-GI Frederick Mellinger, whose strapline stated 'We not only dress Hollywood legends, we create them'. Mellinger invented the first push-up bra, the 'rising star'. Italian company La Perla, founded by Ada Masotti in 1954, also purveyed luxury handcrafted lingerie including teddies, slips and peignoirs.

Going-away clothes achieved a new significance as honeymoons were now frequently taken abroad. In contrast to the full-skirted New Look, Chanel – who had reopened her fashion house in 1954 – continued to design classic two-piece suits with a collarless edge-to-edge jacket and a narrow A-line skirt to the knee, made out of heavily textured tweeds. Easy-to-wear, with a multiplicity of copies on the market, the Chanel suit was an invaluable element of the bride's trousseau. The silhouette was evolving into a longer, leaner line and the moulded midriff was an influential element of all the collections of the Parisian couturiers, such as Dior and Jacques Fath. Hats were a vital element of the going-away outfit. _Vogue_ lists, as the 'prettiest hats in years' in 1953, 'the boat-shaped straw, the topless fez, the chin-tied pill-box, the back-tilted toque, the undulating cartwheel, and a coarse straw hat, the coal-heave, with an undulating brim.'

Trousseau Specialists

This charming Nightdress is an example of several specially designed for your trousseau—expressed in white pure silk Georgette and blue lace

PRICE £17·15·0

Lingerie—Second Floor

LANgham 4444 (Debenhams Ltd.) **Debenham & Freebody** WIGMORE STREET, LONDON, W.1

36

THE QUEEN, MARCH 15, 1950

ABOVE A 1950s advertisement for a nightdress specifically designed as part of a wedding trousseau. The ruched bodice and softly gathered skirt are in white silk georgette and blue lace. Available from the London department store, Debenham & Freebody.

The American Bridal Salon

The USA turned its vast resources from the war effort to addressing the consumer economy and increasing productivity in all aspects of the American way of life. As the deferred weddings of wartime and the immediate post-war years were finally undertaken, the wedding ceremony became big business. The majority of bridal gowns were now manufactured by specialist producers, which involved a visit to a shop rather than a dressmaker for fittings. A store within a store, the bridal salon was a commercial venture operated by department stores, but disguised as a social occasion. Uniformed attendants served the bride and her mother tea or lunch in luxurious surroundings, while various dresses were displayed or modelled well away from the bustle of other shoppers in the store. Furnished with sofas, tables, desks and chandeliers, the salon purported to replicate the experience of buying haute couture, with the event mediated through the bridal-gown specialist rather than the *vendeuse*. Some stores had limited stock, as bridal gowns required considerable storage space, so a Bridal Book illustrating the available designs would be on hand.

If the gown was readymade, it was ordered in the correct size and minor adjustments made. Wedding bureaux provided a one-stop service covering all aspects of the ceremony and the reception, a collaborative endeavour by various departments and staff. The inevitable result was a standardization of style, both in the dresses themselves and the ceremony. The department store provided a variety of props such as lamps, platforms, candlesticks and rugs, which appeared at every wedding. An example of the commercialization of the wedding industry is the description of the 'Lowenstein Catering Company's number one wedding' in Herman Wouk's 1955 novel, *Marjorie Morningstar*:

> There was a choir of five bell-voiced boys
> in white silk robes and white hats with white
> pompoms. There was a broad canopy of
> white lilies on a platform entirely carpeted
> and walled with greenery and white roses.
> There were blazing blue-white arc lights, a
> movie photographer, and a still-photographer.
> There was a rose-strewn staircase for her to
> descend; there was a quite meaningless but
> quite gorgeous archway with gates at the head
> of the staircase, covered and festooned with
> pink roses, through which she was to make her
> entrance. There were banks of gold chairs, five
> hundred of them, jammed solid with guests,
> and with spectators who had read
> the announcement in The Times *and knew*
> the bridegroom or the bride. After the
> ceremony there was as much champagne
> as anyone could drink; and as many hot
> hors d'oeuvres as the greediest guest could
> stuff into himself. There was to be a ten-course
> dinner, beginning with imported salmon,
> featuring rare roast beef, and ending in
> flaming Cherries Jubilee. There was to be
> a seven-piece orchestra, more champagne,
> a midnight supper, and dancing till dawn.

The wedding ceremony, operated as big business, was fuelled by various organizations such as the National Bridal Service (NBS), founded in 1951 by jeweller Jerry Connor. The first organization in the country to train bridal consultants, the NBS eventually expanded into a division called 'Weddings Beautiful' in 1954, which included freelance wedding planners not associated with particular retailers.

LEFT *Modern Brides* model, American Martha Boss, modelling her own bridal gown in 1952. The small bouquet is in keeping with the youthful, simple square-necked dress and face-framing lace veil with a scalloped edge.

OPPOSITE A model wears the latest New York bridal fashions of 1953. Rather than a tiara or a wreath of blossom, the 1950s bride often chose to wear a hat, here seen securing the short, bouffant veil. 'The shorter the veil, the smaller the bouquet' was a rule to balance the silhouette.

The Rock 'n' Roll Wedding

In opposition to the prevailing ethos of sophisticated daywear, youth movements, involving the newly emerging teenager, rejected the sartorial and social aspirations of their parents for a unique style of their own, which included a new musical phenomenon: rock 'n' roll. From the beginning, the musical genre had been viewed with suspicion, the phrase rock'n'roll being a euphemism for sexual activity in black American nightclubs long before it became associated with music. Elvis Presley burst on to the scene in the early 1950s with network television appearances, causing outrage with his youthful gyrations. 'Heartbreak Hotel' in 1956 was his first number-one hit and in November of that year he made his film debut in *Love Me Tender*. Outfitted at Memphis store Lansky for much of his performing life, Presley popularized a version of the 'zoot' suit, an exaggeratedly loose suit associated with jazz musicians, made by the tailoring brothers. For his television debut in 1956, he performed 'Shake, Rattle and Roll' and 'I Got a Woman' wearing a black shirt, white tie and sports coat. The American teenager wore her hair in a ponytail, Tangee lipstick and rolled-up jeans with bobby socks and saddle shoes, while her boyfriend imitated Brando and James Dean in a black leather motorcycle jacket.

Meanwhile, in Britain, young working-class men adopted a style of dress that was a pastiche of Edwardian tailoring from Savile Row, combined with the influence of the American zoot suit. Their girlfriends frenziedly backcombed their hair into beehives, a neat dome sometimes reaching 15 centimetres (6 inches) high, sprayed into a solid helmet with a shellac-based substance called 'lacquer'. Embroidered peasant-style blouses or tight figure-hugging sweaters were worn with cropped 'Capri' pants or a full, mid-calf dirndl or circular skirt, often decorated with an appliquéd poodle, which implied European sophistication. The full skirts were supported by layers of nylon net, or a 'paper' nylon that was stiffened with starch to hold its shape. Eventually a hoop crinoline petticoat was developed, which had channelled tapes threaded with nylon boning in imitation of whalebone petticoats.

Stiletto heels with pointed 'winklepicker' toes were worn with nylon stockings. Seamless stockings were introduced in Britain in 1952, but most women preferred the seamed variety as they were fashioned to fit the shape of the leg rather than steamed into shape.

The rock'n'roll look was interpreted on the wedding day by a short bouffant veil that allowed full height to the hair, with a single rose positioned at the front of the head replacing the tiara or circle of flowers. The groom would sport a DA with his Teddy boy suit: heavily pomaded long hair that was slicked back to form a 'duck's arse' at the back. Jerry Lee Lewis, an American rock 'n' roll singer known as 'the killer', provided the inspiration. He played his classic worldwide hits 'Whole Lotta Shakin' Goin' On' and 'Great Balls Of Fire' on a frenetic boogie woogie piano while standing up, often with one foot on the keyboard. For the singer's marriage (his third) to Myra Brown in 1957, he wore a black suit with leopard-print lapels and pocket flaps; his underage bride wore a neat suit with a small, shaped hat.

BELOW The boned bodice is shaped by three darts and three tiers of spangled scalloped lace are supported by layers of stiffened petticoats in this prom-style dress.

BELOW AND DETAIL LEFT
A prom-style sleeveless wedding dress with a two-tiered lace skirt with scalloped edges, a dropped V-shaped waist and a bateau neckline formed by further lace edging decorated with beading.

COSMETICS

During the 1950s women were admonished not to 'let themselves go', otherwise their man would look elsewhere, which would undermine the whole concept of the nuclear family. It was a woman's duty to put her husband first. Thomas Hine, in his book *Populuxe* (1988), recounts the comments of Mrs Dale Carnegie writing in *Better Homes and Gardens* in 1955:

> The two big steps that women must take are to help their husbands decide where they are going and use their pretty heads to help them get there… Let's face it girls. That wonderful guy in your house – and in mine – is building your house, your happiness and the opportunities that will come to your children.

As such, the wedding was increasingly seen as a passport to respectable suburban wifedom, now considered a full-time job. Cosmetics were a vitally important part of the ritual of being a 1950s woman. The bride would be unlikely to wear, as described by Lindy Woodhead in her book, *War Paint* (2003), the 'Rivers of blood-coloured lipstick and nail polish [that] flowed between Arden, Rubinstein and Revlon in the first half of the 1950s'. Brides were encouraged to be 'natural' on their wedding day, but the going-away outfit demanded dramatic make-up such as that worn by model Dorian Leigh in the Revlon advertising campaign 'Fire and Ice' in 1952. Wearing a Balenciaga-inspired cape falling from one naked shoulder and nails painted a fiery red, the strapline to the press advertisements read, 'Are you made for fire and ice?'; Rubenstein countered with 'Playing with fire, bright-as-blazes lipstick colour'. Nails were polished, leaving the tips and the half-moon unpainted.

Good grooming included a discreet scent. The French couture house Nina Ricci launched its celebrated scent L'Air du Temps in 1948, a light, romantic fragrance popular with the 1950s bride. Hair was cropped into the 'poodle' cut, a style favoured by Elizabeth Taylor and Doris Day. For the more sophisticated, hair was worn in a French pleat. Women now included a weekly visit to the hairdresser for a professional wash and set, and the perm was a popular option. Brides were also advised to take their headdress to the hairdresser, so that the hairstyle could be adjusted accordingly.

Ready-to-Wear

For those brides unable to afford the bespoke wedding dress, the department stores offered a ready-to-wear service. London's Debenham & Freebody had its 'Gainsborough Room', while Harrods and Marshall & Snelgrove both had a bridal salon. *Vogue* regularly provided lists of dressmakers and fabric suppliers for the prospective bride, bringing out a specialist *Brides* magazine in 1957. Ready-to-wear was an increasingly available option as specialist wedding manufacturers such as Pronuptia emerged.

Pronuptia

With the strapline, 'Pronuptia the Love Brand', the French bridalwear company has been supplying the prospective bride and her attendants with middle-to-top-end bridalwear since their inauguration in 1958. Founded by Marie and Henry Micmacher in Paris in response to the success of similar enterprises in America, the design partnership recognized a niche in the European market for ready-to-wear bridal gowns following the post-war boom in weddings. Pronuptia allowed women a choice, enabling them to refuse the hand-me-down dress that so many had been grateful for during the war and post-war eras, when luxurious fabrics were scarce and the closest they got to it was recycled parachute silk.

Targeted at those brides who could not afford made-to-measure gowns, Pronuptia was eager to replicate the same personal service offered by haute couture with the purchase of a mass-produced dress, providing the customer with a personal stylist who remained with her from the initial viewing right through to the wedding day itself, if required.

During the 1950s the brand exploited the new fabrics being developed out of the petrochemical industry, particularly nylon and polyester. Gowns were initially shown to the bride-to-be 'off-the-peg' or viewed through large-scale, photo albums, with the stylist on hand to offer advice. Once the choice was made, measurements were taken and the dress sent for alterations, with a final appointment for the fitting of the finished dress.

The first of many franchises, in 1962 the Pronuptia brand expanded outside of France, opening an outlet in Brussels, followed by branches in other parts of Europe, the USA and Canada. In 1983 the company launched eveningwear and cocktail dress collections. Parisian couturier Jean-Paul Gaultier was invited to collaborate with the brand in 1987, as was Christian Lacroix in 1999.

Recognizing that most men were unlikely to spend a similar amount to the bride on their look for the day, in 1996 the company began to offer morning suits and pageboy outfits for hire. Following a drop in sales in 2008, Pronuptia filed for bankruptcy and was bought out by the French company, Nuptialliance.

Synthetic Fabrics

Many of the new synthetics of the era were synthesized from petrochemicals. They were promoted for their easy-care, wash-and-wear qualities – 'It's a new age in nylon, no ironing, no mending, no wilting' – which often meant a quick rinse and drip dry. However, wedding gowns made from synthetic fibres were considered inferior and, although nylon (polyamide), crimplene (polyester) and orlon (acrylic/polyacrylonitrile) tended not to crease the way that natural fibres did and, unlike nylon, polyester didn't yellow with age, synthetics were only used for mass-produced dresses as they proved sweaty and uncomfortable. In 1957, Lurex was first marketed, often combined with other fibres, including a form of nylon, as in this advert for 'shimmering Ban-Lon nylon brocade touched with gold and silver Lurex'. Machine-made lace was a success story; in cotton or a polyester cotton mix, it was crisp and affordable. Handmade lace was out of the question, pricewise, for most brides.

BELOW Figured silk-satin dress with boat-shaped neckline and elbow-length sleeves, photographed by Norman Parkinson for the cover of the popular *Brides* magazine, 1957. Specialist publications for the prospective bride flourished during this era, as weddings became increasingly commercialized.

ABOVE A draped wedding dress by British ready-to-wear label Frank Usher. The company opened its first showrooms in the mid-1950s and many of the dresses were featured in *Vogue* magazine. The label became famous for its sophisticated and glamorous formalwear.

RIGHT A nylon wedding dress made by upmarket London store Harrods. Nylon had none of its later connotations of cheapness and was considered a wonder fabric when it first permeated the market, advertised as easy to launder, noncreasing and light to wear.

▶ Lacy tiers

Influenced by the all-over lace bodice of the gown worn by film star Grace Kelly on her marriage to Crown Prince Rainier of Monaco in 1956, the material proved a popular choice for many brides, particularly layered into tiers of flouncy frills.

▼ Short veils and skirts

As hemlines headed upward, the veil became shorter and more bouffant, changing the sweeping silhouette of the traditional bride for one of contemporary modern glamour, as in this dress dating from 1958. The short skirt shows off the new-style shoe, the stiletto.

Key looks of the decade

1950s

◀ Bridal jackets

The versatile dual-purpose wedding dress and ballgown appeared in the 1950s, as seen here in a feature from American fashion magazine *Harper's Bazaar*. The jacket or bolero was removed after the ceremony for an evening of dancing.

The V-shaped waist

Extending the line of the bodice into a 'V' lengthens the torso and narrows the waist. Designed by John Cavanagh in pure white duchesse silk satin in 1955, the skirt of this dress is draped into the waist seam to provide fullness on the hips. The headdress by Simone Mirman is a bandeau of white satin with bows.

The Sweetheart line

Hollywood's version of the New Look, the Sweetheart line, was designed by Helen Rose, costumier to the stars and wedding-dress designer of both Elizabeth Taylor and Grace Kelly. The fitted heart-shaped bodice emphasized the waist and was attached to a full skirt.

Bridal gloves

Gloves were worn everywhere in the 1950s, and often paired with short-sleeved or sleeveless gowns for an elegant look. Bridal gloves were available in opera, elbow and wrist lengths, and in tulle, lace or satin, and in a fingerless form.

Ballerina-length dresses

Emulating the New Look silhouette, the 1950s wedding dress was often in the shorter ballerina-length style, just above the ankle, with a circular skirt and stiff petticoats.

Saucer hats and bands

Hats were a vital accessory during the lady-like 1950s, particularly the forward-tilting saucer shape worn low on the forehead. The style influenced the design of the bridal headdress, evident in this wedding ensemble featured in *Harper's Bazaar*.

RONALD PATERSON chooses embroidered organdie for this lovely b

1960s:
Demoiselles and Dandies

OPPOSITE Innovative pattern-cutting constructs a unique combination of Bertha collar and veil, rendered even more unusual by the feathered lining in this photograph by John French for the *Daily Mirror* in 1964.

In the decade of moon boots and the mini, some brides still opted for the traditional wedding gown: full-skirted, with long pointed sleeves and a tightly fitting bodice, in classic materials such as duchesse satin and lace. Even the traditional gown, however, was subject to the fluctuations of contemporary fashion. On her marriage to Anthony Armstrong-Jones in 1960, Princess Margaret, Queen Elizabeth's sister, wore an unadorned wedding gown that reflected the encroaching minimalistic approach to fashion, even though designed by court dressmaker and master of embellishment Norman Hartnell. The bodice was moulded to fit the Princess's tiny, exquisite form by incorporating the stand-up collar and semi-inset sleeves into the bodice. The skirt lengthened into a train at the back, with a waterfall of tulle for the veil. This was one of the last occasions when royal guests were obliged to wear long dresses for a morning ceremony.

The popularity of the sheath dress, first mooted by Parisian couturier Cristobal Balenciaga, did not translate well into bridalwear, but the high-waisted Empire-line styles that followed, which became ever shorter as the decade progressed, imparted an ingénue quality in keeping with the times. Mary Quant was purveying her schoolgirl chic, young girls were known as 'dollybirds' and the 'youthquake' resonated throughout the major fashion capitals of Paris, London and New York. By the 'summer of love' in 1968, the prospective bride had rejected the traditional option, choosing instead to wear a wedding dress that was more in keeping with her own personal style. Many subscribed to alternative culture by resolutely defying convention and wearing an assortment of eclectic garments for the ceremony. Afghan coats, Victorian piano shawls, panne velvet maxiskirts, kaftans, beads and feathers were all mixed with vintage finds from grandmother's attic or from the proliferation of antique markets.

New Departures

Spare, streamlined styles heralded the beginning of the 1960s, a time of looking forward to a future free of constraints: sexually, socially and in fashion. The scaffolding that underpinned the 1950s silhouette was discarded in favour of simple shift dresses that skimmed the body and ended abruptly mid-thigh. For the first time, fashion was being designed, made and sold by the young, for the young, in the newly proliferating boutiques. *Vogue* asked in April 1960, 'What is the Young Idea? Youth's at the prow this summer: setting its own brisk pace in fashion and enthusiasms'. Mary Quant, Foale & Tuffin, John Bates, Gerald McCann and later, Barbara Hulanicki of Biba, were the new fashion entrepreneurs, aided by visionary retailers such as Vanessa Denza of the 21 Shop at London's Woollands department store. Initially, America showed some resistance to Britain's 'youthquake', until fashion buyer Paul Young set up the legendary boutique Paraphernalia in New York and Tiger Morse opened her boutique Teeny Weeny, selling paper

dresses and silver boots. The US fashion establishment, however, considered the Mod look to be an essentially teenage phenomenon, a short-lived look that only impacted on the major urban cities. The generation gap was never more evident than when choosing a wedding dress. *Homes and Gardens* columnist Verity Lambert described the increasing difference in expectations between the bride's mother and her daughter in 1966:

I set off round the shops in advance to see what this season's bride will be wearing. What an eye-opener it is to the uninitiated to find so much space set apart in so many of the big stores for brides! Row upon row of brocade, satin, net, lace and all kinds of white gowns with and without trains waiting to be chosen. White dust sheets are continually being spread upon the carpet for dresses to be tried on with their trains laid out behind them. After several visits I am still trying to persuade her to try on just one of those wedding dresses. 'It would take ten years off my life', she whispers, appalled by what she sees. After many visits she settles for six yards of silk tulle, and only enough white cotton curtain lace to make a skin-tight dolly-rocker, 'for some little woman to make up something really with it'. But what little woman will make anything up that has been left so late? Only one, and down she goes on her hands and knees on the drawing-room floor to cut out her daughter's with-it white curtain lace dolly-rocker.

Couture or bespoke versions of the mini wedding dress were appearing, inspired by the architectural lines of the 'Space Age' collection of 1964 by Parisian couturier André Courrèges. These were constructed from heavily textured fabrics in dazzling white, the concise lines standing away from the contours of the body. White was also the colour of the newly invented tights/pantyhose that were marketed in 1966, and which allowed hemlines to rise even further than 'the 16 inches from the ground' as in a 1961 Wolsey advert for stockings: 'Sheathe those attention-getting 16 inches in the sheer delight of Wolsey nylons and you're sure of being as up to the minute as the Greenwich Time signal.'
Often lacy or patterned, the tights were worn with flat white shoes. Sara Davidson, chronicler of the era in her book *Loose Change*, wore 'a white knit mini-dress, white tights and white pumps, and carried a bouquet of yellow roses' for her wedding in 1966. Her hair had been cut by Jacqueline Kennedy's hairdresser Kenneth Battelle, but the writer rushed home and combed out the 'fixed little spit curls, "tendrils" he called them' for a more natural look.

LEFT Designed by John Bates for his Jean Varon label, this white cotton gabardine and silver vinyl coat and dress was commissioned by influential *Vogue* fashion journalist Marit Allen for her own wedding in 1966.

OPPOSITE Disposable fashion: a white plasticized paper wedding dress designed by James Sterling, with frilled nylon lace cap sleeves. The central panel of faux plastic lace is reminiscent of the wipe-clean plastic tablecloths of the era.

OPPOSITE, FAR RIGHT 'Space Age' fashion from André Courrèges and Paco Rabanne influenced wedding attire, as seen here in this cropped futuristic bridal tunic-dress of chain-mail-effect embroidery by Parisian couturier Guy Laroche, worn with a matching helmet and boots.

Jackie Kennedy also wore a white minidress for her marriage to Greek shipping tycoon Aristotle Onassis in 1968. The ivory gown was not specifically designed as a wedding dress, but appeared in the summer collection of Jackie's favourite couturier of the period, Italian-born Valentino. The demure high-necked dress with scallops of lace inserts across the bodice had matching lace sleeves with long, narrow pearl-buttoned cuffs and a pleated georgette skirt. It was accessorized with a simple bow of white ribbon in her bouffant hair and cream moiré shoes designed by Dal Co for Valentino. Her two wedding dresses, worn with little more than a decade apart, defined the difference in style between the two eras.

Diane von Furstenberg, designer of the iconic wrap dress, wore a gown designed by Marc Bohan for Christian Dior for her wedding to Prince Eduardo Egon von und zu Furstenberg in 1969, which combined the two styles: the formality of an ankle-length gown but worn with a broad-brimmed straw hat with flowers and ribbon streamers. The long frilled skirt had an overskirt of lace embroidered daisies, a flower that came to represent the simplicity and stylization of 1960s fashion. The daisy, with its simple, many-petalled shape and yellow, sun-like heart, is the most long-lasting of wildflowers and is also known as the marguerite (or ox-eye daisy) when garden bred. Used in bouquets at the time, it also proliferated on bonnets, was transformed into jewellery and became the trademark of British designer Mary Quant.

RIGHT AND DETAIL ABOVE
The strapless guipure lace bodice of this cocktail-inspired wedding dress by Christian Dior is encrusted with gemstones. The tulip-shaped skirt is gathered onto the waist, to fall just below the knee.

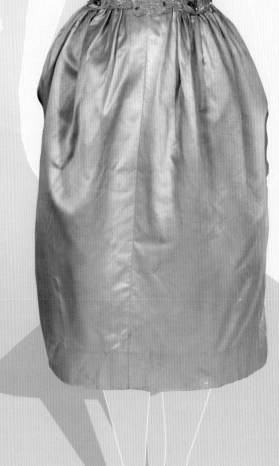

LEFT From Italian couturier Valentino's 1968 spring–summer collection, this silk crepe-de-chine cream minidress, with lace inserts and a small funnel collar, is identical to the one worn by Jacqueline Kennedy for her wedding to Aristotle Onassis in June 1968.

Trains and Veils

With the increase in secular weddings, and in keeping with the simplicity of the silhouette, wedding trains became unfashionable during the 1960s, as did the huge importance placed on the back view of the gown. The view from the steps of a registry office was not the same as that inside a church, as the bride makes her way up the aisle. The veil too was becoming something of an anachronism: the bouffant, back-combed hairstyle of the early 1960s demanded a short, bouffant veil, often secured with a single rose at the front. However, as young women began to adopt one of the sleek, severe geometric styles inspired by Vidal Sassoon, the veil became impractical.

Architect of the five-point cut, the hairdresser explained the style's origins to Marilyn Bender in her book, *The Beautiful People* (1967):

'The Sassoon cut is a matter of evolution, not revolution,' the creator maintains. 'I worked very hard at developing a line. First I took the back and made it short, then gradually longer in front.' Mary Quant asked him to fix the hair of her mannequins so as not to interfere with the high collars she was showing in her collection. 'All I really did was take the pageboy and reverse it, giving elegance to the neck.'

BELOW Photographed by Norman Parkinson for *Vogue* magazine in 1960, this duchesse satin wedding dress is darted into a waist-cinching silhouette, emphasized by the large-scale pleats on the hips. In contrast, the veil is a froth of tulle, attached to a saucer-shaped headdress.

OPPOSITE A hint of formality with a return to the tiara. British-born couturier Sir Edwin Hardy Amies photographs his wedding creations in 1960: one with a full-skirted silhouette and boned, strapless bodice, the other a more contemporary sheath dress, pulled in at the waist with two open darts.

RIGHT Heavy white moiré silk is sculpted into a high-waisted wedding dress and attached train. The inverted pleats are caught with a self-fabric belt decorated with a flat bow from Victor Stiebel's final collection for spring/summer 1963.

Babydolls and Empire Lines

The streamlined mini wedding dress evolved into the 'babydoll' style: a softer, high-waisted silhouette constructed from girlish, pretty materials such as broderie anglaise and spotted cotton with a scalloped hem and cuffs. Even cheesecloth, an inexpensive almost transparent textured cotton muslin, was used. In May 1963, *Vogue* declared, 'The new line is a high line, fresh as baby's first dress but sharp, cool and sophisticated. Ravishing for anyone young and slim... The simple milkmaid looks of the newest wedding dresses look younger than ever: almost like bridesmaid's dresses'.

The youthful bride also wore a child-like flower-strewn bonnet with ribbon ties, or a triangular lace-trimmed headscarf, tied underneath the hair at the back of the head, which *Vogue* described as 'the peasant headscarf that's really nurse's gear', or under the chin as worn by Audrey Hepburn for her marriage to Dr Andrea Dotti in 1969. The high-waisted minidress worn by the actress had long sleeves that ended in a fluted frill and Givenchy's signature stand-away collar. In pale pink, the dress epitomized ingénue wedding style. The bride carried a simple bunch, rather than a formal bouquet, of flowers (see page 123).

The major shoe manufacturers of the time were still producing stilettos or kitten heels with pointed toes for women who were reluctant to embrace the one-inch low-heeled Pilgrim-buckle pump initially designed by Roger Vivier in the previous decade. The 'switched-on' bride bought tap shoes from London-based theatrical costumiers, Anello and Davide. These 'Mary Janes' had

a strap across the instep, a small square heel and round toe, and could be bought in satin or leather and dyed any colour. The bouquet was also simple and unpretentious in style, a small sculptural circle of blooms held together with ribbon, or simply a handful of daisies. Jewellery was conspicuous by its absence; too much jewellery was considered ageing and bourgeois, and the double-ring ceremony was no longer as popular.

Smock tops with a softly gathered skirt, puff sleeves and Peter Pan collars rendered the young bride waif-like, emphasized by the adoption of the child-like pose adopted by models: slightly bow-legged and deliberately gauche. American designer Anne Fogarty extended the baby-doll line to the floor with her high-waisted wedding dress made entirely of *point d'esprit*, a machine-made net with small all-over dots, unlined on the long, tight-fitting sleeves with a double sleeve head. The scoop neck-line was gathered under the bust and held by ribbon, decorated with a small cascade of artificial flowers and matching a small bouquet with long streamers.

Prospective brides not only patronized the specialist shops and salons, but also bought from the non-bridal ranges of leading contemporary designers. John Bates, initially under the label Jean Varon, designed ravishingly pretty Empire-line dresses made of lace and broderie anglaise, as did Nettie Vogues and Annakat. Mexicana produced pin-tucked and pleated white cotton dresses with scalloped bell sleeves and layered flounced skirts that could be bought off-the-peg, making them ideal wedding dresses.

OPPOSITE, FAR LEFT
Designed by John Bates for his Jean Varon label, this light-hearted wedding dress displays the designer's customary joie de vivre, here evidenced in the flirty polka-dot, fit-and-flare skirt and high-waisted bodice, defined with a ribbon bow.

OPPOSITE, LEFT A faux coat-and-dress ensemble, this Empire-line wedding dress has a boat-shaped neckline and a flat ribbon bow featured on the high waist. The lace scalloped-edged 'coat' is attached to the dress, which then forms a train at the back.

RIGHT A pin-tucked high-waisted gown, with a pie-crust frill collar, that falls in soft folds to a frilled lace hem. The slightly billowing sleeves are gathered at the shoulder and cuff, where they are caught with a ribbon bow. The bridesmaid wears a miniature version, but with a dark sash. Photographed for *Vogue* magazine by Norman Parkinson in 1967.

The 'Wedding Bell-villes'

Women's Wear Daily featured Bellville Sassoon wedding dresses in 1967, with the title 'Those Wedding Bell-villes'. Founded in 1953 by former debutante Belinda Bellville, the society dressmaker became renowned for dressing Britain's debutantes for the 'season', a social calendar that included traditional events such as Ascot, Glyndebourne and Henley. By the 1960s Belinda Bellville had become London's foremost couture house, offering a new style of bespoke fashion for the younger market that was unlike that of older, established names such as Norman Hartnell. The first ready-to-wear bridal dresses were made in 1961 for London's most stylish department store, Woollands in Knightsbridge, and for Bergdorf Goodman in New York. London's Royal College of Art graduate David Sassoon had joined Bellville as a designer in 1958; he was subsequently appointed a partner and the label became Bellville Sassoon in 1970.

The label soon had a monopoly on London's society weddings, as debutantes who were dressed by the label for their 'coming-out' ball and the season's parties naturally returned to Bellville Sassoon when they required a wedding dress. As with all upper-class weddings, photographs regularly appeared in the society magazine *Queen*, and even in the national newspaper *The Sunday Times*. Both these publications recorded the wedding of Lady Philippa Wallop, daughter of the Earl and Countess of Portsmouth, to Viscount Chelsea, son of Earl Cadogan, in 1963. The bride's dress followed a simple princess line, with the white raffia flowers embroidered with crystal drops on the sleeves to match the pill-box headdress.

A dedicated bridal workroom was installed in Cadogan Place in 1963 and accounted for a quarter of the company's business. In 1965, British magazine *Woman's Journal* commented:

> The bride was dressed by Belinda Bellville…
> and that means that she is bound to be one
> of the most looked at, talked about and best-
> dressed brides of the year. Belinda Bellville
> brides always are. She's the society brides'
> own designer, their first choice when only the
> most beautiful dress in the world will do.

The Bellville Sassoon style is both romantic and feminine, inspired by the Restoration, Empire, Victorian and Edwardian periods. David Sassoon explains in his book, *The Glamour of Bellville Sassoon* (2009), 'I remember young brides-to-be, typical Dolly birds and Chelsea girls, would come in wearing high boots and mini-skirts but every single one of them wanted a romantic wedding dress'. A blue garter was initially given to the brides alongside the dress, but this was replaced in the 1970s with a small blue bow sewn inside the bodice.

 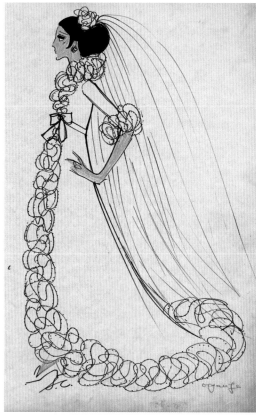

LEFT AND FAR LEFT Illustrations showing two designs by Bellville Sassoon, including the demure Princess-line dress with trumpet sleeves (far left) and a wedding dress with flamenco ruffles dating from 1968 (a version was also made as an evening gown).

OPPOSITE One of Bellville Sassoon's first ready-to-wear dresses featured in *The Sunday Times*, 1962. The sleeves are hemmed with a frothy frill of lace to match the hem of the skirt. The short bouffant veil is secured with a pearl-encrusted pill-box hat worn on the back of the head.

Winter Weddings

Fashion in the 1960s looked toward the past as well as the future, with pre-revolutionary Russia and the medieval aesthetic being referenced by many brides due to the influence of popular films such as *The Lion in Winter* (1968), *Dr Zhivago* (1965) and *Camelot* (1967). These epic love stories all contain romantic scenes set in wintry landscapes against an historical backdrop which influenced wedding style. Winter wedding fashion lends itself to historical detailing far more than dresses designed for the summer months. Earlier eras were also recalled with the use of military detailing such as frogging, usually in black on red or gold on white, with velvet being the ideal choice for cooler weather, either in red or 'winter white'.

On her marriage to Kevin Billington, Lady Rachel Pakenham wore a Russian-inspired pearl white maxi-length coatdress with a broad hem and cuffs circled with white fox fur. Military-style corded frogging held the coat together. The bride's hair was pulled back into a pile of big curls, with tendrils left to frame the face. The veil was secured by the family tiara. The bride's attendant and four bridesmaids wore tent dresses bordered with silver brocade and carried white fur muffs. With a honeymoon in Scotland, the winter trousseau included, 'warmly coloured velvet trouser suits, fur circled maxi-dresses, tall boots and troubadour buckled shoes, light little knitted dresses with long sleeves and surprise stripes'.

The epic love story *Dr Zhivago* starring Omar Sharif and Julie Christie particularly popularized the use of fur, even if faux, with brides opting for fur-trimmed hoods with matching muffs, carried in place of a bouquet. The medieval look was equally appealing to the prospective winter bride, not least because Vanessa Redgrave looked so ravishing in her proposal scene from the musical *Camelot*. She wore a long white over-cape with the typical medieval trumpet sleeves and a white fur capelet around her neck. Her hair was fashioned in a simple partial topknot and left to flow below the shoulders. Although not every bride could arrive at her wedding at the castle on a white horse, she could certainly replicate Guinevere's wedding dress: a heavy gold and silver brocade medieval-style dress with a deep scoop neck and a train/cape hung from the shoulders.

LEFT A medieval-inspired winter wedding ensemble of pastel pink pure virgin wool gabardine by Parisian couturier Pierre Cardin dating from 1967 comprising a *chasuble* (a sleeveless vestment worn by a priest) worn over sleeveless, square-necked gown, which is edged in white mink. A matching hood ties under the chin.

LEFT An illustration of a wedding gown by Pierre Balmain for autumn–winter 1968, featuring an edge-to-edge bodice, trimmed with a band of lace to match the trumpet-shaped sleeves. The domed pill-box hat is secured on short hair.

BELOW A winter wedding outfit by French couturier Jean Patou, from 1967. The heavy duchesse satin is worked into set-in sleeves and cut to fall in sculptural folds at the back. A flapped pocket is sited high on the hips, and the cuffs and hem are trimmed in white mink. Matching shoes are by Andrea for Patou, 1967.

BRIDAL BEAUTY

The beauty correspondent for *Homes and Gardens* in 1966 encouraged a toned-down look for the big day:

This spring, the top fashion look is built around a tender pink lipstick and a satin smooth translucent skin. This is reassuring news for mothers whose daughters are about to be brides. The new lipsticks, in their subtle sugar-almond colours would seem to be designed expressly with brides in mind. Names like Sugar Rose, Spice Pink, Soft-silver Rose and Pink Heaven leave no doubt about their pinkness. Nail varnish should be a very pale edition of your lipstick colour. A naturally pale girl may like to use the tiniest flick of cream rouge under her powder.

Vogue also advised:

Brides are not expected any longer to look ashen-faced, led like sacrifice to the altar, so do wear rouge; it gives a lively and healthy look, especially with white. The dollybird bride ignored such advice and lavishly outlined the eyes with black eyeliner, applied untrimmed false eyelashes above the eyes, painted lashes on below, as seen on model Twiggy, and added a smattering of false freckles with a brown eyebrow pencil. Lips were obliterated with foundation, until Mary Quant produced her 'Bare essentials' cosmetic collection, 'the first great post-atomic breakthrough in make-up, which included "Blot-out" to neutralize lip colour'.

As the silhouette softened over the decade and the mini was replaced with the flowing, bias-cut mididresses of Ossie Clark, hair too became much softer. Allowed to grow out, the Vidal Sassoon five-point 'wash and go' haircut was replaced with curls. A visit to the hairdresser was once again required before the wedding day to practise the fashionable loose chignon, with artful tendrils left to frame the face. These were often constructed with a 'hairpiece' to increase volume or add a cluster of false ringlets.

The Hippie Bride

By the end of the decade, the crisp, futuristic, architectural clothes of the early 1960s had given way to a return to a yearning for the natural and the nostalgic. The archetypal hippie bride was Botticelli's Venus, dancing barefoot through the grass in a floating gown of silk chiffon with flowers entwined in her hair, or a Pre-Raphaelite, heavy-lidded beauty, draped in silk velvet. Partnered by an equally alluring bridegroom in patterned flares and a brocade waistcoat, many parents despaired.

Christopher Gibbs describes the aristocratic vision of Jane Ormsby-Gore in *Vogue* in 1966:

> She scours the Portobello Road and the antique shops searching for handfuls of Venetian lace, rich embroideries, and beautifully made clothes of any age and kind. She has boots of Russian leather, endless shirts of cream and white lace, embroidered velvet coats falling almost to the ankle… huge plumes of ostrich and egret tumbling from floppy 1900 hats, and above all a jewellery box stuffed with glittering treasures… She likes to wear no make-up at all except for the eyes, which she thinks should look as huge and exotic as possible. She likes very short skirts, but also very long ones.

The wedding ceremony was no longer perceived as a commercial opportunity, mediated through the bridal specialist or wedding planner. The counterculture pushed the boundaries of gender to the limit; the sexes were virtually indistinguishable as they plundered exotic cultures for clothing and artefact, identifying with the marginal and the oppressed. Eastern mysticism provided elements of the ceremony as well as aspects of the dress as couples created their own vows and rejected traditional venues in favour of the beach, woods or fields. Bouquets were no longer purchased from a florist. In her eponymous autobiography, actress and singer Marianne Faithfull describes walking through the fields of Cambridge picking wild flowers for her forthcoming marriage to John Dunbar: 'I had started to cry because I'd forgotten to get a bouquet and John went out and picked a big bunch of light May blossoms and gave them to me; they had great long black thorns on them. It was all so enchanted, but as it turned out, it was the wrong kind of magic. It's very bad luck, you see. May blossom belongs to Pan.'

The counterculture was anti-fashion. Haute couture represented consumerist values; in the era of doing your own thing, the idea of being dictated to by a fashion elite in Paris was untenable. The influence of hallucinogenic drugs and hippie guru Timothy Leary's exhortation to 'turn-on, tune-in, and dropout' resulted in young people trekking to India and Morocco rather than planning a wedding ceremony.

Although the hippie movement purported to be free-thinking, concerned with breaking down barriers of class and race, women were not yet liberated in any way. Living together remained a minority choice, and traditional weddings still took place, even among members of the counterculture. 'These days how could anyone contemplate wedlock?' Richard Neville asks in his 1995 autobiography, *Hippie Hippie Shake*, when he hears of his sister's plans to wed:

> After drinks at the Ritz, it was taxis to an elegant address in Mayfair. I had never seen so many chandeliers. The champagne was fizzing; the Fleet Street luminaries were throbbing in black tie and tulle, like extras in a Fred Astaire movie. David's best man was Christopher Booker… 'I don't know why you Underground people bother to rail against modern society,' he remarked, sweeping a glass of bubbly for me from the butler's passing tray.

OPPOSITE Dating from the late 1960s, this Mary Quant wedding dress for her diffusion Ginger Group label has a 1940s-inspired halterneck and lingerie-shaped bodice caught up into a bow.

RIGHT AND DETAILS BELOW Designed by Spanish-born, British-based designer Marisa Martin, this dress dates from the late 1960s to early 1970s. With a boutique in London's Knightsbridge, the designer exemplified the richly embellished hippie-deluxe ethos of the period, alongside designers Bill Gibb and Thea Porter.

Even avant-garde artist Yoko Ono and pop iconoclast John Lennon chose to undertake the ritual. After a civil ceremony in Gibraltar (forgotten passports ruled out France, their first choice), John and Yoko spent their honeymoon in a bedroom in the Hilton Hotel Amsterdam in a very public 'bed-in' to publicize world peace. Sporting matching long hair and tennis shoes, both wore white for the ceremony. Ono styled her knitted minidress with knee socks and a large floppy hat, and Lennon wore a ribbed tailored jacket and turtleneck sweater.

The hippie look soon became commodified by a mass-market fashion industry eager to capitalize on the latest trend. High-end designers and couturiers such as Yves Saint Laurent in Europe and Rudi Gernreich in California purveyed their own version of hippie deluxe, with luxurious kaftans and transparent dresses that were to infiltrate mainstream fashion in the coming decade.

JUST DANDY MENSWEAR

In July 1962 *Vogue* stated: 'Whistle up peacocks. The decorously besponged-bagged gentleman is dead.' Men were finding their sartorial feet and, at the beginning of the decade, although the lounge suit continued to be worn for informal weddings, bridegrooms now felt they had more choice: fashion photographer David Bailey wore a powder blue Shetland sweater for his wedding to French film actress Catherine Deneuve.

The 1950s male silhouette of the upturned triangle was replaced by a slender, narrower line in lightweight fabrics such as mohair, popularized by London retailer John Michael. Meanwhile, in Paris, couturier Pierre Cardin pioneered the concept of the ready-made suit for men that was also affiliated to a recognizable brand. His designer label introduced the first Cardin menswear line in 1961. Among the collection was the collarless jacket, adopted by British pop group the Beatles. Revolutionary retailer John Stephen, with his menswear boutiques lining London's Carnaby Street, introduced flamboyant and outrageous colour, texture, print and pattern to men's fashion, paving the way for the archetypal dandy, who moved on from the 'mod' boutiques of Carnaby Street to the hippie excesses of London's King's Road.

Long-haired, perfectly groomed dandies defied the usual male stereotype and bought their clothes from boutiques such as Granny Takes a Trip, Hung On You, and Mr Fish, described in the Nik Cohn book, *Today There Are No Gentlemen* (1971) as 'a holocaust of see-through voiles, brocades, and spangles, and mini-skirts for men, blinding silks, and flower printed hats'. The aristocratic dandy had his suits made at Blades of Dover Street or Doug Hayward, who only accepted new accounts on personal recommendation. His signature look was slim line, with high vents in the jacket and width at the bottom of the trousers. Tommy Nutter, tailor to the pop stars, also custom-made trouser suits for men's girlfriends.

As the counterculture accelerated throughout the decade, and the era of the dolly bird and the pop star waned, sartorial excesses were eschewed in favour of anti-consumer and anti-fashion statements. Clothes picked up on the hippie trail in Kathmandu or Goa, prayer shirts with bells and beads, and the ubiquitous jeans, now customized with floral panels and worn with a homecrafted tie-dye T-shirt. These were mixed with period and military costume from Ian Fisk's boutique I was Lord Kitchener's Valet, as worn by the Beatles on the cover of the *Sgt Pepper's Lonely Hearts Club Band* album. Even the formal wedding was subverted by the 1960s hippie. The top hat of the morning suit, now usually grey rather than black, was an incongruous sight, perched on top of shoulder-length hair.

LEFT Beatles' luminary John Lennon and avant-garde artist Yoko Ono dressed in white, including matching plimsolls, for their wedding, which took place in Gibraltar in 1969.

OPPOSITE A civil wedding at London's Caxton Hall in 1967 for singer Eric Burdon of the Animals and Angie King. The bride and groom wear full hippie regalia, including an embroidered Afghan coat with high-collared floral print shirt for him and a silk sari for her. She carries a carnation.

Space Age themes

The 'Space Age' fashions of André Courrèges, Pierre Cardin and Paco Rabanne were incorporated into wedding fashion by the use of structured materials such as ribbed Ottoman silk and piqué cotton, combined with plastics and metallic embellishment.

▶ Transparency

A see-through voile wedding dress designed by Torrente in 1968 is imprinted with stylized daisies. Brevity and transparency were increasing phenomena of 1960s fashion, led by Californian designer Rudi Gernreich and Yves Saint Laurent in Paris.

▼ Kaftan styles

The influence of hippie fashions on wedding style: this kaftan-style wedding dress has square-shaped sleeves and a centre-front split skirt edged with decorative braid.

Empire line

The high-waisted Empire line, with the skirt gathered just under the bustline, was a Regency-era favourite revived in the 1960s. Decorative bows and sashes were often positioned to emphasize the central focal point of the dress.

Key looks of the decade
1960s

◀ Pill-box hats

The domed pill-box hat was positioned on the back of the head to allow for the bouffant hairstyles prevalent at the beginning of the decade and secured the equally bouffant tulle veil. The simplicity of the shape complements the uncomplicated silhouette of the era.

Maxis and minis
Wedding dresses inevitably followed the day's hemline fashions, alternating between ultra-short and extra-long, both appearing in a slim, narrow A-line silhouette, often with trumpet- or bell-shaped sleeves.

▲ The headscarf as headdress
Adding to the ingénue appearance of the 1960s bride was the headscarf, a triangle of fabric tied under the chin to match the dress. Here, film star Audrey Hepburn wears one to partner her pale pink Givenchy minidress for her wedding to Andrea Dotti.

Bubble-shaped dress
The bubble sheath dress, with its narrow waist, voluminous skirt and tapering hem, was a popular look from Dior and Balenciaga that evolved from the 1950s 'Tulip' and Givenchy's 'Sack' shapes.

▲ Daisies
The marguerite, more commonly known as the daisy, typified the graphic simplicity of the era and was frequently used in bouquets. Here, a textile rendition of the flower is seen on a gown with matching long train by French designer Jean-Louis Scherrer, dating from 1964.

1970s:
The Barefoot Bride

OPPOSITE A demure
Empire-line dress with a
box-pleat in the centre
front of the bodice,
opposing the inverted
box-pleats on either hip.
Unusually for a wedding
dress, the sleeves are
gathered into buttoned
cuffs. Photographed by
Norman Parkinson for
Brides magazine in
autumn 1970.

Reflecting the state of flux in fashion generally, no one particular style of wedding dress dominated the 1970s. Several diverse looks emerged: the haute hippie of Bill Gibb and Gina Fratini, the mob cap and milkmaid look purveyed by Biba, and later Laura Ashley, and Tommy Nutter's tailoring for Bianca Pérez Morena de Macias on her marriage to Mick Jagger in 1971. The opening of the Barefoot Bride shop in New York City in 1971 supplied those prospective brides who wanted an 'alternative' wedding, which was still popular at the beginning of the decade, with fashionable versions of the hippie look – frothy white broderie-anglaise dresses, large brimmed hats and embroidered kaftans. Scottish-born Bill Gibb designed fairytale dresses that fulfilled every bride-to-be's romantic fantasies, as did Gina Fratini.

A new silhouette in bridalwear, the A-line 'Princess' line, emerged. Daywear also followed this long, lean line, with garments cut close to the body with high armholes to create a narrow torso. The increasing popularity of trousers to replace the mini, and the unpopular midi length, added to this effect. Trousers were high-waisted, narrow on the thigh and flared at the ankle, worn with a high wedge heel or platform shoes to elongate the lower half of the body even further.

The back-to-nature ethos, prevalent during the 1970s, evoked a pastoral idyll redolent of wild flowers, rain-washed hair, and sprigged cotton made up into ruffled pinafores. These could be found at Laura Ashley, whose daywear was frequently appropriated for an informal wedding. Later in the decade, high-end ready-to-wear American designers, including Halston and Calvin Klein, provided a pared-down minimalism in luxurious fabrics that influenced the design of wedding dresses, which subsequently lost some of their hard-edged purity of line to incorporate a softer, draped silhouette.

The Changing Silhouette

Royal weddings continued to provide public excitement. Televised around the world, the nuptials of Queen Elizabeth's daughter Princess Anne and Captain Mark Phillips in London's Westminster Abbey in 1973 had an audience of one hundred million. The pearl-encrusted dress was at the vanguard of the new silhouette, which had evolved from the narrow, high-waisted Empire line of the late 1960s into the princess line, a 'fit and flare' pattern-cutting technique. This provides a flared A-line skirt, dispensing with the waist seam and with width at the hemline. It was first invented by couturier Charles Frederick Worth for a dress designed for the Empress Eugenie in the 1860s.

The demand for ready-to-wear wedding dresses was now overtaking couture, even at such high-end labels as Bellville Sassoon. Ready-to-wear gowns varied in price, from $1,300 for an exclusive gown by American label Christos that retailed through Bergdorf Goodman in 1974, to an Eve Muscio for Milady gown in nylon that retailed at $170. Influenced by the hippie deluxe aesthetic of Bill Gibb and Mary McFadden, wedding-dress designers were incorporating medieval style into their 1970s repertoire. This look included 'Camelot' sleeves, tight at the top and widening to a trumpet shape at the wrist, mirroring the shape of the skirt, which was narrow under the arms and then formed a wide hem. This A line was favoured by one of the preferred American labels for the traditional bride, Christos, who appliquéd hand-clipped French point d'Alençon lace and pearl beading onto silk organza. Founded by Cyprus-born designer Christos Yiannakou, Christos gowns have appeared in Hollywood films, such as *27 Dresses* (2008).

The ingénue look continued to be a theme, particularly with the label Constantino for Aida Bridals. This style retained elements of the 'babydoll' look, with a deep flounce around the hem of the skirt and balloon sleeves (a tight-fitting upper arm that billowed out into a full, gathered lower sleeve caught in with a cuff). Even though bridalwear designer John Burbidge designed a sleeveless wedding dress for President Nixon's daughter Tricia in 1971, very few brides copied the look, preferring long sleeves.

John Burbidge

A prolific designer for the bridal company Priscilla of Boston, from the late 1940s to 1985, John Burbidge was born in 1922 and served for three years in the Army during the Second World War and attended the New England School of Art and Design. He began at Priscilla of Boston by operating a button machine and gradually worked his way up to designing. His technique involved clipping photographs of models from magazines, laying

tracing paper over the cut-outs and then tracing the figures, onto which he added his designs. After creating, in his words, 'hundreds' of sketches and doodles, he would work out the details in muslin. Eventually he achieved status as Priscilla Kidder's favourite designer and was known for his use of certain features, such as bows, bustle backs, puffed sleeves and 'star' bodices.

Burbidge achieved national recognition when he designed the wedding dress worn by President Nixon's daughter, Tricia, in 1971. The dress featured his signature detailing: cut lace, appliquéd over the sheer silk of the outer dress, proliferating at the hemline and worn over an inner opaque sheath dress. The official bridal portrait, by photographer Dick Winburn, was featured on the cover of *Life* magazine on 18 June, 1971.

OPPOSITE FAR LEFT Pierre Cardin's modern approach is evident in the signature seaming and sculptural silhouette of this 1971 robe in pure worsted wool flannel. Patch pockets are the only decoration, and a contrast in texture is provided by the white fox-fur sleeves. The more traditional headdress is replaced with a beret on the back of the head.

OPPOSITE TOP

A couture bridal gown from Pierre Balmain, dating from autumn/winter 1976–77, in which a length of fabric forms a low headband caught on either side of the head with a spray of textile flowers, before extending over the breasts into a draped bodice. It is worn over a low-cut, long-sleeved dress.

OPPOSITE PAGE, BOTTOM Another experimental wedding dress from Balmain for fall/winter 1972–73. The slim-fitting sheath dress extends upwards at the neckline to form a face-framing circular hood. The deeply flounced hemline is made of gathered lace.

TOP LEFT A more severe look from Balmain for spring/summer 1971. The pointed, deep cowl neckline of the dress extends down the back to form a long, heavy train. The nun-like coif and trumpet sleeves add to the monastic, medieval impression of the dress.

ABOVE The triangular peasant headscarf is rendered in tiers of lace ruffles and tied under the chin in this bridal outfit by Balmain for spring/summer 1970. Vertical rows of ruffles are also featured on the high-waisted bodice and sleeves, and around the hem of the lightly gathered skirt.

LEFT Bands of scrolled texture are inset into the stiff folds of this A-line dress by Balmain for autumn/winter 1970–71. The austere silhouette is softened by matching bands on the sleeves and bodice, which are repeated on the collar and headdress.

OPPOSITE Norman Parkinson taking a photograph of the feather-bedecked bride and bridesmaid for *Brides* magazine in autumn 1970. The swansdown bonnets and cape are accessorized with simple posies of flowers and Mary Jane shoes.

BELOW 1970s nostalgia for an earlier age by British label Bellville Sassoon. This medieval-inspired gown, with trailing sleeves and overskirt, has a quilted neckline and waistband that draws in the gathered bodice. The headdress, worn low on the brow, replicates the waterfall frill of the skirt.

ABOVE A mix of ethnic style and haute-hippie from Bellville Sassoon in this gathered tunic worn over a flowing, ankle-length skirt. The tasselled, plaited belt matches the decorative feature on the sleeves, and a shawl replaces the more traditional veil.

The Hippie Bride

During the 1970s, radical feminism was growing, nurtured by the publication of Germaine Greer's groundbreaking book, *The Female Eunuch*, in 1970. In it she rails against the consumerism of the wedding ceremony and marriage in particular. The hippie bride was a reluctant customer of the department store bridal salons or the bespoke seamstress, preferring to do her own thing instead. She dipped into the dressing-up box and her grandmother's attic, and rummaged through antique markets. In 1971, columnist Virginia Graham wrote a feature 'Anyone Want an Heirloom?' in *Homes and Gardens* discussing the service hippies had provided to ordinary people:

> They have provided a repository, so to speak, for all the sartorial paraphernalia left us by our mothers, who inherited it from their mothers… not only have they pounced on all the lace, all those bibs and tuckers and ruchings and veils and shawls and scarves and yard after yard of flouncing, but many other tiresome things as well. Around their darling dirty necks are Granny's feather boas, on their breasts are her cameo brooches, their fingers are deep in her quaint rings, and they carry her ostrich feather fans and her little beaver muffs. Oh, how can we be grateful enough to our dear crazy boys for wanting to wear admiral's full-dress uniforms, and guard officer's crimson silken sashes, and glinting clinking medals won in the Zulu war, which, suspended on petunia ribbons round their necks, lie so prettily on their flowered shirts?

Vicki Howard, in her book *Brides, Inc.*, writes of how wedding-dress manufacturers were perplexed by new trends toward informality during the late 1960s and 1970s: 'A self-consciously anti-materialist celebration, the New Wedding took place out of doors or in a non-commercial space, with handmade or hand-me-down wedding clothes. In response to the less-expensive informal wedding, the industry lobbied for formal weddings, citing them as a solution for rising divorce rates in the postwar period'. She goes on to quote wedding-dress entrepreneur Patricia Kidder's remark that 'if a bride gets married in a short dress in a justice of the peace's office, it seems too quick and easy and not too important. But if the bride and her family go to a lot of trouble arranging a big wedding – and her father has paid a lot of money for it – she'll think twice about running home to mother after the first tiff'.

The hippie wedding included a rejection of all the traditional venues and rituals, including the wedding

vows. Lance Morrow looked back in 1983 at the vogue for self-penned vows in *Time* magazine.

> The 1960s and the '70s were the great epoch of the improvisational, personalized wedding ceremony – preferably performed in a sun-shot meadow, the bride barefoot and vaguely pagan, Chloë going to Daphnis.
>
> The vows concocted for those weddings seem period pieces now. They were oppressively poetic, gushily confessional. They were sweet and intimate and profound and occasionally metaphysical, like a Hallmark card. They were illuminated by moonbeams of Kahlil Gibran ('Sing and dance together and be joyous, but let each one of you be alone') and drenched with fragrances of Rod McKuen.

ABOVE American social activist, Abbie Hoffman, on his marriage to Anita Kushner. The couple sit cross-legged on either side of Linn House, a self styled priest of the Neo-American Church, as he officiates at their wedding ceremony in Central Park, New York.

RIGHT From the Diorling label (Dior's ready-to-wear collection), a youthful bride wears short, cotton, bib-fronted hot pants, which reached the height of popularity in 1971. The ingénue impression is increased with the balloon-sleeved spotted blouse and the upturned brim of the hat.

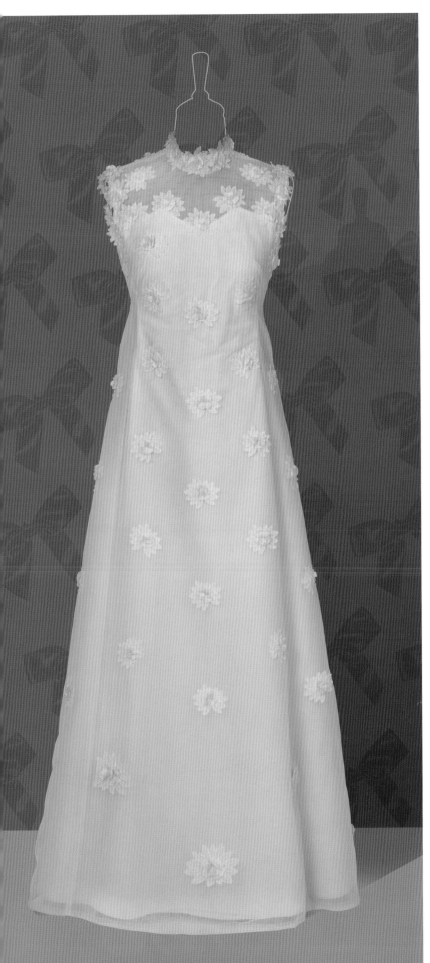

LEFT AND ABOVE Sleeveless wedding gowns became popular in the 1970s. This A line dress has a sweetheart neckline on the acetate underslip, which is overlaid with embroidered flowers on net. The back view shows a flat bow positioned at the high waist, from which the skirt falls in small gathers.

RIGHT Details of appliquéd flowers from the dress. Leaves of cut lace surround handmade silk satin petals.

Fantasy Fashion

For those brides wishing for a hippie-style wedding while retaining an element of formality, or without recourse to grandmother's attic, designers such as Bill Gibb, Gina Fratini and Zandra Rhodes provided the right mix of eclectic eccentricity. Layers of floating printed silk chiffon, gathers, smocking and shirring were all hallmarks of the haute-hippie style of these designers. Although none of them limited their output to wedding gowns, their signature look satisfied all the requirements of the bride who wanted a fairytale fantasy wedding dress.

Unlike the severity of the Princess line, this unstructured silhouette was abstract and loose, with hand-screen-printed flowing forms that frequently ended in handkerchief points or jagged edges. These were inspired by the cut and form of vernacular dress, such as those seen in Max Tilke's book *Costume Patterns and Designs*. It featured flat patterns of wrapped trousers, embroidered waistcoats, peasant shapes, and most particularly the kaftan, of which London retailer and designer Thea Porter was the chief exponent, an example being Porter's 1970 'Faye Dunaway' wedding dress constructed of silk, velvet, organza and lace. Luxe entered couture with Yves Saint Laurent's 1976 collection based on the Ballets Russes, with cascading gypsy skirts and opulent brocades.

These free-flowing garments were worn with equally decorative accessories, including platform shoes that reached fantasy heights, and included layers of coloured leather, often appliquéd with motifs. Pablo & Delia, the Argentinean designers based in London during the 1970s, designed canvas hand-painted boots and floating, free-spirited whimsical dresses, as did Bellville Sassoon. The use of precious jewellery was confined to the middle-aged and bourgeois, as *Vogue* recommended:

Jewellery is silver, real and well worn. Hang silver chains, braid, tassels around your neck; wear fine little rings together and get rid of anything 'chunky'. Collect every choker you see, particularly in coloured Mexican beadwork supporting a verge of suede ribbon fringe, knotted at random. Tangle them up in your ribboned hair.

Chokers adorned the necks of most brides, constructed from flowers, feathers, velvet and snakeskin; Thea Porter created versions fringed with Indian glass beads and embroidered with butterflies. Bridesmaids dressed like the gypsies in Augustus John's paintings, with a raggle-taggle collection of dressing-up clothes.

BOTTOM LEFT A draped and gathered Qiana jersey dress and matching turban by Bill Gibb from 1972 is worn with the decade's platform shoe.

BOTTOM RIGHT Utilizing her signature geometric shapes, Zandra Rhodes has deployed concentric circles in silk-satin on this wedding gown from 1978. The circular veil is cut into the shape of a daisy.

OPPOSITE Chiffon godets in the skirt of this couture chiffon gown by Valentino are responsible for the fullness at the hem. A velvet ribbon secures a silk corsage at the waist. This model was worn by Christina Onassis for her wedding to Alexander Andreadis in 1975.

THE FANTASY BEAUTY LOOK

As straw hats with a big floppy brims worn over rain-straight hair were replaced by loose ripples of shoulder-length hair, hippie locks became more tamed and professionally styled as the decade progressed. Hair was either crimped with irons or, for a more natural look, plaited when wet and then untied when dry. It was fanned out from a centre parting and was often tinted in delicate shades. Minute sections of hair were plaited and woven with flowers or feathers, or threaded with beads. Fantasy fashion demanded fantasy make-up, too. The look was no longer well scrubbed, as *Vogue* informed in 1970:

> *What's happening with make-up is freeing it as surely as art was freed in the Renaissance, and the same ideas are at work. From now, make-up is not your uniform – it is your barometer. You may look painted – preferably for a close-up in a film of A Midsummer Night's Dream, with you playing Titania. The new face is a delicate façade, porcelain pale, and on top of that it is coloured delicately, one colour misting away at the edges to another. Remember eyelashes are hair and meant to look like silky fans.*

Cosmetic manufacturers were now packaging eyeshadows in multicolour compacts. Models like Penelope Tree and Maudie James set the style, with lots of shimmer on eyes and cheeks, eyebrows plucked to a fine, high arch, and bare nails.

LEFT Designed by Gina Fratini, this full-length, two-tiered gown dates from 1970 and includes an attached top that is designed to fall open from the centre-front band. The sleeves are split to fall open with movement, and the edges are hemmed with an undulating satin-stitch.

OPPOSITE RIGHT A smock-type dress by Gina Fratini, with the fullness of the caped sleeves and body gathered into a deep square yoke. The stylized flowers are embroidered in shades of cream and brown.

OPPOSITE LEFT A detail from a cream, silk, smocked and pin-tucked organza wedding gown, edged with nineteenth-century lace, by Gina Fratini from 1970.

Gina Fratini

Born in Kobe, Japan, British designer Gina Fratini was of Irish parentage and her family returned to Britain when she was 12. After studying at London's Royal College of Art, she began her design career by joining the Katherine Dunham dance group as assistant to costume and set designer John Platt. In 1965 she married Renato Fratini and it is this surname that is synonymous with her signature flouncy, full-length, Swiss-dot, cotton voile dresses trimmed with broderie anglaise.

Fratini launched her own label in 1964 and her profile was raised in 1971, when one of her gowns was chosen for Princess Anne to wear for her birthday portrait – a peach-coloured print on voile with a gathered neckline, puffed sleeves and soft, gathered skirt. A wedding dress created by Fratini with a cream silk organza smock top and full skirt, and matching full sleeves with deep lace-trimmed cuffs, lace insets and pin-tucks on the yokes and sleeves, dating from 1970, was featured in the exhibition, 'The Cutting Edge: 50 Years of British Fashion' at the Victoria & Albert Museum, London, in 1997. Gina Fratini closed her business in 1989, but worked as a guest designer for Norman Hartnell until 1990 and continued designing for the royal family.

BELOW A military uniform-inspired wedding suit from Bill Gibb, dating from 1978, in ivory wool. It features a mandarin collar and evenly-spaced rouleau loops and lizard-skin buttons to the waist. The coat splits to reveal the matching, buttoned dress beneath. White work is embroidered on the hem.

RIGHT Dating from 1972, this wedding dress by Bill Gibb, in eau-de-nil satin-backed crepe, features the designer's hallmark of double rows of topstitching along the collar, hem and cuffs. Enamel buttons hold the bodice together, godets of fabric inserted into the waist darts create fullness in the skirt.

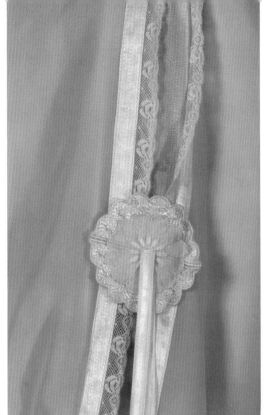

TOP The sleeves of this Rumack & Sample dress are split and edged with satin binding and lace, then caught at the elbow with a rosette of gathered lace threaded with ribbon streamers.

ABOVE The Celtic-inspired embroidery in shades of rose, gold and copper is bordered by coloured braid edged with beads. These extend into long streamers on either side of the dress.

RIGHT A medieval-style gown from Rumack & Sample, a label that specialized in using antique embroidery, trim and buttons on their designs. The yoke of the bodice forms the structure of the dress, from which the skirt and sleeves fall into loose gathers, before the sleeves are pulled into cuffs.

The Retro Bride

'Vintage' was not a commonly used term during the 1970s; instead 'retro' was the word applied to the proliferation of fashions from previous eras that occurred throughout the decade. In 1971, Sotheby's in London auctioned film costumes from the heyday of Hollywood glamour. This coincided with the Odeon style purveyed by the Art Deco shopping paradise, Biba, which offered a sultry siren bride with kohl-rimmed eyes in clinging panne velvet.

As the decade progressed, so too did the references to the past. By the middle of the 1970s the harder-edged 1940s replaced the 1930s as a source of inspiration. Platform shoes, first invented in the 1940s by Salvatore Ferragamo, made another appearance and were even more elevated and extraordinary than before, with contemporary wooden platforms designed by Manolo Blahnik for fashion label Zapata. Cloche hats, turbans and hats with veils all made a comeback, as brides appropriated the printed rayon tea-dress – or its 1970s equivalent, the mid-calf, handkerchief-point, bias-cut dresses of Ossie Clark adorned with luscious patterning by Celia Birtwell. The full-blown wedding dress was also subject to retro influences, particularly the bias-cut dress in silk satin that was resonant of the 1930s, accessorized with a close-fitting veil and a headdress cascading into yards of tulle.

OPPOSITE LEFT A John Bates wedding gown in silk jersey, dating from the late 1970s for his label Jean Varon. The tabard-shaped overdress has an asymmetrical hem decorated with tassels, and is lavishly embellished with sequinned yellow flowers and silver foliage.

OPPOSITE RIGHT Nude-coloured silk-satin is used on the yoke and pearl-buttoned cuffs of this Ophelia dress by Ossie Clark. The reverse, matt side of the fabric is used for the gathered skirt and sleeves.

RIGHT DETAIL Embroidered flower detailing is repeated on the back bodice of this Anna Belinda dress.

RIGHT The overdress was a popular feature of 1970S wedding gowns, particularly when cut to hang in a waterfall point at the front, as in this dress by London label Anna Belinda. The heart-shaped bodice is embroidered with flowers, and held together with rouleau loops.

The Natural Look

The babydoll smocks of the 1960s increased in volume in the 1970s, and unlike the smocks of the previous decade they were worn over billowing skirts, which resulted in a loose, flowing silhouette. As *Vogue* remarked, 'It was a wonderful time to be pregnant.' The Laura Ashley label epitomized the 1970s desire to get back to nature. Her milkmaid-like smock dresses and flounced pinafores evoked images of a nineteenth-century Thomas Hardy heroine, wandering through country lanes on her way to the milking parlour. Although initially not specifically designed for a wedding, the full-blown romantic style of the dresses was soon adopted by prospective brides, and in 1973 the label introduced a dedicated wedding line.

A brand with a similar approach to Laura Ashley was the Gunne Sax clothing label. Founded in the 1960s, and bought by Jessica McClintock in 1969, the company went from producing a single clothing line to an international life-style brand, including bridal wear, for which the designer won the Bridal Information Resource's Retail Choice Award in 1996 and 1997. It was named after the 'gunny sack' or burlap trim – a course, natural fabric woven from jute or flax – that was used on some of the label's earlier dresses. The label is associated with the revival of indigenous American rural or 'prairie' clothes, drawing inspirations from the late nineteenth- and early twentieth-century American fashion. Many of the pinafores and dresses in gingham prints and calico had laced bodices resembling corsets, with gigot (leg-of-mutton) sleeves, a look seen on Katharine Ross in the film *Butch Cassidy and the Sundance Kid* (1969).

Laura Ashley

A genuine cottage industry, Laura Ashley is renowned for starting her business on a kitchen table in London's Pimlico, in the early 1950s. Her inspiration to start printing fabric came when she visited the Victoria & Albert Museum to see an exhibition of traditional handicrafts by the Women's Institute. Particularly interested in patchwork, she was unable to source any Victorian prints for her patches, so decided to design and produce them for herself.

Inspired by the headscarf worn by Audrey Hepburn in the film *Roman Holiday* (1953), Ashley started printing headscarves in 1953, which were sold by mail-order and department stores such as John Lewis. Due to this initial success, her husband, Bernard, left his career in the City to help print fabric full-time – Laura designed the prints and Bernard turned his hand to building printing equipment. In 1955 they formed their first company, Ashley Mountney, moving to bigger premises in Kent before finally relocating to Wales where Laura had spent her childhood.

The first Laura Ashley dress appeared in 1966; by the following year the signature look of the label – ankle-length, flounced and frilled dresses in tiny sprigged prints – was established and was to remain virtually unchanged throughout the following two decades. The first stand-alone Laura Ashley shop opened in Kensington, London, in 1968, followed by others in various cities. The distinctive shop, with a green frontage and stripped pine interior, was allowed to appear in only the most picturesque of venues, such as Bath and Shrewsbury in England and Paris and San Francisco abroad.

Although synthetic fabrics had made an impact on the high street, Ashley was a traditionalist and a romantic, and she was passionate about natural fabrics. The dresses were invariably made of cotton and featured a fitted bodice with a scooped neckline trimmed with a lace insert. Skirts were full and ankle length, and billowing sleeves were tightly gathered into deep cuffs at the wrist, edged with lace or a frill. Even mobcaps were *de rigueur* (worn like serving wenches from the kitchens of *Upstairs, Downstairs*, a BBC series of the time). Pinafore dresses were also popular: a full cotton dress with a fine cotton lawn pinafore, bib top and full skirt fitted to a waistband and tied in a bow at the back. The 'Little Bo Peep' look was created by wearing a white, layered dress, its capped sleeves edged in cotton lace with an overdress like a pinafore (apron), printed and layered to the floor.

Bridesmaids were also dressed by Laura Ashley. The designer retrieved and reproduced archive prints from the Georgian and Victorian period, demure floral designs that emulated early block prints. The Laura Ashley price-point was inexpensive, even for daywear, so the label was often bought instead of more expensive dresses that offered a similar look. Elizabeth Vining pointed out on the Victoria & Albert Museum website that 'I wanted a Gina Fratini dress costing £112 from Harrods. The Laura Ashley option was a bargain £12 for two dresses. It was a white, multi-tiered, cotton and lace panelled dress, with a floral printed cotton pinafore worn on top'.

The Laura Ashley label continued to offer a version of pastoral nostalgia throughout the following decades, providing sailor suits for the pageboys and bridesmaids dresses that reflected the desire for a seemingly gentler, more romantic era. Their 1986 catalogue of wedding-dress styles included: 'Swiss dot, cotton lawn dresses with pin-tucked, fitted bodice; lace inserts; high, fitted collars (like innocent choir boys) with full sleeves gathered into deep cuffs, buttoned tight to the wrists. Fully gathered skirts dropping to the ankle'. The male version of the look was a grandfather shirt of checked flannel worn with a Fair Isle waistcoat.

OPPOSITE AND INSET
A demure Biba cotton wedding dress, designed to be worn with a mob cap and bare feet. The gathers are placed on the bust-line rather than under it, making this an unsuitable style for anyone with a womanly figure. The high neckline and gathered puff sleeves add to its child-like appeal, while the short sleeves of the matching coat (inset) form a caped effect, giving an almost ecclesiastical appearance to this demure wedding outfit.

LEFT AND DETAIL BELOW
Leading exponent of the milkmaid look, this cotton dress by Laura Ashley features all the requisite details that represent 1970s rural romanticism: the frilled yoke of panelled lace insertion, a sashed waist, a flounced hem and gathered deeply-cuffed sleeves.

Daywear Brides

The international economic oil-price crisis of the period, combined with a less formal approach to social events, resulted in many brides underplaying their wedding and dressing down for the ceremony in daytime clothes. In Britain the early years of the decade saw to the thee-day working week and widespread social discontent that resulted in quieter weddings. They were often confined to a secular ceremony with a small reception at home, or dinner for a few friends and relatives in a hotel.

Marriage was beginning to be perceived as less important, as couples increasingly began to live together. There was something inappropriate and curiously old-fashioned about the idea of a traditional wedding with a big bouquet, a train and a tiara, and it did not resonate with the times. Some prospective brides eschewed the accoutrements of the 'big day' for reasons of economy or taste, and chose an off-the-peg dress from a contemporary designer to wear as a wedding dress. Liz Tilberis, then a fashion assistant at British *Vogue* and later editor of the American edition of *Harper's Bazaar*, bought her dress from a sample sale at British designer Jean Muir – a mid-calf, cream-coloured, satin-backed, crepe jersey, with a pin-tucked bodice and rouleau fabric buttons, which she wore with matching hand-dyed wedge sandals. For her going-away outfit Tilberis chose a pair of white cotton trousers and a blue satin blazer with red buttons. In her autobiography *No Time to Die*, she describes the confusion of styles then evident: 'My frightfully proper English relations in top hat and tails; the *Vogue* lot in extravagant printed Kenzo dresses, with plastic cherry earrings and platform shoes; my bridesmaids in Liberty florals and turbans fastened with pink cloth roses, wearing fake eyelashes, cheeks painted with little red clown circles; and Andrew's bearded artist friends from Leeds in jeans'.

The Tailored Wedding Suit

For the first time, trousers became a mainstay of the fashionable female wardrobe in the 1970s, apart from a brief period during the 1940s when women wore trousers for practical reasons. Although Sylvia Ayton and Foale & Tuffin had designed trousers for women in the early part of the 1960s, and Yves Saint Laurent had produced his iconic 'Le Smoking' in 1966, new attitudes to informality needed to develop before they could be recognized as acceptable wear for women. It was not unknown for women to be refused entry to some restaurants and hotels when wearing trousers, and they continued to be resisted by male bosses in the work place until the 1970s.

Yves Saint Laurent introduced gangster-inspired trouser suits in 1971, heralding a 1940s revival that added width to the shoulders and nipped in the waist.

Ralph Lauren developed his men's flat-front trouser for women in 1971. He also designed the clothes worn by Diane Keaton in Woody Allen's film *Annie Hall* (1977), sparking a vogue for women wearing an oversize version of male loose jackets and baggy trousers – not a purely androgynous look, as the effect emphasized the woman's femininity and fragility.

It was the custom for London tailor Tommy Nutter to cut and fit a suit for the girlfriends of his male clients, which included pop royalty such as the Beatles and David Bowie. When Mick Jagger married his Nicaraguan girlfriend Bianca Pérez-Morena de Macias in 1971, the tailor not only crafted Jagger's three-piece suit, with its signature wide lapels and flared jacket, accessorized with sneakers and floppy-collared print shirt, he also made a suit for the bride. Often mistakenly identified as a trouser suit, the bride's single-breasted jacket was matched with a maxi-skirt and a wide-brimmed hat with an attached tulle veil.

BELOW LEFT A viscose tunic-style daywear bridal dress by British designer Janice Wainwright has a gently gathered low neckline and long, transparent sleeves. Although constructed as one piece, the decorative borders below the waist and at the hem give the illusion of a two-piece suit.

BELOW DETAILS The eye of the embroidered peacock feather is delicately deployed as an all-over, multidirectional design and then stylized to create a shell-like border.

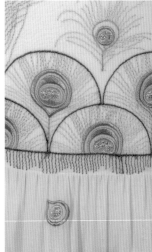

LEFT AND DETAILS ABOVE
Matt and glossy nude-pink satin is used for the yoke of this maxi-skirted wedding suit by Paul Nichols. The fitted and darted jacket is fastened with rouleau loops, and the back flares into a train-like peplum.

BELOW London tailor Tommy Nutter was responsible for the three-piece suit worn by British rock singer Mick Jagger and the matching skirt suit of his new wife Bianca for their wedding in St Tropez in 1971.

THE GROOM'S ATTIRE

As with womenswear, there was a multiplicity of looks for the 1970s bridegroom. These included lightweight, mohair, narrow-shouldered suits by French designer Pierre Cardin as well as the tailored excesses of Tommy Nutter and Tom Gilbey, where the width of the lapels was matched by the width of the tie. The traditional grey tail coat and trousers were suitable for only the most formal of weddings. If morning dress was worn, discreet eccentricities were incorporated into the garment – a flash of moiré lining, or a wider lapel bound in a contrasting colour.

European design was making headway on the international stage, with designers such as Piero de Monzi, Walter Albini and Ted Lapidus incorporating checks and stripes into menswear. In the US, Bill Blass offered sporty sophistication, Sal Cesarani combined fine European tailoring with unexpected touches and colour, while Ralph Lauren created casual classics that won him a Coty award for menswear in 1970. The great dandy of American literature, Jay Gatsby, whose wardrobe of cream-coloured suits and pastel shirts in the 1974 film *The Great Gatsby* was designed by Ralph Lauren, proved influential for a summer wedding, just as Mia Farrow as Daisy, wearing beaded chemise dresses recalled the flapper styles of the 1920s. The hippie beard disappeared, to be replaced by the moustache, epitomizing groomed, dandyish glamour.

Fluidity in Fashion

The disco scene and the glitter-ball fashions of New York's Studio 54 had little direct influence on wedding fashion – very few prospective brides chose to go up the aisle wearing a sequinned boob tube and hotpants. However Roy Halston Frowick, America's foremost designer of the 1970s and darling of the disco set, produced easy-to-wear fluid dresses in double jersey that inspired a more relaxed silhouette and infiltrated wedding-gown fashion, replacing the structured A-line silhouette of the early 1970s. This elegant, more grown-up look was in stark contrast the back-to-nature ethos of the hippies and the use of natural materials, and was due, in part, to the new synthetic materials now emerging.

Qiana, a name selected from a computerized combination of random letters, was the 'miracle fibre' launched by DuPont in 1968, 30 years after the invention of nylon. It revolutionized the textile industry and was hailed as the fabric of the future. Claiming to have qualities superior to the most luxurious silk fabrics, Qiana gave the appearance of silk – from the lustre of its surface yarn to its lightweight, drape and colour – but was also wrinkle resistant, drip-dry and could be machine washed. The fluidity of the fabric was its chief property. Bridalwear designers, such as Bill Schad, Miss Hilda and Bridal Originals in particular, featured Qiana, utilizing its draping qualities for high-waisted Empire line dresses with softly gathered skirts, capes and batwing sleeves. Extended trains of Qiana, some as much as 6 metres (20 feet) in length were draped around the body in a Grecian, sculptural style, forming a circle of fabric around the feet of the bride.

The end of the 1970s was a watershed for fashion, when American ready-to-wear designers, such as Calvin Klein and Diane von Furstenberg, produced modern sportswear-influenced clothes that stripped away the last remnants of the ephemera of fantasy fashion. British street style had little mainstream resonance internationally and the pre-Raphaelite beauty of the earlier part of the decade was now replaced with a new feminine ideal – sporty, healthy, clean cut and unadorned.

OPPOSITE The coming trend for urban sophistication can be seen in this bridal outfit from Jean-Louis Scherrer's autumn/winter 1976–77 haute couture runway show. It is in stark contrast to the milkmaid prettiness that was popular in the earlier part of the decade.

RIGHT British ready-to-wear label Frank Usher originated in 1944, and continues to offer a bridal service – Frank Usher Destination Bridal – which is tailored toward weddings abroad. This 1970s silk, draped, goddess dress is typical of their elegant styling.

Leg-of-mutton sleeves
Also called gigot sleeves, the full gathers and long, many-buttoned cuffs of these neo-Edwardian sleeves lent the appropriate ingénue effect to the milkmaid and mobcap wedding styles of the early 1970s.

▶ Fantasy
Model Angie Bowie wears an embellished, full-length, knitted coat with wide, trumpet sleeves over a draped jersey dress that dates from 1977. The fantasy feathers are by Japanese designer Yuki Torimaru.

Key looks of the decade

1970s

◀ Ethnic influences
Other cultures provided the inspiration for folkloric embellishment and handcrafted detailing that were popular counter-culture and alternative wedding styles, as seen in this lavishly embroidered tunic and skirt from 1971.

The Princess line
Finding renewed popularity in the 1970s, the Princess line was originally created by the couturier Charles Worth in the nineteenth century. The garment is cut with two seams down the front of the dress, which incorporates both the bust and waist darts and provides fit and flare to form an A-line shape.

Punk influences

The anti-establishment punk revolution of 1976, led by Vivienne Westwood and Malcolm McLaren, went from street style to catwalk with this slashed and safety-pinned couture version of a wedding dress by Zandra Rhodes, complete with gold stitching and outsize corsage.

Revival styles

Retro styles proliferated throughout the decade, from the turn-of-the-century Edwardian looks through the 1930s bias-cut dress to the masculine shapes and androgyny of the 1940s.

▲ Trouser suits

The influence of Yves Saint Laurent's 1966 'Le Smoking', and the move toward feminism can be seen in this androgynous wedding suit of 1975. The jacket is fitted to the waist and the trousers flared at the ankle, providing an elegant, elongated silhouette.

◀ Romantic looks

Matching outfits for the bride and groom, from the ready-to-wear spring/summer 1976 collection of French fashion house Yves Saint Laurent. The off-the-shoulder neckline and loose, draped body of the bride's gown references the muumuu that, together with the kaftan, were popular items of leisurewear during the era.

1980s:
Taffeta and Tiaras

The marriage of Lady Diana Spencer to Charles, Prince of Wales, in 1981 set the paradigm for fairytale finery, and influenced the style of wedding dresses for the decade to come. A magical cloud of paper taffeta, with a double-frilled neckline and billowing sleeves, the gown represented a return to full-blown embellishment and heralded a Victorian revival. The cathedral train, the veil, the big bouquet and the diamond tiara were all reinstated as the focal point of the wedding. Although women dressed for success in the boardroom in big-shouldered power suits, they succumbed to the romantic ideal of enormous puffed sleeves and waist-cinching sashes on their wedding day.

Mainstream fashion underwent change almost overnight when Christian Lacroix, while at the couture house Patou, introduced the *pouf*, or puffball, skirt in 1987, thus inverting the fashion silhouette by widening the skirt and narrowing the shoulders. Under his own label, Lacroix plundered historical styles as well as his native Provence for his eclectic imaginings and translated them into wedding gowns for cash-rich customers.

The strength of the American dollar resulted in a surfeit of disposable income, increasing the demand for couture; weddings were yet another opportunity to display the affluence and avid consumerism so typical of the era. Once more, weddings became grand in scale and aspirational, theatrical spectacles. The ceremony was subsumed by the social occasion with lengthy preparations for the day, including the American custom of the 'rehearsal' dinner. Usually a formal occasion requiring a full-length evening gown, this was not an opportunity to rehearse the vows, but a social occasion for friends and family to be introduced.

The return to formality reinstated the morning suit for the groom, and the number of bridesmaids increased exponentially. Wedding gifts were no longer personal – they comprised household equipment as the newlyweds entered married life in the 'designer' decade. The trousseau became an outmoded concept; the bride was no longer presented by her parents with a gift of clothes and lingerie to see her through the first months of marriage.

A Fairytale Princess

When the Archbishop of Canterbury, Dr Robert Runcie, intoned from the lectern of St Paul's Cathedral, 'This is the stuff that fairytales are made of', he could well have been speaking of the bride's dress. On top of this, there was a 100-strong guard of honour from the First Battalion Welsh Guards, 3,500 people in the congregation and 750 million people all over the world watching the ceremony on television. Two million spectators lined the route of Diana's procession from Clarence House, with 4,000 police and 2,200 military officers on hand to manage the crowds.

Months of feverish speculation occurred before the dress designer was finally chosen. To the surprise of many, a relatively inexperienced couple were given the commission: David and Elizabeth Emanuel. The dress featured a wide, double-flounce collar and elbow-length sleeves, a boned bodice and an enormously full skirt over crinoline petticoats. The 7.6 metre (25 foot) detachable train was folded into the horse-drawn carriage with difficulty, which meant the dress looked crumpled when Diana finally alighted on the steps of St Paul's. Spectators and commentators criticized its appearance, not realizing that creasing was a feature of the material from which it was made – paper taffeta.

Great care was taken to source the components of the wedding gown in Britain. The dress was constructed from three different types of fabric, including high-quality taffeta made from silk produced on Lullingstone Silk Farm in Dorset, which was then woven by traditional Suffolk silk weavers Stephen Walters & Sons. Lace that was originally presented by the Royal School of Needlework to Queen Mary was augmented with lace from Nottingham manufacturer Roger Watson, onto which Elizabeth Emanuel and her mother hand-embroidered more than 10,000 pearls and sequins. The sequinned hand embroidery on the veiling was by S Lock Ltd. Cotton bobbin net for the lace and knitted silk tulle for the petticoats were manufactured by Nottingham lace company John Heathcoate.

The tiara that held the veil in place was a Spencer family heirloom, a circlet of scrolling acanthus leaves and star flowers with diamonds. The bride wore

RIGHT An informal photograph taken behind the scenes at Buckingham Palace by Patrick Litchfield, following Diana's marriage to Prince Charles. It includes Her Majesty, The Queen and bridesmaids India Hicks, Sarah-Jane Gaselee and Clementine Hambro.

matching ivory silk and lace slippers by Clive Shilton, and the traditional large bouquet was of gardenias. The bridesmaids' flower-and-ivy circlets and flower baskets were by Edward Goodyear. A useful addition, and one well worth copying, was a matching pochette and umbrella in case of rain. As with all royal bridegrooms, Prince Charles wore his service uniform, the Royal Navy Commander's full dress uniform. Inside the cathedral, Prince of Wales' feathers and flowers festooned every pillar and cameramen were stationed around, broadcasting the occasion to the world.

BELOW LEFT The relatively inexperienced designers David and Elizabeth Emanuel were appointed to create Lady Diana Spencer's wedding gown. They faced fierce competition from more established couture houses, such as Norman Hartnell, to win the design commission of the decade.

BELOW The Prince and Princess of Wales stand together after the ceremony outside the portals of St Paul's Cathedral in London. The Princess's formal wedding gown and traditional bouquet marked an end to the romantic, pastoral-inspired prettiness of the 1970s.

Wedding Gown of The Lady Diana Spencer

OPPOSITE The train of the wedding gown extended the length of the steps leading up to the entrance of St Paul's Cathedral, during Lady Diana Spencer's arrival for her wedding to Prince Charles on 29 July 1981.

The Duchess in Duchesse Satin

British designer Lindka Cierach was chosen to design the wedding dress for the other British royal nuptials of the decade, that of Sarah Ferguson to Prince Andrew in 1986. As for previous royal weddings, thousands of people lined the streets of London from Clarence House to Westminster Abbey, where the ceremony was to be held. It was watched by a worldwide television audience of 500 million. Inside the Abbey, 2,000 people, including 17 members of foreign royalty, the US First Lady Nancy Reagan, Prime Minister Margaret Thatcher and assorted celebrities, watched the bride make her four-minute walk up the blue-carpeted aisle on the arm of her father, Sir Ronald Ferguson.

The Victorian-inspired gown was fashioned of ivory duchesse satin imported from Italy. The full skirt was shaped into a slightly dropped V-shaped waistline from which the gored skirt flowed to the hem, forming a train at the back. Elaborate embroidery and bugle beads adorned the bodice, and the slightly gathered sleevehead was accented with ribbon bows. A large bow at the bustle flowed into a 5 metre (17 foot) long train with the initials A and S intertwined in beadwork. The bride's veil was attached to a perfumed coronet of gardenias, replaced with a tiara before the couple emerged from the chapel. The Duke of York wore the ceremonial day dress of a naval lieutenant and the young pages, including Prince William, were dressed in sailor's outfits, complete with boater hats. The four bridesmaids, all children, wore pale peach ballerina-length dresses trimmed in lace with ruffles and a bow decorating the back, flowered wreaths in their hair and they carried wooden hoops festooned with flowers.

A turn-of-the-century Landau carried the newly betrothed couple to Buckingham Palace, where the bride and groom appeared on the balcony before enjoying a traditional wedding breakfast of lobster, lamb and a 1.8 metre (6 foot) high white wedding cake embellished with pastel sugar flowers. Later, 300 guests converged at Claridges Hotel for another party before the couple departed for their honeymoon in the Azores.

RIGHT AND BELOW The wedding of Sarah Ferguson to Prince Andrew took place on the 23 July 1986. The gown, designed by Lindka Cierach, had a pointed bodice, which narrowed the waist, and an excess of fabric at the sleevehead that also made the waist appear smaller. The lace-bordered train flowed from a fan-shaped bow at the back and was embroidered with thistles, bees and hearts, as well as anchors and waves, in seed pearls, gemstones, sequins and diamanté.

Formal and Froufrou

Socially aspirational 1980s wedding etiquette included a variety of defining criteria for levels of formality, which in turn influenced the choice of wedding dress. A formal wedding required the dress to have a train and a long veil. The American magazine *Modern Bride* categorized the different types of wedding as: formal daytime, semi-formal evening, formal evening, semi-formal daytime, semi-formal evening and informal daytime and evening. The bride's choice of gown for an informal wedding embraced the increasing popularity of the sleeveless wedding dress, accessorized with a hair ornament or hat rather than a tiara. In America, the hour that separates a formal evening wedding and a formal day wedding is 6 pm; however, in Europe no wedding ceremony may be conducted after that hour.

The wedding gown for any formal wedding in this period was inspired by the froufrou of Princess Diana's wedding dress, and the crinoline skirt became the most desired silhouette at the beginning of the decade. Unlike its 1950s counterpart there were no structured underpinnings, such as stiffened petticoats or wired 'cages', to retain the shape and the fabric was allowed to fall to the ground in folds. The skirt was pleated or gathered onto the bodice or, for a more streamlined look, cut into shaped panels to skim over the hips before widening out to provide fullness at the hem. Sleeve styles were extreme, referencing the emphasis on the shoulderpad in daywear, and also inspired by Victorian and Edwardian features such as gigot sleeves with puffed and gathered armholes.

In Britain, David and Elizabeth Emanuel were the leading proponents of the full-blown crinoline; other British designers tended to be more restrained. Frank Usher, a ready-to-wear label originating in the 1940s, produced more understated wedding gowns, and British-born Victor Edelstein and Catherine Walker (both favourite designers of Princess Diana) offered bespoke wedding dress services that purveyed a refined and elegant glamour. In America, Ron LoVece, Ada Athanassiou, Paula Varsalona and Frank Masandrea all designed traditional wedding dresses evoking romance and feminine fantasy.

The recession-hit 1970s had produced a lull in the bridal business, but following this fall in demand, manufacturers and designers were now flourishing again. American designer Frank Masandrea used the hiatus in wedding gown sales in the 1970s to produce a ready-to-wear sportswear line, but re-established his bridal business with Paul Diamond in 1983. He recalled his early career in *Women's Wear Daily* in 1985: 'I've been through barefoot brides, brides in love beads. We've gone from the anything-goes mood of the Sixties to a very traditional luxury look.' He goes on to describe the upturn in the demand as being a result of 'something in the wind', adding, 'Women had gotten secure enough that they could have corporate jobs and wear sportswear during the day, but on their wedding day they really wanted to look like a bride.'

BELOW LEFT The V-shaped bodice is accentuated with a pin-tucked centre piece, forming a stomacher, an eighteenth-century device that holds the bodice in place. This historical reference can also be seen in the short, puffed sleeves. Dating from 1987, the dress was designed by Tatters, on London's Fulham Road, one of Princess Diana's favourite design houses.

BELOW RIGHT A detail showing the hand-made roses combined with spiraling, small, pleated frills that form the floral décolletage of the dress.

OPPOSITE Dating from the beginning of the decade, this dress, photographed by Norman Parkinson for *Brides* magazine in 1980, features unstructured, free-flowing layers of frills and a demure high-necked bodice in soft chiffon.

LEFT AND OPPOSITE
The late 1980s was a period of historical revivalism, as the grandeur of past ages was appropriated for theatrical-style wedding gowns. Dating from 1987, British designer Victor Edelstein refers to the late eighteenth century with this lace dress, featuring a pleated satin cross-over bodice that extends to the back of the waist to form a ruched bow. The peplumed overskirt descends into a short train.

Jewelled Headdresses and Tiaras

In this age of bejewelled and glamorous excess, the full-length train and the sparkling tiara made a comeback. David Sassoon recounts in his book, *The Glamour of Belville Sassoon*:

> *The security arrangements are such that we often never see the tiara until the morning of the wedding, when it goes straight up to the workroom to have the veil mounted and attached, which is an art in itself. Some of the jewellery we are invited to use is quite spectacular – brought round to us directly from the bank vault. As well as family tiaras, we sometimes work with precious family veils. If these are to be used, they need specialist handling and go off to the Royal School of Needlework to be carefully cleaned, and if necessary, repaired.*

Not all tiaras are family heirlooms; their popularity in the 1980s resulted in contemporary jewellery designers including tiaras in their jewellery collections. American-born jeweller Frances Bendixson was inspired to make her first tiara when Prince Charles and Lady Diana

LEFT Erik Mortensen took over as creative director of the House of Balmain on the couturier's retirement in 1982. This design, dating from the 1983–84 autumn/winter collection, features white mink-trimmed double sleeves and diagonal jewelled beading on the tabard-like bodice with a jewelled bandeau-style headdress. The bride carries a matching fur muff.

BELOW The embroidered and tasseled outsize sash is the main feature of this sketched wedding dress with ornamental headdress by Erik Mortensen for Balmain, dating from 1982.

Spencer announced their engagement. Like many other contemporary jewellers, Bendixon achieves the look of court jewels with materials such as twisted silver and gold wire threaded with precious and semiprecious stones; many pieces can be converted into necklaces.

As an item of jewellery the tiara is also subject to the whims and vagaries of fashion. During the 1980s it was worn with a knowing sense of irony by post-punk television presenters, teenage girls and film stars alike. Irish-born Slim Barrett moved to London in 1983 having studied fine art in Galway, Ireland. He has since carved out a reputation in contemporary jewellery design, with high-profile works commissioned by Versace, for whom he designed and made the Flame tiara and the Twisted fairy crown. He also designed the diamond coronet for Victoria Adams' marriage to David Beckham in 1999.

For those that don't have a 'family fender' or can't afford a modern collectable, there are many manufacturers of crystal and pearl tiaras and crowns, such as Butler & Wilson, a costume jeweller on London's South Moulton Street that supplies tiaras made from sparkling diamanté and delicate seed pearls.

BELOW Models at a Parisian fashion show in 1989. The tulle veils loop around the face and are secured with sprays of flowers. The large rhinestone earrings are typical of the period, when outsize costume jewellery assumed a new importance.

Glitz and the 'Glamazon' Bride

Wedding dress manufacturers, such as Priscilla of Boston and John Burbidge, continued to produce traditional gowns to high production values. However, throughout the decade of glitz and glamour, and in tune with the excess of the era, some brides demanded more sparkling embellishment. Silk duchesse satin was now prohibitively expensive, so synthetic fabrics, such as acetate satin that mimicked its subtle shine, were substituted. Influenced by the 'body-con' dresses of designers such as Hervé Léger and Azzedine Alaïa, romantic, Victorian-inspired gowns were abandoned in favour of figure-hugging, show-stopping numbers that revealed every curve and generally ended in a fishtail train. These shimmering, sequinned and pearl-beaded satin acetate gowns were extremely detailed, requiring hours of handsewing – a skill usually outsourced to underpaid overseas labour.

Extra glitter was supplied by veiling, constructed from synthetic tulles with names like 'Glamour' and 'Meteorite'. These were positioned on big, back-combed, teased hair, as seen in *Dynasty*, the influential television series that featured power-hungry femme fatales. An alternative view was offered by the doyenne of American etiquette and tasteful entertaining, Martha Stewart, who published her book *Weddings* in 1987. Providing defining exemplars of the perfect wedding – at home, the yacht club, the farmhouse and the summerhouse – Stewart advised on all aspects of the ceremony, from the gown to the catering and the acceptable typeface font for the invitations.

BELOW Queen of knitwear, Sonia Rykiel, features her signature dark-edged textile rosette on the shoulder of this 1988, fine-gauge knitted, two-piece wedding outfit. It appeared at the finale of the designer's ready-to-wear spring/summer 1988 fashion show in Paris.

BEAUTY 1980s STYLE

The fashion ideal diverged in the 1980s between the 'glamazon' with the big hair and heavy maquillage that went with the showgirl type of wedding gown (all sparkle and hairspray) and the athletic girl-next-door, with a natural look and short hair, exemplified by Princess Diana and models such as Christy Turlington and Linda Evangelista who cropped her long locks in the late 1980s.

Make-up for the bride was skilful, subtle and understated, and included clearly marked brows and gloss, rather than lip-stick – the classic 1980s red lip was usually eschewed for a more obviously pretty pastel shade for the wedding day.

OPPOSITE The bride in this sketch for a couture gown looks like a bejewelled mermaid. It is by Erik Mortensen for Balmain and dates from the spring/summer 1984–85 collection. The embellished sheath dress extends into a hooded headdress and explodes into a fishtail skirt.

RIGHT Model Abyan wears an accordion-pleated, Empire-line, chiffon dress with embroidered bodice and fluted sleeves from Pierre Balmain in 1989. More layers of pleated chiffon ascend to form a train from the Castilian-inspired hat.

BELOW Couture fantasy, sketched by Erik Mortensen for Balmain's spring/summer 1986 collection. A long, slim sheath dress with fishtail hem is rendered extraordinary by a finely pleated hat/veil combination. A square of fabric is angled to fall in a point at the front, suspended from a horizontal headpiece.

The Couture Wedding Dress

Opulence, luxury and embellishment were key looks for the 1980s bride, inspired in part by the revitalization of the once moribund haute-couture industry. This was the result of the power of a strong dollar at the beginning of the decade, the rise in the price of ready-to-wear and the influx of clients from the Arab states. In addition, American high society was in the throes of a period of excessive and conspicuous consumption, under the aegis of Nancy Reagan. Wife of the then-president, she was eager to reinstate formal entertaining, following the 'dress down' years of the Carter administration.

The first catwalk collection of Christian Lacroix in 1987 was also credited with reinstating the relevance of couture. Born in Arles, France, the designer initially gained recognition when, in his position as head designer at the couture house Patou, he introduced the puffball skirt in 1987. With its almost circular shape, he brought change to the silhouette, disarming power dressing and promoting whimsy and romance instead. The success and international influence of the collection led fashion entrepreneur Jean-Jacques Picart and businessman Bernard Arnault to create the twenty-fourth couture house in Paris, with Lacroix at the helm. Nicholas Coleridge witnessed the first collection by Christian Lacroix couture on the catwalk. In his 1989 book, *The Fashion Conspiracy*, he records his response:

> *Gasp and the world gasps with you. The models that processed along the catwalk wore clothes with proportions so strange, so topsy-turvy that they defied conventional logic… There were enormous cloche hats pinned with gilded twigs and bulrushes, and skirts made out of pony skin, silver fox and black Persian lamb. There were jackets embroidered with Camargue motifs and coats made out of red duchesse satin.*

Traditionally, a couture show concludes with a wedding dress, and this show was no exception. The model, Marie Seznec, appeared on the runway in an eighteenth-century-inspired dress featuring a 'stomacher' – a boned or stiffened triangular section of fabric inserted into the bodice that ends in a rounded point just below the waist, helping keep the carriage upright. This pre-revolutionary style historically includes front lacing, decorated with ribbon bows of decreasing sizes called *echelles*. The Lacroix version replaced the ribbon bows with gilded pieces of jewellery. The quilted satin underskirt was revealed by the draped overskirt, known as a *polonaise*, gathered up at one side into

ABOVE Most famous for his eighteenth-century-inspired *pouf* silhouette, Lacroix also combined a range of eclectic references in his work. Here, in his debut couture collection of 1987, the ornate, white, crewel embroidery work on black is inspired by the costumes of Spanish matadors.

OPPOSITE LEFT A froufrou of layers of net tulle, strewn with yellow and pink flowers, creates a frothy, overblown creation. This ready-to-wear wedding dress, by Christian Lacroix, is being modelled by Marie Seznec at the finale of the designer's autumn/winter 1988–89 catwalk show.

rich folds and pleats. The oval-shaped veil of lace was positioned to fall to the shoulders.

Although Lacroix was renowned for his ebullient juxtaposition of brilliant colour – purple, mimosa, orange, pink and emerald green – couture customers frequently had the catwalk designs made in white to wear as a wedding dress. Bridal gowns were, and continue to be, of vital importance to the commercial success of haute couture, utilizing the skilled embroidery and beading ateliers to the full. In Coleridge's *The Fashion Conspiracy,* British designer Alistair Blair remembers the first wedding dress to pass the $100,000 mark. The fashion debut of Christian Lacroix in July 1987 preceded the October stock market crash by three months, and wedding dresses provided commercial stability in unstable times. The Lacroix label made up to 70 couture wedding gowns a year from an output of 200 garments.

The bespoke process of couture was also deployed for another favourite theme of the 1980s: the riding habit, which was essentially an Edwardian look. Karl Lagerfeld tailored silk-satin jackets with a boned and corseted bodice and a peplum drawn up into an oversized bow above a bustled skirt, for the House of Chanel. Replacing the train and veil, the riding habit was accessorized with a small top hat in white, perched at the front of the head and decorated with a band of tulle left to float down the back of the gown. Lagerfeld designed his first bridal collection for Chanel in 1983; it was a version of Chanel's edge-to-edge cardigan jacket, but made in silk satin and edged with rows of frilled tulle rather than braid. Lagerfeld's bridal collections are known for their spectacular and innovative design and he has recently collaborated with the Spanish designer Rosa Clará.

ABOVE French fashion model and muse, Inès de la Fressange, wearing an extraordinary combination of a tailored metallic silver dress overlaid with a crinoline made from semicircles of net tulle. The whole outfit is finished off with an outsize silver bow at the hem. From the 1987 spring/summer haute couture line by Karl Lagerfeld for Chanel.

Carolina Herrera

Born María Carolina Josefina Pacanins y Niño in Caracas, Venezuela, Herrera, the Marchioness of Torre Casa, had a privileged upbringing, attending her first couture show when she was 13 years old. As a socialite in New York in the 1970s, she spent evenings at Studio 54 with friends Bianca Jagger and Andy Warhol. In 1981, encouraged by her friend and *Vogue* editor Diana Vreeland, she went into business and formed Carolina Herrera Limited. The couture line offered elegant, meticulously made clothes in luxurious materials that epitomized her own personal style of understated glamour.

This aesthetic can also be found in her bridalwear designs, which she launched in 1987. Herrera's hallmark is a sculptural silhouette in sumptuous fabrics with restrained embellishment. This is particularly evident in her most famous commission, the clover-scattered organdy wedding dress for Caroline Kennedy. Herrera opened her flagship store on Madison Avenue in 2000, followed by an affordable diffusion line, CH Carolina Herrera, in 2002.

Emanuel Ungaro

The renaissance of haute couture in the 1980s signalled the arrival of Italian-born Emanuel Ungaro as one of the 'big five' of the couture houses, alongside Chanel, Dior, Givenchy and Yves Saint Laurent. Originally one of the 1960s pioneers of the new haute couture, together with André Courrèges and Paco Rabanne, Ungaro opened his couture house in 1965 with the assistance of Swiss artist Sonja Knapp and Elena Bruna Fassio. He made his mark with a precision-cut and unadorned silhouette, entirely in keeping with 1960s minimalism, shortening skirts to unprecedented heights and using vivid colours.

During the 1980s the designer's aesthetic underwent a radical change as he introduced colourful, ultra-feminine dresses that draped and wrapped around the body in a mix of vibrant prints. These tapped into the desire of the era for lavish occasionwear, resulting in international recognition for the brand and a high profile in America. His wedding dresses in this period were constructed of draped, pale pastel crepe, fastened with fabric flowers,

BELOW The late President Kennedy's daughter, Caroline Kennedy, posing with her uncle, Ted Kennedy. She wore a gown by Carolina Herrera on her wedding in 1986. The simple puff sleeves and flower-strewn bodice, with a plain round neckline, go against the prevailing ethos of design excess and shows an elegant restraint that is typical of the designer.

and he was hugely successful with his 'New Baroque' look of puffy sleeves and flounced skirts. He was a favourite of New York's 'shiny-set', socially prominent leaders of fashion such as the late Nan Kempner, and as such much in demand for bespoke bridal gowns of exquisite workmanship, beautiful fabrics, finishing and details – the couture dress has to be as beautiful on the inside as well as the outside.

As is customary, Ungaro ended every runway show with a bridal gown – an opportunity for the designer to present extreme ideas that could be adjusted to the taste of the client. Emanuel Ungaro retired in 2005.

British Designers

A new wave of British designers, including John Galliano and Rifat Ozbek, provided the fashionable bride with an alternative to full-blown Victoriana, and yet were equally romantic. Ozbek was the first British designer to enjoy an international reputation with his signature look of high-waisted trousers, swirling coats, lavishly embroidered boleros and military-inspired jackets.

John Galliano graduated from London's Central St Martins in 1984 with a collection labelled 'Les Incroyables', inspired by the clothes of the French revolution. His innovative cutting techniques included bias-cut slip dresses, which translated into elegant wedding dresses. In 1999 Galliano was appointed creative director of Christian Dior in Paris, where he continued to include bridal gowns in his repertoire. Those brides who eschewed the demureness of the Victorian-inspired dress could now opt for the near nudity of the strapless gown. Traditionally, the bride had been required to cover her shoulders for the ceremony, but with the increased secularization of the event it now became socially acceptable to leave the shoulders uncovered. In 2010 actress Penelope Cruz wore a strapless Galliano design for her marriage to Javier Bardem.

BELOW LEFT Experimenting with shape and form, this ruched, body-sculpted skirt flares into stiffened, armour-like shoulder pleats of duchesse satin. It is from the finale of the haute couture spring/ summer 1986 collection by French designer Emanuel Ungaro.

BELOW RIGHT The gathered and pleated duchesse satin of this wedding gown, from Ungaro's haute couture spring/summer 1987 collection, exemplifies the 1980s propensity for over-design, from the outsize pleated ruff of the collar to the pleated sleeves and hobble skirt.

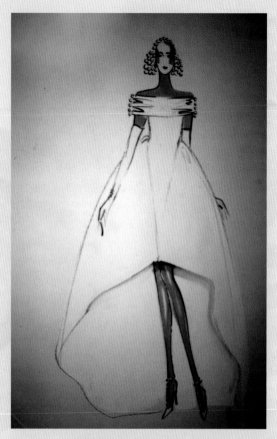

LEFT A frequently seen feature, shown in this 1987 Erik Mortensen for Balmain design, was a hemline that was shorter at the front than the back, where it naturally formed a short train. A broad-banded neckline, revealing bare shoulders, was also an increasingly popular trend and evidence of a transition from covered shoulders to the fashion for strapless gowns in the 1990s.

BELOW The wide circular hem of this simple skater-style dress, by Erik Mortensen for Balmain in 1987–88 is edged with a border of white mink and has an elevated front.

THE DESIGNER FLORIST

Traditional big bouquets were back in style in the 1980s. Victorian overtones were provided by the inclusion of rock ferns and ivy to classic all-white flowers, such as stephanotis, freesias and white roses. It was also an era of innovation. Floristry was now subject to the creative eye of the designer; a spring wedding might include delphiniums, sweet peas and lilies of the valley tied with vintage ribbons and lace, or a dramatic one-off design of unusual combinations – white orchids with corkscrew willow, sprayed silver. Bridesmaid's bouquets were generally more colourful and informal, in keeping with the youth of the attendants. They might be posies of blue salvia, sweet peas and pansies or flower baskets containing rose petals in colours that coordinated with the sashes of the dress.

With a formal wedding the florist was responsible for the flowers in the church, which would continue the theme: sprays of flowers twined with ivy and ferns tied to the end of the pew for a country wedding, or a minimalist display of orchids or calla lilies positioned by the chancel rail. The florist also designed the centrepieces for the tables.

RIGHT Printed pattern is rarely used for bridal gowns, but Yves Saint Laurent makes an exception here using rose-printed fabric for a swathed, body-conscious dress, with the fullness pulled onto one hip and tied in a bow, from 1987. The bouquet is a simple sheaf of matching brilliant blooms.

THE GROOM'S SUIT

The Victorian revival in wedding style included the reinstatement of the morning suit, together with the top hat. Elizabeth Hawes, in the book *Weddings* by Martha Stewart, recommends: 'A morning suit is worn at a formal morning wedding, up to and including a pre-launch event; white tie is worn at a very formal late-afternoon or evening event; and a tuxedo whenever it suits the mood'. She also advises:

> *Rental tuxes can be horrendous – true penguin garb, shiny, ill fitting, and obviously the 'borrowed' item of the wedding ritual. And there is something demoralizing about renting a tux for your own wedding, especially as the bride is spending vast sums on a confection that is likely to be worn only once.*

The alternative was one of the 'designer' suits that were proliferating as the interest in fashionable menswear grew. Italian designer Giorgio Armani dominated the 1980s menswear market, reducing the padding and interlinings of traditional tailoring techniques to produce an unstructured, double-breasted jacket with long lapels and loose-fitting trousers. By using cloth generally allocated to womenswear, such as wool crepe, Armani softened the male silhouette even further. Produced in pastel shades for summer, his signature look of crumpled linen, sleeves pushed up in the style of Don Johnson in the television series *Miami Vice*, adorned many bridegrooms. Film also influenced male fashion: Armani designed the costumes for Richard Gere in *American Gigolo* (1980) and Manhattan tailor Allan Flusser designed the suits for Michael Douglas as Gordon Gekko in *Wall Street* (1987). British designer Paul Smith popularized the suit for the 'yuppie' (young urban professional) set, juxtaposing classic tailoring with details such as brightly patterned linings.

The opulence and extravagance evident in womenswear also appeared in menswear, particularly in the Mannerist-inspired prints, bold colour and luxurious materials of Italian designer Gianni Versace, who launched his first menswear collection in 1975. In the 1980s, the designer introduced a new silhouette for men – a longer, slimmer jacket with minimal buttons worn over draped trousers.

Specialist Bridal Houses

The department-store bridal salon was in decline during the 1980s, but specialist shops were booming with the rise of the independent bridal consultant and the proliferation of high-end, ready-to-wear designers. Taffeta ballroom gowns by Richard Glasgow with off-the-shoulder sleeves, unique antique laces from Pat Kerr (the designer of the bridal gown in the Estée Lauder advertisement for the perfume 'Beautiful') and intricate beadwork from Bianchi were some of the many options on offer. The Bridal Building on New York's Seventh Avenue provided 24 floors and thousands of cut-price wedding gowns for the prospective bride, but most preferred the more leisurely experience of visiting a designer boutique.

This was a more time-consuming exercise, involving two or three fittings, with the gown taking 10–16 weeks to make from the initial consultation. The first fitting was called a 'virgin' fitting for measurements, after which the gown was designed and cut. At the second and third fittings, adjustments were made – often because the bride had decided to lose weight. Labels such as Mary McFadden, Carolina Herrera and Oscar de la Renta also offered a bespoke bridal service.

JLM Couture

A long-standing label that has adjusted over time to the fluctuations in the bridal market by introducing new lines at different price-points, JLM was also one of the first to be alert to the fact that many bridal attendants wanted dresses with a fashionable edge that could also be worn on other occasions. Originally named Jim Hjelm's Private Collection, Ltd, JLM was founded by long-time bridal gown designer Jim Hjelm in 1985. Born in Worcester, Massachusetts, the designer attended the New England School of Design before working for the major bridal label the House of Bianchi in Boston. In 1962, Hjelm took a position with a rival bridal house Priscilla of Boston, where he stayed for 19 years. In 1980, Hjelm moved to New York, becoming a designer for Galina-Bouquet, Inc. After several years at Galina, and 25 years in the bridal industry, Hjelm decided to launch his own label with business partner Joseph L Murphy. The company went public in 1987 – and Jim Hjelm's Private Collection became the only publicly held bridal house in the industry.

OPPOSITE Italian fashion designer Giorgio Armani challenged the traditional techniques of English tailoring by deconstructing the jacket and creating a fluid silhouette at odds with the then formal man's suit.

The label specialized in traditional wedding gowns, known as 'heirloom' pieces, following the Sweetheart line and featuring nets, silks and antique-like laces in luxurious fabrics. Following the 1990s downturn in the economy, the company's price point proved too expensive compared with other bridal ready-to-wear manufacturers, such as Armani, Anne Klein and Donna Karan. To offset the drop in demand, Hjelm introduced the JH Collection, which used synthetic fibres and, in 1992, the Contemporary Classic division to produce gowns with less embellishment and simpler styling. To this end, Lazaro Perez was appointed and the gowns marketed under his name. In 1993, the company launched a line of less-expensive dresses under the New Traditions label.

Convinced that there was a market for fashionable bridesmaids' dresses designed to be worn beyond the wedding day, Murphy introduced fashion-led styles in muted colours in 1994 under the Occasions label. By the late 1990s, the company was comprised of a number of labels, only one of which was Jim Hjelm, and the business was subsequently renamed JLM Couture Inc. In 1997, with Perez and McMillan designing expensive bridal gowns for the company, JLM quickly moved up the ranks of the upper end of the bridal gown business.

ABOVE Ronald Reagan escorts his daughter, Patti, in her wedding dress, designed by Mariana Zaharoff, who also created the influential clothes for *Dynasty* and *Dallas*.

BELOW Mary McFadden's spring/summer 1984 collection, featuring the unique pleated silk Marii technique, which she patented in 1975.

Boned bodices
The stomacher, or plastron, of the eighteenth century – a boned or stiffened triangular piece of fabric inserted into the bodice and ending in a rounded point – was a popular feature of 1980s bridal gowns. It maintained posture and also created the impression of a narrow waist.

▶ Froufrou and frills
Exemplified by Zandra Rhodes, the era's propensity for layers of frills and lavish use of fabric reached an apogee at the beginning of the decade.

Key looks of the decade

1980s

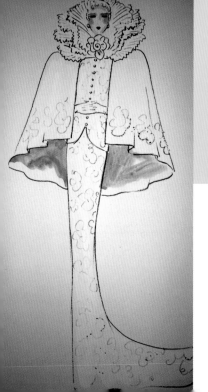

◀ Flamboyant fantasy
Haute couture explored the limits of futuristic fantasy, deploying the ateliers for ever more outrageous headdresses and caped configurations, seen here in this bridal gown by Erik Mortenesen for couture house Balmain for 1985.

Puffy sleeves
Wide shoulders were the defining feature of 1980s fashion. In wedding attire, where hard-edged shoulderpads would not have been so appropriate, this width was translated into the puffed sleeve. Usually gathered at the sleevehead, with a subtle amount of padding, they were secured at the elbow or wrist in a deep lace-edged frill.

◀ Body-sculpted bridal
The silhouette of the wedding gown changed radically at the end of the decade, with the introduction of the gym-honed figure. Rather than copy the bandage dresses of mainstream fashion, a similar effect was often achieved with ruching or draping, as in this sequinned example by Helen Anderson from 1988.

Long trains
The increasing formality and extravagance of the 1980s wedding ceremony demanded a return to Edwardian opulence, and the train once again became an important expression of status and expenditure.

Rosettes and ruffles
An era of lavish embellishment, ruffles appeared in both occasionwear and wedding dresses. They were either structured in an architectural waterfall in heavyweight satin, or light and airy in silk chiffon.

▲ Dropped 'V' waists
A typically formal wedding dress of 1988. The dropped V-waistline, usually designed with a modified crinoline skirt and décolleté neckline was made popular by the gown worn by Sarah Ferguson at her marriage to Prince Andrew in 1987.

1990s to Now:
Today's Designers

At the beginning of the 1990s, the ornate bridal gown, with the billowing crinoline skirt falling from a narrow waist and full, puffed sleeves, gave way to a long, narrow streamlined sheath dress or a classical columnar shape structured in architectural heavy duchesse satin. This pared-down simplicity of wedding style by designers such as Vera Wang and Narciso Rodriguez, who designed the influential bias-cut shift for Carolyn Bessette for her marriage to John F Kennedy Jr in 1996, was in keeping with the minimalism of mainstream fashion. With wedding ceremonies more often taking place in hotels or specialist venues, and not confined to either a registry office or a place of worship, it became increasingly acceptable to display more flesh, resulting in a vogue for strapless gowns which remains one of the most significant trends in wedding-dress design. Sexuality is now more overt; where once bridal attire represented virginity and purity, now fashionable wedding dresses are cut to display the undulating curves of the bride, emphasizing the décolleté and following the line of the body to end in a fishtail flick at the hem.

Alongside the eschewing of extraneous detailing, another trend emerged: the fantasy gown – the specialty of couturiers such as Vivienne Westwood and British designer John Galliano, who as well as designing for his own label is also creative director at Parisian couture house Christian Dior. Traditionally the final outfit on the catwalk, the couture bridal dress became an option for the prospective bride who was prepared to spend more money than ever before and who was inspired by a multiplicity of sources, from the ever-burgeoning print media to films such as *Sex and the City* (2007), which showcased the best of wedding attire from leading couturiers and designers.

Traditional accoutrements such as the train, veil and the tiara have also undergone changes since the 1990s. They have been relinquished by some brides in favour of more dramatic accessories, such as the exploding heart tiara of the Argentinian jeweller Otazu or the Swarovski-encrusted veil from Mexican designer Alberto Rodriguez. Rather than adding a separate train to the gown, designers now have a propensity to extend the length of the dress so that it pools at the bride's feet in a short train, creating a statuesque, goddess-like look.

The Modern Wedding Service

The wedding industry underwent a massive expansion at the turn of the twenty-first century, fuelled in part by the ubiquity of the wedding ceremony in popular culture. Beginning in 1994 with the release of the British film *Four Weddings and a Funeral*, other films followed with the wedding ceremony as a central plot device – *The Runaway Bride*, *My Best Friend's Wedding*, a remake of *Father of the Bride* and *The Wedding Planner*, to name a few. Weddings became the subject of numerous reality television programmes, from surprise ceremonies to prize-winning competitions. Today the US wedding industry geared up to exploit the ever-increasing custom of partners reaffirming their wedding vows. With celebrities such as model and actress Heidi Klum and musician Seal renewing their vows on a yearly basis, 'vow renewal packages' offer yet another opportunity for bridal designers to produce that special dress. Full-on formality is the norm for the turn-of-the-century bride. As the demographic shifted from the 20-year-old ingénue to the more mature woman of 30 – the average age of a bride in 2000 – a couple is now prepared to invest both time and money in protracted nuptials, bridal showers, extensive 'hen' and 'stag' parties, and a honeymoon that is regarded as the 'holiday of a lifetime'. The day before the wedding there is a bridesmaid's luncheon, hosted by close family members of the bride, followed by a rehearsal dinner in the evening.

When so much expense is incurred in the social aspect of the wedding, a bespoke bridal gown is a natural choice. The luxury wedding dress has become a flourishing niche market, barely challenged by the discount and chain retailers selling off-the-rack mass-produced lines. Brides-to-be are invited by one of the proliferating wedding-advice websites such as the Knot (theknot.com) to design their own 'bridal avatar', and can source their wedding dress on an iPhone. However, the real-life wedding planner continues to provide a personal service, and most brides prefer the more thrilling experience of visiting a 'bricks and mortar' boutique or bridal salon, or, increasingly, sourcing their very own vintage dress.

The Bride Abroad

Throughout the 1990s, it became an increasingly popular option to hold the wedding ceremony in some exotic location. British bridal house Berketex launched a range of wedding dresses called Affiniti in response to the number of wedding ceremonies being held abroad. These short dresses with matching jackets were a practical solution to the problem of packing a full-length traditional wedding dress. However, as beach weddings increased in popularity, formality gave way to a more relaxed approach. Indigenous clothing – the sarong-style dress, the white broderie-anglaise kaftan (accessorized with a white lace parasol and by Allegra Hicks) and even the bikini (in white satin, designed by Vivienne Westwood) was worn to exchange vows by the sea. Bouquets of local flowers such as hibiscus, bougainvillea and orchids were carried and bare feet completed the look.

BELOW Movie star Renée Zellweger wearing a wedding gown representative of the style of foremost American designer Carolina Herrera for her short-lived marriage to singer Kenny Chesney at Cruz Bay Beach, Virgin Islands, in 2005.

OPPOSITE Sarah Jessica Parker in the fashion-led movie *Sex and the City* (2007) as Carrie Bradshaw wearing designer Vivienne Westwood's champagne silk wedding dress – known as the Gold Label Lily. The gown features the designer's signature corset infrastructure.

LEFT Fairytale fantasy from John Galliano for French fashion house Christian Dior, 2005-6. The dress features tremblant wings in lieu of a train and a boned corset overlaid with embroidered silk tulle which ends in an oversize bow. The Faerie Queene wears a velvet and gilt crown, shot with stars, designed by milliner Stephen Jones.

From Catwalk to Aisle

Narciso Rodriguez was a relatively unknown designer when he was commissioned to design the wedding dress for Carolyn Bessette on her marriage to John F Kennedy Jr in 1996. The simple, streamlined, bias-cut, white sheath dress was a triumph of understated chic, and set the style for the following decade as bridalwear design became an ever-accelerating business.

Many independent designer labels responded to requests from the prospective bride-to-be for a dress adapted from runway collections; this prompted Alice Temperley to introduce a dedicated bridal line. Other top designers specialized in wedding gowns and then subsequently launched a ready-to-wear collection, as was the case with American designer Vera Wang, who has remained at the forefront of bridal design since the implementation of her label in 1990. Wang's aesthetic of pared-down simplicity responded to the vogue for bridal understatement that was beginning to appear at the end of the 1980s, when the silhouette shifted from the romantic full-skirted crinoline to the classical columnar shape of the Empire-line and sheath dress. Dating from the nineteenth century, the Empire-line *robe en chemise* replaced the panniers and bustles of the previous era with simple high-waisted dresses in white muslin or calico, sometimes dampened to cling to the body in imitation of the folds and drapery of Greek statues.

British designer John Galliano referenced the eighteenth century for inspiration, and his neoclassical wedding gowns have a seductive aura of déshabillé. Vivienne Westwood also reworked the silhouettes of the seventeenth and eighteenth centuries, but with the buxom heroines featured in the paintings of Jean-Antoine Watteau and François Boucher rather than the sylph-like waif of Galliano's muses. Westwood first introduced the corset into outerwear in 1987, and prospective brides used Westwood's main-line dresses of boned corsets and swagged skirts as bridal gowns before the designer launched her first dedicated bridal collection for Liberty of London in 1993. The 1940s-inspired matching trouser suits with large satin lapels in cream wool were in tune with the times but untypical of Westwood, who went on to incorporate her signature boned bodices and lavishly swathed skirts into her bridal ranges.

TOP John Galliano for Dior epitomizes the power of cultural research in presenting his collections. The oriental essence of this wedding gown from 2007 lies in the origami-like folds of stiff taffeta in the bodice and skirt.

RIGHT The simplicity of the draped and fitted bodice and full skirt of this taffeta wedding gown from Vivienne Westwood's ready-to-wear collection of 1997 is imbued with an element of subversion in the use of the ornate blindfold.

FAR LEFT Typical of 1990s style, this dress by Bellville Sassoon shows the move toward overtly sexy, body-hugging styles, the silhouette formed by the back-laced corset and the hourglass shape emphasized by the fishtail skirt.

LEFT British designer Joe Casely-Hayford has produced his own-brand label for men and women since the mid-1980s. This ivory raw-silk dress, decorated with pearls, metal rivets, chains and studs, wittily plays on the loss of freedom symbolized by the wedding ceremony.

Styles for a Contemporary Market

There is currently an unprecedented diversity in wedding dress styles. For brides who wish to engage with a more avant-garde experience, extreme couture – such as Viktor & Rolf's knitted dress with oversized cardigan, Roksanda Ilincic's wayward flying ruffles, Yumi Katsura's kimono styles or the shimmering Lurex burka from Haider Ackermann – provide an alternative to the traditional gown. Alber Elbaz at Lanvin is at the top end of the market, with ready-to-wear wedding gowns made from the most luxurious fabrics: washed silk satin, mousseline, charmeuse and gazar, fashioned into frilled and layered dresses. Matthew Williamson forsakes his signature colourful prints for Empire-line, white-on-white, peacock feather-figured fabric. Even American style institution, J Crew, the original preppy label, now offer bridalwear in ruffled silk organza among their checked shirts and cosy cashmere sweaters.

Since the turn of the twenty-first century the style of wedding dresses has become as diverse as the venues in which they appear: a Marie Antoinette-inspired froth of lace, pin-tucks and frills for a wedding in a Long Island garden, with vows spoken under a wisteria and honeysuckle pagoda; or a column of bias-cut silk by Vera Wang for a formal wedding in one of Scotland's historic castles. Designers are also finding solutions for the problem of wearing a dress that would lend enough formality to the ceremony, while still being appropriate for later festivities. Giambattista Valli's wedding dress for shoe designer Charlotte Dellal in 2010 had a tulle-swathed bodice with a multilayered skirt of rows of tiny frills, which transformed into a sleek, smooth silhouette once the tiers at the waist were removed. Landscape artist Miranda Brooks chose an Oscar de la Renta dress for her wedding, with a bustled overskirt that was later dispensed with for dancing.

Fashion trends are now subsumed to personal preferences and considerations of body type rather than the latest look – a prospective bride who is curvaceous may be attracted to the figure-hugging curves of an Oscar de la Renta dress, while a romantic who yearns for a fantasy fairytale wedding may embrace the fragile femininity of an Alberta Ferretti wedding gown. Renowned for her delicate beaded dresses, Italian designer Ferretti produced her first bridal couture line in 2010. With a limited edition of 14 dresses, each named after flowers, the lightweight and airy gowns each required 30 to 40 hours of hand-sewing and embroidery and were constructed of 80 metres (88 yards) of tulle, silk Mikado, cabochon and platinum threads.

American contemporary designers such as Phillip Lim, Thakoon Panichgul and Jason Wu have all deployed their modern, streamlined aesthetic to bridalwear, while others such as Zac Posen respond to a specific request from a favoured customer. Posen fashioned a skintight sleeveless dress that expanded into a massive fishtail skirt just below the knees for top model Coco Rocha for her marriage to British artist James Conran held in the gardens of a Gothic revival castle in France's Loire Valley in 2010.

Contemporary bridal gowns are almost invariably strapless, either cut straight across the top of the bodice for a tubular sheath dress or shaped into a Sweetheart line, which is then balanced with a full skirt, a signature style of New York label MGNY – Madeline Gardner New York. The strapless bodice requires only a short veil, and one that encloses the shoulders is usually deemed sufficient coverage for the bride's appearance in church. Inevitably, couture gowns reflect the designer's current collections and personal aesthetic.

RIGHT An unusual hit of colour for the runway wedding finale. This haute couture gown by Emanual Ungaro for fall/winter 1996–97 represents the exquisite skills of the embroidery atelier. Colourful blooms are embroidered onto figured silk taffeta under- and overskirts, with larger flowers appliquéd to form a waistband. Tiny posies form the buttons for the severely-shaped lace bodice.

Anne Barge

American designer Anne Barge spent much of her childhood accompanying her mother, an accomplished pianist and organist, to the many wedding ceremonies for which she played. As an adult, while teaching in Atlanta, Georgia, Barge visited a trunk show (a touring show of a designer's collection, usually held in a department store with the designer present), held by Priscilla of Boston. After showing her sketchbooks to the designer she was offered a job as an apprentice with the company. Following a period working in fashion show production, display and retail management, Barge opened her own boutique, Anne Barge for Brides, in 1981, in the chic, upscale Buckhead district of Atlanta; she went on to offer a bespoke service with individually designed gowns. New York bridal manufacturers Kleinfeld acquired the Anne Barge store in 1994, while Barge continued to manage and buy for the Saks Fifth Avenue bridal salons.

In 1996, British entrepreneur Richard Branson appointed Barge as managing director at Virgin Bride. Barge introduced American and European designers to the UK, together with an understated ethos that contrasted with the then romantic, traditional look of the British bride. The designer also added adult bridesmaids' dresses to the range, something of a novelty at the time. Finally, in 1999, Barge launched the Anne Barge Bridal Collection, combining classic designs with luxurious fabrics and museum-quality beading and embroidery. With an atelier above Atlanta's Four Seasons Hotel, the line is represented in Neiman Marcus and stores throughout the US, UK, Spain and Japan.

RIGHT A classically simple A-line dress from Anne Barge's autumn 2007 collection. The strapless bodice, now a wedding gown staple, is beaded, and the skirt is banded in horizontal stripes of silk-satin that broaden toward the hem and emphasize the narrowness of the waist.

Collette Dinnigan

Phillipa Lepley

Born in South Africa, raised in New Zealand, and with a thriving business based in Australia, designer Collette Dinnigan has a global view of the fashion industry, particularly since she has shown her collections in Paris since 1996. Dinnigan initially concentrated on designing and manufacturing lingerie – silk pyjamas and French knickers that incorporated antique lace. Although the line proved difficult to sell in Australia, it was successful in high-end stores in Europe and the US, selling to Barneys and Harvey Nichols, which prompted the designer to launch a small clothing collection in 2000. Currently with stores in the UK, the United States, Europe, the Middle East and Asia selling her fashion label, Dinnigan has added a dedicated bridal range of hand-beaded and hand-finished couture gowns. Her magical 'Snow White' collection employed cutwork, appliqué and exquisite beadwork, while her spring-inspired 2009 'Secret Garden' collection featured styles in French lace, organdy and draped jersey, embellished with dragonfly and daisy motifs.

London-based designer Phillipa Lepley has garnered a reputation for structured bodices and corsetry softened with layers of tulle, lace, organza and chiffon – simplicity combined with exquisite detail. Trained at the London College of Fashion, born in Nottingham and now based in Fulham, Lepley set up her studio in 1988. The designer prides herself on creating a perfectly proportioned dress for each customer using what she calls 'the mathematics of design'. Rather than following fashionable trends, the designer prefers to create a timeless classic for the bride who wants to look her best and not have the dress wear her. Lepley's wedding gowns are form-fitting, floor-sweeping affairs, with subtle embellishment to add interest and individuality – a layer of lace or sequinned net, a wrap decorated with textile roses, a diamanté jacket or embroidered flowers running down the bodice. The 2010 season was called 'My Nirvana', and included all the elements of her signature style of romantic femininity, alongside her 'mathematical obsession with proportion'.

FAR LEFT A neo-Grecian, simply draped wedding dress, the fullness of which is pulled in with a jewel-clasped belt that matches the shoulder ornamentation. The style, from Australia-based designer Collette Dinnigan's 2010 ready-to-wear collection, is titled 'Dew Drops'.

LEFT Fresh, youthful and relying on draping and cutting for dramatic effect, this gown from British designer Phillipa Lepley's 'Garden Roses' collection of 2011 exemplifies the designer's signature style.

Monique Lhullier

Retaining a traditionally romantic approach to bridal attire, while also promoting a modern aesthetic with a sleeveless an A-line silhouette the Los Angeles-based Filipino-born fashion designer Monique Lhullier is at the high-end of the bridal market. Of mixed French and Spanish-Cebuana descent, Lhullier studied at Lausanne, Switzerland, after which she enrolled at the Fashion Institute of Design and Merchandising (FIDM) in California, where she met her future husband, Tom Bugbee. It was the process of designing her own wedding that cemented her vision for her future firm, and in 1996 she launched her first bridal collection with a loan from her father.

Lhullier has a remarkable celebrity clientele. In 2005, she designed a gown for pop singer Britney Spears' wedding to Kevin Federline and subsequent commissions have included gowns for Kristen Stewart, Kelly Clarkson, Natalie Imbruglia and Sarah Gore; she designed the wedding dress worn by Hilary Duff in the film *A Cinderella Story* (2004).

Marchesa

British-born Georgina Chapman, who co-founded the Marchesa label with Keren Craig, launched this high-end fashion label in 2004. Since then the exquisitely embellished gowns in opulent fabrics have graced Hollywood's red carpets. Named after the infamous *fin de siècle* socialite and femme fatale, Marchesa Luisa Casati, the design partners created a capsule bridal collection in 2010, unveiled exclusively at Bergdorf Goodman in New York. The bridal collection features Marchesa's signature deft manipulation of fabric and extensive ornamentation, including Grecian draping, delicate embroidery and laser-cut waterfalls of organdy and heavily perforated lace.

OPPOSITE FAR LEFT Luxurious detailing is the hallmark of designer Monique Lhuillier, as seen in this gown from the spring 2011 collection, in which picot-edged flowers centred with seed pearls are appliquéd to a boned, mesh bodice.

OPPOSITE LEFT A juxtaposition of a crinolined overskirt printed with gilded broken stripes and the flower-strewn shoulder straps combine in an exquisite wedding dress and veil from Lhuillier's 2011 collection.

RIGHT A mille-feuille explosion of silk chiffon, circular, pleated frills spirals down a simple sheath dress in ever-increasing circles on this gown from Marchesa's ready-to-wear autumn/winter 2010 collection.

Bruce Oldfield

With three decades of high-end fashion behind him, British designer Bruce Oldfield has been creating eveingwear for some of the world's most famous and elegantly dressed women, from Hollywood actresses and pop stars to international royalty. Known for classic, simple elegance with a contemporary twist, his beautifully structured clothes combine lightness and fluidity with sumptuous fabrics and intricate detailing. Among his clientele, past and present, are the late Diana, Princess of Wales, Queen Rania of Jordan, Anjelica Huston, Charlotte Rampling, J K Rowling, Helen Mirren, Rihanna, Taylor Swift and Sienna Miller.

Brought up and educated in the care of children's charity, Barnardo's, for whom he remains vice president. Oldfield studied fashion at Ravensbourne College before going on to St Martins School of Art, from which he graduated in 1973. In 1975 the Bruce Oldfield label was launched alongside his first ready-to-wear collections for European and American stores. Oldfield started the couture line in 1978, and in 1984 he opened his first shop selling to an international clientele.

In 1990 Oldfield was awarded the Order of the British Empire (OBE) for services to the fashion industry; he also has honorary fellowships to the Royal College of Art and the universities of Durham and Sheffield.

The designer opened his first flagship bridal boutique in London's Beauchamp Place in 2010, offering a collection of couture, custom-made and ready-to-wear gowns as well as dresses for the mother and bridesmaids and exquisite accessories for the entire party. In this one-stop shop, the bride can choose coordinating shoes and bags as well as items from an exquisite collection of vintage accessories.

BELOW 'Leonora', designed by Bruce Oldfield in 2010, is a sleeveless tulle couture dress with an embroidered bodice. Appliquéd horizontal strips of alternating duchesse satin and zibeline encircle the fluted skirt.

OPPOSITE An Oldfield strapless, form-fitting, couture silk tulle dress, titled 'Flora', features sequinned embroidery on the overdress and a draped fishtail skirt that elegantly pools to the floor in a small train.

Alice Temperley

Renowned for the exquisite embellishment and range of decorative techniques of her main fashion line it was a natural progression for British designer Alice Temperley to launch a dedicated bridal line in 2009. Following her graduation from London's Royal College of Art, where Temperley studied fabric technology and print, the designer launched her fashion label in 2000 with her husband, Lars Von Bennigsen, during London Fashion Week. Working out of her Notting Hill studio in a cobbled mews off west London's boutique-filled Ledbury Road, the designer exemplifies a typically British style, combining an eclectic bo-ho look with embellished elegance. Scarlett Johansson, Gwyneth Paltrow, Jennifer Aniston, Kate Winslet, Claudia Schiffer and Catherine Zeta-Jones have all been photographed in her hand-embellished creations.

TOP FAR LEFT The cleverly shaped seaming on the embellished bodice of Temperley's 2010 'Ellette' dress has an inverted 'V' at the waist. The boat neckline and capped sleeves have a fresh, ingénue appeal.

BOTTOM FAR LEFT From the same season, this 'Jessamine' dress also has Temperley's signature hallmark of an undemanding silhouette. The Empire-line dress with a deep 'V' neckline has delicate lace sleeves that button up to the elbow and a long circular train with a lace scalloped edge.

BOTTOM LEFT A flattering fall of bias-cut silk crepe in this 'Jean' dress by Temperley references the styles of the 1930s in the goddess poise of the model and the small, neat head. The cut lace-work of the caped bodice is edged in a contrasting texture and is typical of the designer's innovative fabric treatments.

OPPOSITE LEFT Along with the strapless gown, the asymmetrical one-shouldered dress has achieved growing popularity, seen here in this detail from a 2007 gown by Vera Wang.

OPPOSITE RIGHT With typical minimal seaming and darting, this bias-cut, silk-satin dress by Vera Wang has a simple bandeau neckline. Decoration is limited to a cluster of silk chiffon bows on the hip.

Vera Wang

One of the best-known names in the luxury wedding market, Vera Wang was prompted to start the company by her unsuccessful search for the right dress for her own wedding. The business was launched in 1990 out of a salon in the upscale Carlyle Hotel on Madison Avenue in New York. Wang's success in the competitive world of bridal fashion was due in part to her skill at elevating the whole consumer experience to encompass all aspects of the ceremony and an image of exclusivity and luxury.

With a philosophy of 'less is more', Wang's interpretation of the wedding dress offered 1990s brides an alternative to the excesses of 1980s flounces. The designer won the commission of the decade in 2010 when she was asked to design the dress for Chelsea Clinton's nuptials. The dress was a strapless, raw-edged, laser-cut, swirling silk-organza ball skirt and train, with a diagonally draped bodice in silk tulle, accented by an embellished belt. (For the reception, Chelsea changed into a Grecian silk tulle Vera Wang gown with a criss-cross back, accessorized with a narrow, grosgrain, black belt.) Wang, a friend of the Clinton family, also designed all the bridesmaids' dresses, which were strapless, bias-cut, lavender chiffon gowns with a side drape and contrasting plum bow. The groom wore a Burberry tux.

The Wedding Planner

OPPOSITE An authentic vintage dress is ideal for those who want to wear something completely original on their big day. This original Edwardian vintage wedding dress is from the Vintage Wedding Dress Company, who also carry vintage-inspired contemporary designs in their 'Decades' collection.

A vintage-inspired wedding is a rare opportunity for the modern bride to set the scene and star in her very own costume drama. Inspired by the feminine froth and frills of the films such as *My Fair Lady* and television drama series *Downton Abbey*, an Edwardian wedding can either be a summer picnic set under the low-hanging branches of a spreading cedar tree, with the men in striped blazers and boaters and the women with parasols, or a sumptuous banquet, eaten in the evening by flattering candlelight. During the 1920s the bright young things wore their bridal gowns short. With bobbed hair and knee-length rows of pearls, the flapper bride displayed an insouciant joyfulness with flying feathers and fringes as she danced the Charleston and the Turkey Trot at the reception. The sinuous contours of a 1930s bias-cut, silk-satin bridal gown, resonant of the silver-screen stars of Hollywood's heyday, can be set amid the Art Deco background of a Fred Astaire and Ginger Rogers movie – cocktails and caviar among the glass and mirrors of the boudoir. The Second World War bride with connotations of 'make do and mend' ingenuity could still enjoy the Lindy Hop in her floral tea-dress and seamed stockings.

For the gown, make the most of an hourglass figure by choosing a 1950s wasp-waisted dress with a heart-shaped bodice and full skirt that enhances voluptuous curves. If fashion icon Audrey Hepburn is more your style, the ballerina-length skirt and bateau neckline of the gamine film star suits a slender figure. For contemporary bo-ho style, be inspired by the barefoot bride of the early 1970s, floating across a wild-flower meadow wearing layers of Gina Fratini broderie anglais or a Laura Ashley sprigged cotton smock. Further ideas for planning a period-style wedding can be found on following pages – as a vintage-inspired bride you have the opportunity to bring the past and present together and reunite romance with tradition.

Edwardian Weddings
Lace, Leisure and Luxury

The Edwardian-themed wedding could include the more relaxed leisure activities of that near-mythical period of endless summers and lazy days. Think of E M Forster's Lucy Honeychurch in *A Room With a View* playing tennis in the grounds of her home, Windy Corner, dressed in linens and lace, or cricket played on the sun-soaked fields that witnessed the doomed love affair between the aristocratic daughter of the house and the estate farmer in *The Go-Between*. An Edwardian wedding might encompass a picnic with tables set under the branches of a cedar tree, as described by Consuela Vanderbilt in her book, *The Glitter and the Gold* (1952):

> *The tea table was set up under the trees. It was a lovely sight, with masses of luscious apricots and peaches to adorn it. There were also pyramids of strawberries and raspberries; bowls brimful of Devonshire cream; pitchers of iced coffee, scones to be eaten with various jams, and cakes with sugared icing.*

Although a picnic is perfect for a summer wedding, a spring or autumn affair needs to have an interior venue, and the winter months are particularly suitable for the candle-lit extended wining and dining required. Create 'candlescapes' with candles of various heights and thicknesses to reflect off the cut-glass and polished silver of a long table. Set this with artfully arranged ferns and trailing ivy in autumn and full-blown pink and white peonies in spring or early summer. Source vintage linen tablecloths edged in drawn-thread work or tatting – a lucky find might be a monogrammed set of napkins that match your initials. Invitations must be handwritten, and miniature fans inscribed with the guests' names make unusual place settings.

Find a gilt-mirrored venue, and place palm trees in Chinese vases around the orchestra to create a 'palm court', the music of which should be heard but not seen throughout the meal. In true Edwardian fashion, this consists of several courses and ends with port and cigars. The French chef Auguste Escoffier was much revered at the time, both in America and Europe, and the dinner could begin with his *purée de pommes parmentier* with *croûton de huitre* (a leek and potato soup with oyster croutons). A fish course, possibly salmon with a mousseline sauce, would be followed by an entree of a soufflé, with a palate-clearing sorbet to precede a main course of roast meat. A green salad would then be served separately, followed by cheese, a dessert such as champagne-and-primrose jelly (the Edwardians loved their jellies, both sweet and savoury), and finally a 'savoury' – again designed to clear the palate, consisting of Angels on Horseback or Welsh rarebit.

The Cake

The first recipe for a wedding cake was published in 1655, made for the Manners family of Belvoir, one of the great English aristocratic families. It included the use of yeast, and was bound in a pastry case. The modern recipe probably dates back to the eighteenth century, when yeast would have been discarded, and ingredients included flour, currants and spice mixed with butter, sugar and eggs. By the twentieth century the wedding cake was no longer home-baked, and the royal-iced, three-tiered cake became the tour de force of the confectionery trade; traditionally, the top tier was kept to be presented at the christening of the firstborn.

By the Edwardian period, the piped decoration, which involved hours of dedicated labour, included cupids, flowers, love birds, scrolls and cornucopias surrounded with flowers, often with a vase of flowers on top. *Mrs Beeton's Book of Household Management* (1906 edition) includes a tiered wedding cake with pillars or columns supporting the tiers, rather than solid blocks of wood.

Films to See for Inspiration

A Room With a View, starring Helena Bonham
    Carter (1985)
My Fair Lady, starring Audrey Hepburn and
    Rex Harrison (1964)
The Go-Between, starring Julie Christie and
    Alan Bates (1971)

Reading List

The Shooting Party by Isabel Colegate (1980)
The House of Mirth by Edith Wharton (1905)
Howards End by E M Forster (1910)

The Vows

'Fidelity' by D H Lawrence (1913)

Ideal to read at the ceremony, or take turns reading as part of the vows, the first line begins, 'Man and woman are like the earth, that brings forth flowers, in summer, and love, but underneath is rock.'

The First Dance

Dancing became popular during the years preceding the First World War. The phonograph provided informal entertainment in the evening as the guests rolled back the carpet and danced the tango, turkey trot and hesitation waltz. A wedding reception in an Edwardian hotel such as the Ritz in London and the Alexandria in Los Angeles might include a palm-court orchestra, comprising piano, violin, flute, clarinet and cello and playing popular music of the time, such as 'Nights of Gladness', 'Temptation Rag', 'Lady of the Lake', 'Folies Bergères' and 'Mee-ow'. The orchestra would be seen and not heard, placed behind a bank of potted palms.

CLOCKWISE FROM ABOVE
A film still from *A Room with a View*; Audrey Hepburn in *My Fair Lady*; an Edison concert phonograph, 1913; a turn-of-the-century wedding reception; the reception room at the Ritz-Carlton, New York, circa 1915.

Fine Dining

A more formal wedding would require a traditional Edwardian dinner or luncheon party. This would include ornate table settings of Meissen or Sèvres china, silver, cut-glass and a highly decorative central epergne filled with flowers, which often obscured the guests sitting opposite. Food was plentiful and elaborately served, piled up vertically on the table and usually raised on stands to give height. A grand dinner might consist of 30 courses, including both sweet and savoury jellies constructed like miniature castles, turtle soup, lobster, sirloins of beef and game, if in season, accompanied by rich sauces. Menus were handwritten for every meal, and placed between each pair of guests, and an evening meal would be eaten by candlelight.

1920s Weddings
Cocktails, White Flannels and Orchids

The Roaring Twenties, fuelled by a postwar desire to 'seize the day', were also a time of Prohibition, when selling and drinking alcohol was illegal. It was the era of the speakeasy, where bootleg liquor was poured from teapots and fortunes were made by gangsters such as Al Capone who fuelled this illicit trade. The cocktail was invented to hide the poor quality of home-brewed hooch, the favourite being Champagne Punch, but Sidecars, Mint Juleps, Brandy Sours, Charleston Bracers, Martinis, Orange Gin Sparkles, Palm Beach Specials and Locomotives were also popular.

The exquisite beaded and fringed dresses of couturiers such as Lanvin and Lelong were simple in silhouette. The long veil worn for the wedding ceremony was discarded for the evening of dancing that followed. The syncopated rhythm of the Charleston, popularized by the Broadway show *Runnin' Wild*, joined the Bunny Hug and the Turkey Trot as one of the new dance crazes that hit America in the 1920s.

Fashions in interiors and domestic artefacts were beginning to be influenced by Art Deco. Originating in Paris with the Exposition Internationale des Arts Décoratifs et Industriels Modernes in 1925, the movement came to dominate decorative design over the next two decades, resulting in a highly distinctive pattern of geometric, angular shapes and forms in strong, intense colours. Most cities will have an available venue that dates from the Art Deco period, Odeon style, or alternatively, a summer wedding, held outside, could be styled along the lines of one of Jay Gatsby's day-long parties, with canvas laid down for the dancing, an orchestra, the men in white flannels and a 'tray of cocktails floating through the twilight'.

The highly ornate decorative quality of Art Deco incorporated stylized sunbursts and flowers, frozen fountains, and zigzag ornamentation that appeared on all product design and in the graphic arts. Invitations and place settings can reflect the style of the period by adopting the appropriate fonts: Classic Regular by Monotype and ITC Mona Lisa Recut were both invented in the 1920s.

At the same time, decorators such as Syrie Maugham were embracing the concept of the all-white interior. Her signature use of mirrors, glass and silvered surfaces can be incorporated into a 1920s themed wedding to great effect. Maugham even designed cutlery with white porcelain handles to complement white linen napery, white orchids, and plain white china. Table decorations included white plaster ornaments in the shape of shells, palm fronds and dolphins.

Films to See for Inspiration

The Boyfriend, starring Twiggy (1971)
The Great Gatsby, starring Robert Redford and
Mia Farrow (1974)
The Roaring Twenties, starring James Cagney (1939)
Thoroughly Modern Millie, starring Julie Andrews (1967)

Reading List

*Cheerio! A Book of Punches & Cocktails, How to Mix
Them* by Charles, formerly of Delmonicos (1928)
The Great Gatsby by F Scott Fitzgerald (1925)
The Green Hat by Michael Arlen (1924)
Syrie Maugham: Staging the Glamorous Interior by
Pauline C Metcalf (2010)

The First Dance

'Always' (1925) and 'Blue Skies' (1926) by Irving Berlin
'Someone to Watch Over Me' (1926) and 'Embraceable
You' (1928) by George Gershwin

American-Italian Food

The Prohibition, which went into effect in America on
16 January 1920, had a deleterious effect on American
cuisine, putting hundreds of restaurants and hotels out
of business and spurring the growth of the speakeasy,
where an American version of Italian food was served.
Suggestions for dishes include meatballs, rich meat
sauces, veal cutlets cooked with Parmesan or lemon,
clams stuffed with buttered herbed crumbs, shrimp with
wine and garlic, and mozzarella in torn chunks to be
eaten as an appetizer.

Cocktails and Canapés

Popular canapés from the era such as stuffed eggs
and cabbage rolls would probably not appeal to
contemporary tastes; neither would Gatsby's party fare
of spiced baked hams, harlequin salads and pastry
pigs and turkeys. The following list of appetizers and
hors d'oeuvres is culled from *Mrs Allen on Cooking,
Menus, Service*, by Ida C Bailey Allen (1924):

*Foods that begin a meal:
Canapés, hot and cold, cocktails (fruit, oysters,
clam, lobster, crabmeat), relishes (olives, pickle,
radish roses, plain/stuffed celery, pickled pears
or peaches, salted nuts). Cold canapés include
caviar, sardine and anchovy, Indian (chutney-
based), smoked salmon and stuffed eggs. Hot
canapés include oyster toast, shrimp or lobster
toast and mushroom toast. Other savoury
appetizers: sardines in aspic, stuffed pimientos,
Swedish loaf, anchovy toast, jellied anchovy
moulds, salmon and caviar rolls, finnan haddie
shells, and savoury cheese balls.*

The New York hotel, the Waldorf Astoria, served the
following menu, which can be found in *The Waldorf
Astoria Cookbook* by Ted James and Rosalind Cole
(1981), in 1924 in honour of the then president of the
United States, Calvin Coolidge.

Canapé of Anchovies
Cream of Celery with Toasties
Celery Olives
Aiguillette of Striped Bass Joinville
Potatoes à la Hollandaise
Medallion of Spring Lamb, Chasseur
Asparagus Tips au Gratin
***
Breast of Chicken à la Rose
Waldorf Salad, Mayonnaise
***
Venetian Ice Cream
Assorted Cakes Coffee
Apollinaris White Rock

The Cake

Tiered cakes were poplar in the 1920s, with the
traditional hard royal icing. The top layer
featured a bride and groom cake topper, first
seen in the late nineteenth century. These miniature
figures, representing the newlyweds, were initially
homemade from materials such as plaster or gum
paste. Commercially made cake toppers began to
become widely available in this time period, and they
were created in a variety of materials such as porcelain
and wood, later Bakelite, and eventually plastic.
Generally the bride and groom were dressed in formal
attire, and the cake topper was considered a special
keepsake from the wedding; some of the most sought-
after were made in Germany in the 1920s and 1930s.

The Vows

'I Carry Your Heart With Me' by e e cummings (1913)

A poem concerning profound love, the verse is easily
spoken aloud and understood by an audience, and
contains the repeating lines 'I carry your heart with me
(I carry it in my heart)'. The poem was set to music by
Michael Hedges, with backing vocals sung by David
Crosby and Graham Nash.

FROM TOP Orchid blossom,
a favourite 1920s flower; a
Sidecar cocktail; Mia Farrow
and Robert Redford playing
Daisy and Jay in a still from
The Great Gatsby; a flapper
with a backless dress,
holding peacock feathers; an
antique roadster.

1930s Weddings
Silk Stockings, Zazou and Sequins

An era of elegance, the apogee of Art Deco style, characterized the 1930s: columns of faceted mirrored glass, crystal chandeliers, marble surfaces, slithers of bias-cut satin, and calla lilies in black vases. Only shades of green such as shagreen, eau de nil and emerald were allowed to temper the black and white interiors. Monochrome furnishings were matched by the groom's white tie and black tails (think Fred Astaire flying around the dance floor in *Top Hat*). Cole Porter satirized the trend in his lyrics for the song 'That Black & White Baby of Mine':

> *She's got a black and white dress,*
> *A black and white hat,*
> *A black and white doggie and*
> *A black and white cat...*
> *She's got a black and white shack*
> *And a new Cadillac*

Christian Dior labelled the fashions of the 1930s as 'zazou', a word that perfectly sums up the spirit of the era, elegant yet fast moving and lively, adjectives that can be applied to the 1930s themed wedding. Elegance is provided with monochrome table settings; starched white damask cloths overlaid with black, white china placed on a mirror-tile, which can also be used beneath a series of black glass vases holding white tulips to add to the effect. Emerald green linen napkins, providing the only element of colour, can be placed within faux jade and bone napkin rings. Liveliness comes from the sound of cocktails being shaken and the tuxedoed waiters serving black caviar on silver platters. Be inspired by fashion illustrator Erte or the graphic artist Adolphe Mouron (known as Cassandre) for imagery on the invitations and for place settings.

Because this was the age of speed, try to find a custom-built pale grey Sedanca-de-Ville Rolls Royce with an electrically operated glass partition in which to travel to the reception. Otherwise catch the Eurostar instead of the 1930s Le Train Bleu for a honeymoon at Saint-Jean-Cap-Ferrat on the Côte d'Azure, or fly down to Rio like Fred Astaire and Ginger Rogers in *Flying Down to Rio* (1933).

Films to See for Inspiration

Bringing up Baby, starring Cary Grant and Katharine Hepburn (1938)

Gone With the Wind, starring Vivien Leigh and Clark Gable (1939)

It Happened One Night, starring Claudette Colbert and Clark Gable (1934)

Top Hat, starring Fred Astaire and Ginger Rogers (1935)

Reading List

A Handful of Dust by Evelyn Waugh (1934)

Brideshead Revisited: The Sacred and Profane Memories of Captain Charles Ryder by Evelyn Waugh (1945)

Murder on the Orient Express by Agatha Christie (1934)

Private Lives, a play by Noel Coward (1930)

The First Dance

'Night and Day' by Cole Porter (1932)

'They Can't Take That Away From Me' by George and Ira Gershwin (1937)

Cocktails and Canapés

Cocktails and canapés were a popular choice to follow a late afternoon wedding – the Mint Julep, Gibson, Manhattan and the Martini served from a mirror-fronted Art Deco bar, with waiters in tuxedos carrying silver trays of canapés to the sound of Cole Porter. The renowned decorator Elsie de Wolfe served green and white food and drink at her soirées: watercress sandwiches along with the Lady Mendl cocktail, a combination of Cointreau, gin and grapefruit juice. Glass-topped tables decorated with vases of dyed green tulips (as seen in stage-star Gertrude Lawrence's apartment, along with sequinned curtains) make an appropriate setting for silver bowls of caviar and sour cream, and platters of blinis.

The Manhattan

Combine 2¼ measures of American rye whiskey, 1 measure sweet red vermouth and a dash of bitters. Strain into a chilled cocktail glass and garnish with a maraschino cherry.

The Cake

The centrepiece of the table, the wedding cake, was still made in the traditional mode, with three or more tiers of dazzling white icing and the black-and-white figures on top.

The Vows

'Live You by Love Confined' from *The Magnetic Mountain* by Cecil Day-Lewis (1933)

CLOCKWISE FROM TOP
Manhatten cocktail; Rolls Royce Phantom II; Fred and Ginger in *Top Hat*; a 1930s black-and-white, marble-floored interior; Mint Juleps.

1940s Weddings
Costumes, Corsages and the Lindy Hop

A time of austerity and heightened emotion, the 1940s wartime wedding usually left little time for preparation. Formality was forgotten (unless you were a member of the aristocracy or high society) and as Anne-Scott James wrote in her book *In The Mink* (1952), 'However hard you try to reconcile fashion with war, the two don't mix.'

Venues were likely to be a village hall, a hotel in the city or even a dance hall. The music of the big bands was popular, and American GIs in Britain introduced a new style of dancing, the Jitterbug – a wild and acrobatic jive. Most wartime brides wore their service uniform or a tailored 'costume'; similar suits with pencil or box-pleated skirts can be sourced from vintage outlets. Fine tweed or wool gabardine could be worn for a winter wedding or a fitted linen suit with a textile corsage on the lapel for a summer ceremony. A vintage floral patterned tea-dress makes the Lindy Hop easier to perform, and looks especially effective when worn with wedge-heeled shoes and seamed stockings. For the ceremony, a small straw hat with veil perched in front of a 1940s 'updo', the Victory Roll, accessorized with short gloves, completes the effect.

Food rationing restricted the wedding feast and relatives and friends pooled their food coupons. Town rations varied greatly to what was available in the country, making a rural repast easier to recreate than a frugal town wedding. This lyrical evocation of a late summer feast, perfectly suited to a country wedding, appears in the H E Bates' novel *A Moment in Time* (1964) set during the Battle of Britain.

> *We sat at two long tables laid in the big barn and on the tables, as Tom had faithfully promised, there were lighted candles. A third table, holding spare plates and dishes and hams and legs of pork and so for extra cutting, stood cross-wise to the other two. The great span of oak roof, supported by massive posts not much less than a yard thick, gave the whole barn that church-like atmosphere I found so satisfying…*

He goes on to describe how sheaves of wheat and barley and oats had been tied to the posts, something that could be recreated for a 1940s country wedding, giving the feel of a harvest festival. Stand vases of flowers – dahlias, asters, cornflowers and sunflowers – down the middle of the tables, with ears of barley tucked between, and add jugs of beer and cider.

Films to See for Inspiration

Brief Encounter, starring Trevor Howard and Celia
    Johnson (1945)
Maytime in Mayfair, starring Anna Neagle and Michael
    Wilding (1949)
Mrs Miniver, starring Greer Garson and Walter Pidgeon
    (1942)
Yanks, starring Richard Gere, Lisa Eichhorn and
    Vanessa Redgrave (1979)

Reading List

A Moment in Time by H E Bates (1964)
The End of the Affair by Graham Greene (1951)
The Girls of Slender Means by Muriel Spark (1963)

The First Dance

'Bewitched, Bothered and Bewildered' from the musical
    Pal Joey by Rodgers and Hart (1940)
'Have I Told You Lately That I Love You?' by Scotty and
    Lulu Belle Wiseman (1945)
'Love Letters' by Dick Haymes (1945)

An Austerity-Style Luncheon

The Ministry of Food was set up in England under Lord
Woolton which exhorted people to 'Dig for Victory'
and turn pasture land, flowerbeds and parks into
vegetable plots. Rather than offering Lord Woolten Pie,
an unappetizing dish of mixed vegetables and oatmeal
invented by London's Savoy Hotel, a wedding buffet
of simple 'finger-food', would be in keeping with the
austerity of the period. Patriotism was evident, so try
miniature flags grouped in vases and bunting decorating
the table and room. .

The Cake

In Britain the traditional tiered wedding cake was
unobtainable, as sugar was rationed to 225 grams
(8 ounces), so it became acceptable to house a much
smaller version of the wedding cake
in a cardboard structure covered
in white satin. A contemporary
alternative would be a simple
sponge cake, and following the
patriotic theme you could use red,
white and blue frosting. Unaffected
by food rationing, the traditional
tiered wedding cake continued to
be served at American weddings.

The Vows

'The Life That I Have' by
    Leo Marks (1943)

Written by Special Operations
Executive (SOE) Leo Marks, the
poem was written for a girlfriend
killed in an air crash. However it
became widely known when it used
it as key for a secret code for an SOE (Special
Operations Executive) agent, Violette
Szabo, when she went on an almost
suicidal mission during the war. The
famous first lines are:

> *The life that I have*
> *Is all that I have*
> *And the life that I have*
> *Is yours…*

CLOCKWISE FROM TOP
A sailor and his partner
jitterbugging in the 1940s;
pink dahlias; a still from
the film *Brief Encounter*; an
illustration of a wedding cake
on the cover of the score
for 'The Wedding Waltz' by
Hugh Charles and Sonny
Miller, from 1945.

1950s Weddings

Champagne, Roses and Sinatra

The feelings of optimism after the Second World War were summed up by French couturier and originator of the New Look, Christian Dior, as 'the return of an ideal of civilized happiness'. The reinstating of the importance of the wedding ceremony symbolized the hopes and dreams for a future secure from strife, which had at its heart the family. As women were encouraged to leave their jobs and pour their energies into nurturing the nuclear family, the purchase of a wedding dress was once again seen as every young girl's dream and the gateway to fulfilled womanhood. The curvy girl was in ascendance; she appeared ladylike but voluptuous and her outfits were coordinated, with matching handbag, gloves and shoes.

The television series *Mad Men*, which begins its story in 1959, reflects the prevailing styles and social mores of the era and the importance placed on decorum, elegance and etiquette. Weddings once more became social events requiring forward planning, with coordinating details such as matching invitations, napkins and matchbooks. Ceremonies were held in church, chapels or cathedrals, and it was during the 1950s that the marquee erected in the bride's garden or the grounds of a country hotel or country club became a popular venue for the reception. 'Traditional' and 'classic' were the bywords; Wedgewood china, white roses, cut-glass and silver service were set on white damask cloths.

For the more modern 1950s couple, the decor had to be Mid-Century Modern. Following their example, discard the old-fashioned tablecloth and set the Harlequin, Fiesta or Midwinter's Stylecraft range of brightly coloured tableware on clean uncluttered surfaces. Breakthroughs in 1950s graphic design resulted in layers of flat colour, sometimes deliberately 'off-register', and this style instantly evokes the period when used for place settings or invitations, particularly when combined with the Festival Tilting Font, designed by Phillip Boydell in 1950. The official typeface for the Festival of Britain, the font is elongated, thin and three-dimensional, and leans slightly to the right, creating a subtle sense of movement. Brighten up interiors by using 1950s textile designs, abstract patterns of kinetic art and space-age sputnik motifs in saxe-blue, mustard and orange by designers such as Lucienne Day and Robert Stewart. The 1950s wedding was a sophisticated affair, so dance to the sound of Sinatra, downing Champagne cocktails and Whisky Sours, and nibbling on canapés, but forgo the endless cigarettes.

Films to See For Inspiration

Father of the Bride, starring Elizabeth Taylor (1950)
Funny Face, starring Audrey Hepburn (1957)
High Society, starring Grace Kelly, Frank Sinatra and
    Bing Crosby (1956)
Mad Men, starring Christina Hendricks and John Hamm
    (2007–11)

Reading List

The Best of Everything by Rona Jaffe (1958)
The Constance Spry Cookery Book by Constance Spry
    and Rosemary Hume (1956)
Party Flowers by Constance Spry (1955)

The First Dance

'At Long Last Love' (1957) and 'True Love' (1956),
    both sung by Frank Sinatra
'Unforgettable' by Nat King Cole (1952)

Banquet Fit for a Queen

In postwar Britain, unusual or exotic ingredients began
to be imported from abroad such as the avocado,
often served with crabmeat. Servicemen returning from
the war and the advent of foreign travel introduced
new ingredients into the kitchen such as spaghetti
and pizza. In America, Betty Crocker published her
influential *Betty Crocker's Picture Cook Book* (1950),
which included recipes for Pigs in Blankets and
Chicken Tomato Aspic, a clear savoury jelly that was
a popular and overused substance of the era. Food
was overdecorated, elaborate and fussy; ring moulds
of canned soup and strange combinations of 'salads'
such as iceberg lettuce, marshmallows and tuna fish
appeared. For a 1950s themed wedding, choose smart
little canapés or classic dishes such as a whole
salmon, Beef Stroganoff or Coronation Chicken.
Still a popular choice for a summer wedding
today, Coronation Chicken was invented in
1953 by Rosemary Hume (although the credit
is generally taken by her colleague, the society
florist Constance Spry) to serve at the Queen's
coronation banquet. A dish of cold poached
chicken, bathed in a spice-scented mayonnaise,
it is best accompanied by a rice salad and a spicy
white wine or dry rosé.

The Cake

An authentic 1950s wedding cake followed the
tradition of multi-tiers with white frosting, culminating
in a topper of the bride and groom, often positioned
under a floral arch. However, 1950s-style cake could be
composed of popular motifs from the era, such as the
poodle, representing European chic, or the shape of a
pointed boomerang, a form found on fabric designs,
coffee tables and corporate logos.

The Vows

'A Dedication to My Wife' by
T S Eliot (1958)

Originally drafted in 1955 as an
introduction to T S Eliot's last play
The Elder Statesman, the poem was
a rare declaration of his feelings for
his second wife, Valerie, ending with:

> But this dedication is for others to read:
> These are private words addressed
> to you in public.

CLOCKWISE FROM TOP A
1956 Ford Thunderbird; a
little white chapel – the ideal
wedding venue; two 'Teddy
boys' from 1955 showing off
dressy waistcoat-and-jacket
styles; Champagne cocktail.

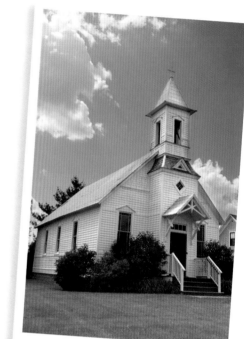

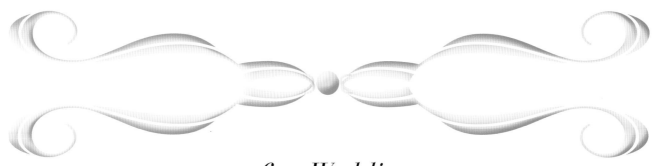

1960s Weddings
Mods, Minis and Pop Music

The wedding ceremony became ever more secular during the late 1960s as pop stars descended the steps of registry offices in velvet miniskirts and daisy-strewn bonnets. Britain's *Punch* magazine conveyed the general response to the Mod wedding with the publication of a poem by E S Turner, *The Milestone*, in 1967:

> *O Mother, dear, we're having a ball,*
> *And the bubbly wine is flowing.*
> *For I've been married at Caxton Hall,*
> *With my navel showing.*

As a 'with it' couple, you and your guests can frug (a dance that evolved from the Chicken) the night away to music by British groups such as the Beatles, the Rolling Stones and the Small Faces mixed with the sounds of American soul from Wilson Pickett and James Brown. 'Pop' art cast a witty, colourful aspect onto 1960s interiors and eye-dazzling 'Op' art by artists such as Victor Vasarely and Bridget Riley shimmered on the walls as well as on the clothes. This effect can be incorporated into a wedding interior by screen-printing fabric with a similar optical-illusion appearance for stapling onto screens and covering tables. Add to the visual confusion by using strobe lights to play over raised platforms where your guests can gyrate to the music, preferably in a mocked-up outsize birdcage.

Invitations printed with the speech-bubble graphics of Roy Lichtenstein will add to the theme, include place settings decorated with thought balloons, for guests to write in later, inspired by the artist's narrative boxes and Pop Art canvases. Decorate the tables with simple pots of still-growing white daises or tall vases of multicoloured gerbera. Instead of a traditional guestbook, install an iconic red Valentine Olivetti typewriter, designed in 1969 by Ettore Sottsass for the guests to write their comments. The favourite form of transport in 'Swinging London' was the Mini Cooper, launched in 1961; so why not park one in the corner of the venue as a background for the photographs?

Films to See for Inspiration

Blow-Up, starring David Hemmings and Vanessa
  Redgrave (1966)
Darling, starring Laurence Harvey and Julie Christie
  (1965)
Georgy Girl, starring Lynn Redgrave, Charlotte
  Rampling and Alan Bates (1966)
The Graduate, starring Dustin Hoffman and Anne
  Bancroft (1967)
Smashing Time, starring Rita Tushingham and Lynn
  Redgrave (1967)

Reading List

Couples by John Updike (1968)
Here We go Round the Mulberry Bush by Hunter
  Davies (1965)
The Kandy-Kolored Tangerine-Flake Streamline Baby,
  collection of essays by Tom Wolfe (1965)

The First Dance

'A Groovy Kind of Love' sung by the Mindbenders
  (1965)
'The Look of Love' by Burt Bacharach and sung by
  Dusty Springfield (1967)
'When a Man Loves a Woman' by Percy Sledge (1966)

French Provincial Cooking

European cuisine found in the influential cookery
books of Julia Child and Elizabeth David became
popular during the 1960s. Consider David's *French
Provincial Cooking*, (1960) for recipes for *Poule à La
Crème et a L'Estragon* (cold chicken with cream and
tarragon sauce) and *Mousse au Chocolat à L'Orange*
(chocolate and orange mousse). Julia Child's
Mastering the Art of French Cooking appeared in 1961,
a best-seller that capitalized on the American interest
in French culture in the early 1960s. For Op and Pop
Art themed additions to the menu, decorate white
glazed cupcakes with targets, bull's-eyes and stripes,
and pile multicoloured candy in glass jars with
barley sugar twists.

The Cake

Although the wedding cake continued to be traditional
in style, made up of two or three decorated tiers, in
Britain the fruit-filled mixture was now more likely to
be a plain or citrus-flavoured sponge cake, a trend
that had begun in America in the eighteenth century
with the introduction of finely milled flour and baking
powder. The darker traditional fruitcake was still served,
but more generally considered to be 'the groom's'.

The Vows

'Love Is...' by Adrian Henri (1968)

One of the Liverpool poets, Adrian Henri was also a
painter and his work became known worldwide. In this
poem he allows the definition of love to be as broad
and individual as the couple, listing various options on
what love is before ending:

> Love is you and love is me
> Love is prison and love is free
> Love's what's there when you are away from me
> Love is...

CLOCKWISE FROM TOP
Psychedelic sounds of the
'60s; dancing the frug; posy
of daisies; a couple with
their Mini MK II in 1968;
hippie style with headband
and wildflowers..

1970s Weddings
The Bo-ho Bride and the Disco Diva

The prospective bride and groom planning a 1970s themed wedding can take their pick from the unfettered and unalloyed personal expression of the early 1970s hippie wedding to the glamorous sequinned excesses of New York's notorious Studio 54 and subsequent 'disco fever'. The hippie wedding combined counter-culture values with a back-to-nature ethos, rejecting the formal banquet for brown rice and the bespoke wedding dress for a Victorian nightgown and a piano shawl. Current preoccupations with eco-friendly 'green' activities and sustainability make this an ideal option for the contemporary bride.

Replace the formal marquee with a conical Native American tipi or a Mongolian yurt, set up in an apple orchard, with an open fire for cooking. Decorate with homemade bunting and use handcrafted corn-dollies as table decorations. Spread striped Moroccan dhurries and kelims over hay bales and hang wind chimes from the trees, then set the stage with pressed-tin Moroccan lanterns. Music can be provided from a gypsy band or banjo or fiddle for dancing.

The counter-culture fostered anti-establishment views that emerged in music, movies and television programmes of the time, limiting the number of films that evoke the lighter side of the 1970s, until *Saturday Night Fever* was released in 1977, which had an iconic soundtrack by the Bee Gees and starred John Travolta in a white three-piece suit with flared trousers. Encourage guests to perfect the *Saturday Night Fever* line dance on a flashing underlit floor.

Although it might be impractical to have four tonnes of glitter dumped in a four-inch layer on the floor of your wedding venue, as happened at Studio 54 (described by the owner Ian Schrager as 'like standing on stardust'), you can suspend a giant disco ball, don the sequins and turn on the strobe light for a similar effect. Dance to Donna Summer and her iconic anthem 'I Feel Love' (1977) while wearing spandex leggings or abbreviated hotpants and high-heeled wedges, false eyelashes and lipgloss. Continue the theme of 'glitter and gloss' by using a lowercase font such as Dreamland Stars by dustBUST in metallic lettering on your invitations and placecards.

Disco Banquet

In complete contrast, food for a disco-themed wedding should be all artifice and gloss. It was the era of the Black Forest gateau. Add silver confectionery balls to the surface of cupcakes for a disco effect and serve Steak Diane, another 1970s classic recipe, with bowls of chunky french fries.

The Cake

A traditional wedding cake would seem out of place in a bo-ho neo-hippie wedding; double-chocolate brownies or a spiced carrot cake would be perfect. For a cake themed along disco-lines, try a centrepiece of *croquembouche* – profiteroles piled-high and decorated with caramelized spun-sugar for the requisite shimmer and shine.

The Vows

A traditional Native American or Eastern wedding prayer would be ideal for a bo-ho wedding. A favourite is the 'Apache Wedding Blessing', said to have been written by Albert Maltz for the movie *Broken Arrow*, however other sources claim the words were adapted from 'Wedding Braids' by Stan Davis. The prayer usually begins 'Now you will feel no rain, for each of you will be a shelter to the other…'.

Films to See for Inspiration

Love Story, starring Ali MacGraw and
    Ryan O'Neal (1970)
Saturday Night Fever, starring John Travolta
    and Karen Lynn Gorney (1977)

Reading List

Hippie Hippie Shake by Richard Neville (1995)
The Whole Earth Catalog by Stewart Brand
    (1968–1972)

The First Dance

'Heart of Gold' by Neil Young (1972)
'How Deep is your Love' by the Bee Gees (1977)
'You're the First, the Last, My Everything' by Barry
    White (1975)
'Your Song' by Elton John (1971)

Health-Conscious Buffet

Concern for the purity and provenance of food was part of the hippie desire for an anti-consumer and authentic way of living. Vegetarianism if not veganism was the norm, an ethos that embraced not only brown rice and tofu, but included experimenting with the fragrant herbs and spices of other cultures, such as Moroccan tagines and couscous, vegetable curries, quinoa and lentil-based dahl. For a contemporary hippie feast, set out trestle tables with salads of edible flowers, delicate rice pilafs and vegetable terrines. Drink cider from coloured blown-glass beakers and decorate the table with wildflower-filled pottery jugs.

CLOCKWISE FROM TOP LEFT
A poster for the 1977 hit
Saturday Night Fever; disco
ball; Moroccan-style interior;
a traditional yurt..

1980s Weddings
Gold, Glitter and Gardenias

Tradition, etiquette and formality were the hallmarks of the 1980s wedding. Influenced by the pomp and circumstance of the royal nuptials of Charles and Diana, the wedding ceremony assumed a social importance last seen in the 1950s. The global hit television series *Dynasty* unleashed a desire for glitz and the glamour, which exemplified an era of lavish interiors, elaborate food and 'occasion' dressing. Look to the richly embellished and decadent interiors of Gianni Versace for inspiration (particularly his former mansion, now a hotel the Casa Casuarinas, in Florida's Miami Beach). Employ a judicious amount of animal-print, like that other master of 1980s excess, Roberto Cavalli, perhaps edging the invitations with a border of printed leopardskin. Choose wineglasses rimmed in gold and mass exotic blooms in ornate cachepots. Arrange gilded candlesticks on a marble-topped table, either real or a paint effect, a popular decorative device of the period. Place settings for the female guests could be miniature minaudières, tiny jewelled handbags, with the name of the guests picked out in Swarovski crystals. In her eponymous best-selling book of 1987, Martha Stewart lays down the rules in detail, from how to organize the best acoustics for musicians playing outdoors to the most effective ambient lighting. She also records the minutiae of social correctness. Here are her recommendations for the perfect 1980s invitations:

> *Tiffany's since its founding 140 years ago has remained a citadel of good taste... Most of their advice is based on the word of Amy Vanderbilt, which has changed little in many decades. One requests "the honour of your presence" at a religious ceremony, but for a wedding at home, in a club or hotel – in other words a social occasion – the proper phrase is 'the pleasure of your company'... an RSVP must be written in the lower right-hand corner.*

Weddings could now be captured on video. With the introduction of the first consumer camcorders by Sony, the 1980s wedding could be recorded for posterity, albeit with poor quality sound and image. If you choose to wear the oversized crinoline dress of the time, a big car is required. British dressmaker Bruce Oldfield, a favourite designer of Princess Diana, recommended the Daimler Vanden Plas Princess; as he records on his website, 'the huge passenger area has been carrying princesses, film stars and brides for the last 60 years.'

Films to See for Inspiration

Pretty in Pink, starring Molly Ringwald (1986)
Wall Street, starring Michael Douglas
    and Charlie Sheen (1987)
Working Girl, starring Melanie Griffith
    and Harrison Ford (1988)

Reading List

The Bonfire of Vanities by Tom Wolfe (1987)
Martha Stewart Weddings by Elizabeth Hawes (1987)
Princess Daisy by Judith Krantz (1980)

The First Dance

'Hello' by Lionel Richie (1984)
'One Moment in Time' by Whitney Houston (1987)
'Up Where We Belong' by Joe Cocker and Jennifer
    Warnes (1982)

Summer Buffet

Food was luxurious but simple with the emphasis placed on fresh ingredients, lightly cooked to preserve their natural flavours. This was due to the far-reaching influence of *nouvelle cuisine*, a description of the culinary skills of French chefs Paul Bocuse, Alain Chapel and Michel Guérard. They replaced the heavy sauces of classic French cuisine such as espagnole and béchamel, thickened with a flour-based roux, with fresh herbs, high-quality butter, lemon juice and vinegar. Red meat was replaced by lobster, scallops, fish, game and steamed green vegetables and salads.

The Cake

At the beginning of the 1980s the four-tier cake was standard; by the end of the decade five tiers were the norm, or even seven or eight. A revival in the art of sugarcraft resulted in complex decorative detailing not seen since the Edwardian era, while the use of a new material, sugar paste – a plastic flexible medium – could be modelled into a variety of decorative effects that were rolled out, cut and moulded. This revolutionized cake decoration, lending itself to realistic, life-like flowers and foliage. The drawback was that sugar paste could not withstand the weight of a many-tiered cake as well as royal icing could, so confectioners and bakers experimented with different forms, even reproducing idiosyncratic shapes personal to the bride and groom: a boat, a guitar or a building. There was also more variety in the cake mixture, with chocolate or a simple génoise sponge replacing the traditional fruit mix. The French tradition of *croquembouche* – a pyramid of cream puffs held together with caramel or chocolate – also became popular.

The Vows

'Something' by Mary Barnet

Lauded for the integrity of her writing, her poetry has been called 'carefully tailored pearls'. This poem ends 'my breath in your presence is the deepest of kisses… Life, I love you too much.'

CLOCKWISE FROM TOP
An extravagant five-tiered wedding cake; a still from the film *Pretty in Pink*; the wedding of Krystal to Blake in *Dynasty*, 1981; a cascade bouquet of lilies and roses.

Shopping Guide

There are many advantages to choosing a vintage wedding dress rather than a modern version, key among them is that they are unique one-off pieces that no one else will have, and often feature exquisite details and workmanship for a fraction of the price that you'd pay for a comparable modern dress. You are also able to wear the dress as soon as you've bought it, so long as you aren't intending to alter it. An alternative option is to buy a retro-look reproduction or have one custom-made. Many contemporary designs reference earlier eras, and there are bridal salons that specialize in reproduction dresses, such as the Vintage Wedding Dress Company's vintage-inspired 'Decades' collection. If you sew, or have a seamstress, there are also vintage and retro sewing patterns available.

When searching for an authentic vintage dress, there are a few ground rules and tips to keep in mind, which will help you find the best pieces for you. See as many different styles as you can from a cross-section of eras. There really is no substitute for the experience gained from seeing and handling vintage pieces.

Where to Buy

Specialist vintage wedding fashion fairs and markets are a great opportunity to meet a lot of dealers and see a huge variety of classic vintage clothing gathered together in one place. Specialist shops and viewings at major auction houses are also excellent places to see high-quality pieces. Here you can familiarize yourself with clothes from different periods and the work of specific designers. Your local vintage boutique or antique shop may have beautiful dresses that have not been created for weddings but which would make lovely choices. Many thrift stores carry a good stock of wedding dresses from more recent eras, such as the 1970s and 1980s.

Online auctions such as eBay can be particularly useful as any wedding dresses on sale are likely to be on offer from the owner or the owner's family. Although sellers are unlikely to be vintage dealers, the provenance is assured in these cases, and they will have details of the history of the piece as well as interesting stories about the bride and the wedding day. Unfortunately there are many more modern dresses than vintage pieces on

offer and there is no way of seeing the item to check its condition. Always email the seller about measurements, stains, repairs, alterations, etc, and ask to see the label if it hasn't been shown.

Buying Tips
- Never buy a stained garment with the hope that it will come out with washing or dry cleaning. If the mark's been there for a long time, it probably isn't going to shift. Get a full description of stains, such as rust, mildew or sweat, as well as any odours.
- Avoid pieces that need extensive repairs. Vintage fabrics are difficult to match with modern ones, so it's unlikely you will be able to patch or repair successfully.
- Always check the item thoroughly for condition. Hold it up to the light to reveal any moth holes or deterioration in embroidery or lace. Check both sides of the fabric for scorches, tears, mended areas, missing beadwork or embellishments and for disintegration of any type. Any professional seller will automatically point out tears or other signs of damage, but always ask.

- Choose a dress from an era that best suits your body shape and personal style; otherwise you may feel as if you are wearing a costume rather than a piece that makes you look and feel great. This will also help you focus on your aim, rather than trying to pick what you like from of a century's worth of designs.
- Work out your budget before you shop. Couture dresses claim the highest prices, but the price also depends on the designer, age, workmanship, condition and size; you may accept an unauthenticated piece if the detailing is remarkably rare or beautiful.
- Because they are worn for one day only, vintage wedding dresses are usually found in near mint condition. Many sellers use standard descriptions to indicate the condition of the garment: mint is rare and perfect, probably never worn; near mint indicates light wear, as in evening dresses; excellent means it is sound with some wear but no flaws; very good indicates minor flaws or stains but otherwise high quality; good means that it is wearable but shows some deterioration.

Sizing

Because most clothing up to the 1960s was home- or dressmaker-made, there may be no size labels in pieces before this period. Each piece was bespoke, made for a specific person's shape, so for that dress to fit you perfectly you have to be that same size.

You will not wear your regular dress size in a vintage dress. Thanks to better nutrition and exercise habits, women today are taller and bigger than ever before, so there's no substitute for trying the item on. If this isn't possible, ask for the seller to provide exact measurements, not only including length, waist and bust measurements but also the hip, cuff, sleeve length, neck opening, from nape to waist, back shoulder to shoulder, waist to hem, shoulder to hem, the circumference of the hemline, and any potentially restrictive areas, like under the upper arm. Since many dresses were worn with a corset, you may want to wear one when shopping. It is also a good idea to get professionally measured; some specialized bridal shops offer a full measuring service, or ask your local tailor or alterations service.

Expect the dress to be one or two sizes smaller, but be advised that waist measurements were proportionately smaller, too. Most vintage dresses only run up to a size 10 or 12 (US 6 or 8) and are shorter than average in length; if you don't fit within this range you may want to consider other options. In general, 1920s fashions generally suit the small and slight of figure; 1950s clothes are created along the hourglass line so they fit the curvaceous, though waists are very small; 1960s fashions are best on the tall and leggy.

Repairs and Alterations

Be aware of what can and can't be altered in a vintage piece. For example, embellished fabrics are more expensive to alter than plain fabrics, as the beads or crystals often have to be removed or repositioned. The fabric often has flaws, such as small tears or stains, which may make it difficult to assess unless you are a professional, although if you are choosing vintage this can be part of its charm. Complex alterations or repairs can take up to three months and may be expensive.

Styles of the Era

Consider your shape when deciding on a vintage gown from a particular era. For example, a 1950s New Look design suits an hourglass figure, whereas a 1960s column or A-line dress is better for the boyish. Try on a selection of different dresses to get a good idea of the look you want, as well as what will suit you.

If you aren't sure of the date of the dress, ask the seller. Construction methods and the silhouette of the garment are good indicators of time period – for example, garments were much more fitted before 1960. The underlying structure will also offer clues on whether the piece is couture or ready-to-wear, and the value and age. Many couture pieces are works of art, highly hand-constructed or hand-embellished and made of the finest materials available at the time. Because these items will never be created again, and the level of artistry involved can never be repeated due to cost and expertise limitations, couture items are highly covetable, particularly those showing exquisite handworked beading or embroidery, unique hand-dyed colours, luxury fabrics or unique techniques.

Care and Storage

If you are ever in doubt about whether a piece should be washed, consult a professional dealer for advice, especially if you suspect the piece may be rare or you are unsure of the fragility of its materials.

- Do not ever use a washing machine or dryer, and think carefully about pressing any item as it can press stains into the fabric. Steaming is usually a good option but only for robust fabrics.
- Always clean an item before storing. Some stains, such as sweat, perfume and alcohol may be invisible at first but will darken with time if not removed.
- Dry cleaning is damaging to many fabrics, and may require the removal of labels or accessories, which may devalue the piece
- Never wash a 1920s sequin dress, as the sequins are made of gelatine, and will dissolve in the water!
- Don't store anything in plastic. Wrap it in acid-free tissue and keep it in a cardboard box. Check the dress's condition each year and repack so the folds are in different places.

ABOVE LEFT TO RIGHT

A selection of original vintage wedding dresses from the Vintage Wedding Dress Company; left to right: 1920s, 1930s, 1940s, 1950s, 1960s and 1970s. The company also carries exquisite designer vintage pieces by Dior, YSL, Chanel and Givenchy alongside unmarked one-off pieces and new collections, for handbags, jewellery, headpieces, veils and shrugs.

Sources and Suppliers

UNITED KINGDOM

Abigail's Vintage Bridal
www.abigailsvintagebridal.co.uk
Based in the East Midlands, Abigail has a private store for the viewing of vintage wedding gowns and fittings. The dresses are cleaned and restored before you see them and are chosen for their distinguishing features from particular decades. You can bring your own vintage dress to have it restored. Abigail also stocks vintage jewellery to compliment whichever dress you choose to buy.

Elizabeth Avey
128 Junction Road
Tufnell Park
London N19 5LB
www.elizabethavey.co.uk
Elizabeth Avey opened her first boutique in 1988: three stores later and she is still very much in demand. She offers a wealth of experience and a strong passion for beautiful and original vintage wedding dresses. There is an emphasis on quality of service and customer care.

Fur Coat No Knickers
Top Floor, Kingly Court
Carnaby Street
London W1B 5PW
www.furcoatnoknickers.co.uk
This beautiful shop is full of vintage wedding dresses that can be fitted to your size. A service is provided to search for your perfect vintage wedding dress, and made-to-measure is also available, with dresses made in your choice of fabric. The shop is packed with finishing touches for the special day: veils, bags, costume jewellery and tiaras, to name a few.

The Goddess Room
Meridian Point
Greystones
Co. Wicklow
Ireland
www.thegoddessroom.net
The Goddess Room's Vintage Bridal collection provides both formal and informal wedding dresses, each garment having a unique quality to it. Bespoke gowns and headpieces from the 1930s onwards are also available. One-to-one viewings available by appointment.

Halfpenny
Camden Mews
London NW1
www.halfpennylondon.com/bridal
(By appointment only)
Halfpenny stocks vintage wedding dresses and creations by Kate Halfpenny – fashion stylist to the stars, known for her bespoke dresses and styling skills; she has also begun to make bespoke diamond and precious stone rings for all occasions. There are so many creations and wonders available that you are bound not to be disappointed.

Hope and Harlequin
31 Sydney Street
Brighton BN1 4EP
www.hopeandharlequin.com
Hope and Harlequin sell vintage wedding dresses and made-to-order gowns. Owner, Louise Hill, carefully sources the collection of vintage dresses from the UK and across the world. The vintage bridal collection is constantly changing and there's always something fresh in stock. Best of all the dresses are cleaned, restored and altered in-house. Made-to-order dresses, using vintage patterns, take around five months to make.

Love Miss Daisy
PO Box 270
York YO42 9AA
(Full address available when booking an appointment through: terri@lovemissdaisy.com)
www.lovemissdaisy.com
Stockist of vintage wedding dresses and much more. Love Miss Daisy reminds you that in buying a vintage wedding dress you are buying a 'slice of fashion history', making your gown seem that much more exciting. The vintage wedding gowns are all hand-picked and one-off, and are ideally priced for the credit-crunch bride.

Love Vintage
Email: info@love-vintage.co.uk
www.love-vintage.co.uk
A website specializing in beautiful, vintage-inspired wedding bouquets, along with hand-made accessories such as wedding favours, table decorations and hair decorations, most of which make the perfect keepsake.

My Sugarland
402–4 St John Street
London EC1V 4NJ
www.mysugarland.co.uk
My Sugarland stocks vintage wedding dresses, along with all the other accessories needed for the perfect vintage wedding look. Vintage bags, shoes and jewellery are on display for trying on with your dress, and a wide range of hats is also available – ideal for the mother of the bride.

Retrostuff
Admiral Vernon Arcade
Unit 70, 141 Portobello Road
London W11 2DY
www.retrostuff-etc.com
Retrostuff Etc stocks vintage wedding gowns from the 1900s to the 1970s. If your size isn't available there is a dressmaker to hand who can amend the dresses and make any stylistic changes you may require. Phone before you go and describe the type of dress you are looking for so you won't be disappointed when you visit.

Vintage Flair
www.vintage-flair.co.uk
Vintage Flair is a company based in the southeast of England which loans out vintage china, primarily within the counties of Essex and Kent but also outside of these areas. If you have a specific colour or a special request for your event, owners Elizabeth and Ellen will do their utmost to match it, and are keen to be as flexible as possible to meet your needs.

The Vintage Wedding Dress Company
Bloomsbury
London WC1
(Full address available when you book an appointment)
www.thevintageweddingdresscompany.com
Years of experience in fashion led renowned stylist Charlie Brear to set up The Vintage Wedding Dress Company. She has produced accessories for Matthew Williamson and even sold under her own name at Matches. She sources dresses from Paris and London and across the world, and stocks pieces from the Victorian era right through to the early 1970s. The dresses are all beautifully cleaned and restored.

NORTH AMERICA

Cabaret Vintage

672 Queen Street
West Toronto
Ontario, Canada
www.cabaretvintage.com

Cabaret Vintage stocks vintage wedding dresses, along with The Cabaret Collection, a collection of new gowns based on the styles of popular vintage pieces sold previously. The website features articles by brides who have bought their dresses from here, complete with wedding photographs showing the beautiful gowns being worn.

Dorotheas Closet Vintage

1733 Grand Avenue
Des Moines
IA 50309
USA
www.dorotheasclosetvintage.com

Dorotheas Closet Vintage stocks a whole range of vintage clothing and has a Bridal section of dresses from the 1920s to the 1960s. It also stocks vintage hats and hairpieces to complete the perfect vintage wedding style.

The Frock

www.thefrock.com

The Frock is a website that sells a truly spectacular array of vintage wedding dresses, 1900s to the 1980s, from designers such as Pierre Balmain, Elizabeth Arden, Oscar de la Renta, Christian Dior and Valentino.

The Paper Bag Princess

287 Davenport Road
Toronto
Ontario M5R 1J9
Canada
www.thepaperbagprincess.com

Elizabeth Mason founded The Paper Bag Princess Vintage Couture in 1992. There is a large stock of vintage bridal wear, neatly displayed and organized in a large showroom. The company also custom-makes vintage style gowns.

Posh Girl Vintage

www.poshgirlvintage.com

This is a family-run website (based in South California) that specializes in vintage wedding dresses from the 1950s and '60s, although if the owners find a special dress from another decade they will stock this as well. Posh

Girl Vintage cites Audrey Hepburn as its inspiration, hence the concentration on 1950s and '60s dresses.

Some Things Old, Some Things New

2924 East Broadway
Tucson, Arizona
USA
www.somethingsoldandnew.com

Some-Things Old, Some-Things New is a locally owned boutique with a spacious fitting area that allows all members of the bridal party to help choose the dress. Along with a large variety of dresses, lingerie and purses are also held in stock, enabling you to find everything you need for your perfect bridal outfit in one store. The boutique claims that appointments are unnecessary – a rare claim for a bridal shop!

Unique Vintage

2013 W Magnolia Boulevard
Burbank, CA 91506
USA
www.unique-vintage.com

Unique Vintage stocks a variety of vintage wedding dresses from the 1940s and '50s. It also stocks regular wedding dresses, so if you are just looking for a wedding dress with that vintage style, this may be a good place to start.

AUSTRALIA

Johanna Johnson

89 Glenmore Road
Paddington
Sydney
NSW 2021
www.johannajohnson.com

Johanna Johnson supplies vintage-style wedding dresses, basing her designs on the glamour of the golden era of Hollywood. Despite international demand for her dresses, there are plenty of different styles available from which to choose.

The Vintage Clothing Shop

Shop 7, St James Arcade
80 Castlereagh Street
Sydney
NSW 2000
www.thevintageclothingshop.com

Although The Vintage Clothing Shop does not specialize in wedding dresses, it sells a range of vintage accessories and antique lace to

complete your look – it's not too expensive either. With a wealth of choice, you're sure to find something to add that vintage style to your big day.

BLOGS AND ARTICLES

The 50s Style Wedding Blog

50s-style-wedding.blogspot.com

La Belle Bride

www.labellebride.com

Deco Bride

decobride.com

Little Miss Wedding

www.littlemisswedding.co.uk/vintage-wedding-ideas

Love my Dress

www.lovemydress.net/blog

Offbeat bride

offbeatbride.com/tag/retro-wedding

One Wedding

www.onewedding.co.uk/ideas/retro-wedding-theme/

A great article detailing how to give your wedding that retro theme, including ideas on what sort of food to have, the cake and decorations, and car hire.

Poptastic Bride

poptasticbride.com/2010/04/retro-bridal-shoes

Pretty Chicky

prettychicky.com/tag/vintage

Retro Wedding Themes Are a Throwback to Good Times

www.weddingfavourskingdom.co.uk/tips/retro-wedding-themes-are-a-throwback-to-good-times/

This article takes an historical look at the 'good old days' of weddings, exploring fine details such as place settings, frames, bottle-stoppers, flowers, and modes of transport.

Ruffled Blog

ruffledblog.com

Glossary of Fabrics

Batiste: an opaque, delicate, lightweight fabric, chosen for its smoothness, which makes it useful as a lining for linen garments. It is very soft, drapes beautifully and may be woven from cotton, polyester, linen, silk or a blend such as polycotton.

Bengaline: a woven vertical rib with a raised surface effect, like a fine ripple. It is created with a silk warp and a worsted or cotton weft.

Brocade: may be mistaken for embroidery owing to its decorative surface, but brocade is woven on a loom bringing in an extra weft which does the figuring and illuminates the floral pattern. Traditionally woven in silk, it is now produced in synthetics. The word brocade is now used loosely to describe any jacquard-woven design.

Charmeuse: a smooth, lightweight fabric that can be woven from silk, cotton, rayon and synthetics. Silk fabrics will always demand a higher price than other yarns; at the other end of the spectrum synthetic yarns should be among the cheapest.

Chiffon: a fine, lightweight, transparent fabric, with a smoothness and drape that make it suitable for use in veils. It may be woven in silk, rayon, cotton or from a synthetic fibre such as nylon.

Crushed velvet: popular in the early 1970s, this fabric has been run between rollers, sending the pile in various directions to give it an irregular, waved effect. The pile can be made from silk, cotton or synthetic yarns and can be imitated on a knitting machine.

Damask: originally a silk fabric made in Damascus, it is now woven in silk, cotton, linen or synthetic yarns. A floral pattern defined by a smooth and lustrous surface is created with a sateen weave, a structure that crams the weft threads together, allowing the light to bounce off the surface of the weave and enhance the pattern. Because of the dense weaving this can be heavy.

Duchesse satin: a lightweight, glossy satin with the threads closely woven together to form a smooth and lustrous surface. Produced in silk or rayon.

Dupion: a crisp silk fabric, woven with irregular slubs (soft lumps) in the yarn, creating a textured surface.

Eyelet: a cotton or linen fabric with embroidered circles that have the centres cut away to create a very small bound hole. This is quite often used as an edging and was very popular in the 1960s.

Faille: a fine, soft rib silk fabric. The ribs are vertical, but not prominent.

Gazar: A loosely woven silk with a crisp finish, derived from the Arabic word *qazz*, or raw silk.

Georgette: a very sheer, lightweight fabric, woven from silk, cotton or synthetic yarns.

Gros de Londre: a fine silk warp creates a horizontal, flat ribbed fabric with alternate thick and thin stripes. The thickness of the weft yarn determines the stripe, which can also be created with worsted or cotton.

Illusion: a fine netting that gives an ethereal, gossamer effect. (See also maline and tulle.)

Jacquard: a fabric woven on a Jacquard loom, which is capable of producing a sophisticated and intricate design. It can be woven with silk, cotton or a synthetic yarn.

Lamé: woven with metallic threads that catch the light to give an impression of liquid silver and gold. It drapes and folds like molten metal.

Linen: a crisp, cool, lightweight fabric woven from fibres of the flax plant, which holds its shape well but can crease easily unless dressed with starch. It may be mixed with synthetic yarns to make it more manageable.

Maline: a very fine net that holds its form and can be used as a veil or to stiffen petticoats.

Marquisette: a soft, transparent net that gives an illusion of weightlessness.

Moiré: a rib woven silk that is finished by being run through rollers. This process crushes the rib in different directions and gives the fabric it a 'water mark' effect.

Net: see maline, tulle and illusion.

Organdy: a light, fine, white cotton fabric. It has a stiff, wiry, translucent finish and is often used for details such as cuffs and collars.

Organza: a transparent fabric that is heavier and stiffer than organdy and holds its form well, making dramatic shapes. It is woven from rayon.

Ottoman: particularly suitable for the architectural shapes of the 1950s, this is a heavy warp-ribbed fabric, with broad ribs that run vertically.

Paper taffeta: a very crisp silk taffeta that folds and creases like paper, hence its name. Princess Diana's wedding dress was made from paper taffeta; the quality of the fabric was not appreciated and misjudged as having creased badly.

Peau de soie: a fine, soft, high-quality silk fabric with a low-lustre effect.

Pique: a soft cotton fabric with a fine, subtle, horizontal stripe created in the weave structure. Because of its more robust nature it may be utilized in cuffs and collars.

Point d'esprit: also known as Swiss dot, this is a finely spun cotton in a plain weave with a raised circular woven spot that sits on the surface and is spaced in an irregular pattern to cover the whole fabric. Used frequently for wedding veils in the 1960s.

Satin: Densely woven silk with a smooth surface that reflects the light. Frequently found as ribbon.

Shantung: Plain woven silk that creates a crisp fabric. The tussah silk thread has an irregular quality to it, created in the spinning process and forming slubs (soft lumps) in the fabric as it is woven. The character of the fabric is so highly prized that some mills try to emulate the 'shantung effect' using rayon or synthetics. However, high-end designers prefer the authentic tussah silk.

Silk-faced satin: see duchesse satin.

Taffeta: a plain, smooth, closely woven silk fabric that satisfyingly holds a good shape by utilizing its characteristics of crispness and being lightweight.

Tissue taffeta: a thin, almost transparent taffeta created by using very finely spun silk or synthetic threads.

Tulle: a sheer fabric, also known as net, illusion or maline, with a mesh-like structure creating very fine hexagonal holes. May be produced in silk, nylon or rayon. Most wedding veils are made in this fabric.

Velvet: a thick fabric with a short-cut pile. With its raised surface of soft-cut fibres, it creates a warm, plush fabric, soft to the touch and suitable for winter weddings. Silk velvet is the most expensive, but velvets made of cotton, rayon or synthetic fibres are cheaper.

Velveteen: a raised fabric similar to velvet, made from cotton or rayon, in which the pile is created via the weft rather than the warp – a technical differentiation that is only of concern in terms of aesthetic choice and cost.

Zibeline: a heavy silk with a twill weave.

Glossary of Lace

No fabric is more closely associated with bridal finery than lace. The bride-to-be is customarily asked on visiting the couturier or dressmaker if she has 'family lace' she would like incorporated into the design of her wedding dress. Dating back, at least, to the fifteenth century and possibly much earlier, lace has long held a unique place in the pantheon of luxurious fabrics and proved so valuable that it became a form of currency; during the Renaissance, for example, Venetians were, by law, forbidden to wear their own art and all Venetian lace was exported for gold. Often named from its town of origin, such as Chantilly or Alençon, lace was traditionally made from silk or linen threads using either a bobbin or a needle. The threads were so fine that they were almost impossible to see with the naked eye and had to be manipulated by touch.

Alençon lace: originating in the French town of Alençon in about 1665, following a ban on the import of foreign lace, this became the most elaborate needlepoint lace made in France. Its outstanding feature is the outlining of the edge of each design in cord – known as the cordonnet and originally made of horsehair covered with buttonhole stitch – which provides a three-dimensional effect.

Bobbin lace: a lace constructed with bobbins and a pillow, also called 'pillow lace'. The bobbins, originally made from bone, and later wood or plastic, hold a series of threads that are then woven together following a pattern marked by pins on the pillow. The pillow once contained oat straw or sawdust; contemporary lacemakers use Styrofoam or Ethafoam.

Brussels lace: a type of bobbin lace, originating in the town of Brussels, which is made in pieces, with the flowers and other designs made separate from the ground, or réseau. Brussels lace dates back to the fifteenth century, and was first mentioned in England in a list of presents given to the Princess Mary at New Year in 1543. The réseau has a distinctive, hexagonal pattern, and the designs have either a standard woven texture, resembling fabric, or a more open style that looks more like a netted ground. This allows for shading, an effect that is found in more recent designs.

Chantilly lace: dating back to the seventeenth century and taking its name from its town of origin in France, this lace is reknowned for its fine ground and richly detailed pattern, which is outlined in a flat cordonnet (strand). Black silk Chantilly lace was especially poplular, particularly for mourning-wear.

Crocheted lace: a form of crochet that uses fine threads, decorative patterns and varying hole sizes to give a 'lacy' effect. Easier and quicker to make than traditional lace, it was not originally considered a true lace.

Cut work: also known as whitework, cut work involves removing threads from a woven background and then wrapping or filling the remaining holes with embroidery.

Guipure lace: a usually heavy lace in which the elements of the pattern are connected by fine threads, or brides, rather than being supported on a net ground. Often layered with overlapping motifs to form a deep and intriguing texture, this lace is now constructed on a water-soluble or heat-resistant base material that is then removed.

Honiton lace: a bobbin lace made in England at Honiton, Devonshire, from the seventeenth century onwards. Most people, however, associate this term with the lace made in Honiton in the nineteenth century, in which strong floral motifs are joined to an often-spotted net background. Queen Victoria inserted a chemisette of Honiton lace in her wedding dress in an attempt to support the British lace industry.

Knitted lace: a style of knitting that incorporated holes into the design to create a lacy effect.

Knotted lace: known by a variety of names including Armenian lace, Nazareth lace and dandella, this ancient and inexpensive lace is still crafted in the Eastern Mediterranean. Made using only a needle and thread, the technique involves tying a series of knots.

Machine-made lace: first produced on a development of the stocking frame, invented by John Heathcoat in 1809. By reproducing basic twists and turns, Heathcoat created a diamond-shaped net on which a design could be embroidered. From this point on the handmade hexagonal réseau (ground) was only made upon request and the designs were appliquéd directly onto the machine-made net. This resulted in the designs becoming more spread out and less connected, and, because the net is not cut away behind the appliquéd design, the net can be seen on the back of the design.

Needle lace: a lace made using a needle and thread. It is the most flexible of the lace-making arts and considered by some to be the highest form. In an early form of needle lace, developed in the fifteenth century and known as Punto in Aria (meaning 'stitches in the air'), outline stitches were basted onto a temporary backing comprising a parchment pattern and layers of fabric. A simple button-hole stitch was then used to cover and connect the pattern threads. The connecting stitches between the motifs were called 'brides' as these 'married' the motifs.

Point d'Angleterre: an intentially misleading term used in England and France to describe Brussels lace. Following a ban in England, in 1662, on the import of foreign lace, English lace merchants, unable to source lace of a high enough quality from British manufacturers, resorted to smuggling it from Brussels, calling it Point d'Angleterre, or 'English point', in order to deceive the authorities. France, under similar import restrictions, also started to sell Brussels lace using this name, and to this day all Brussels lace is called Point d'Angleterre in France.

Point Duchesse (Duchess point): the term for a type of Belgian lace that does not have a ground, or réseau. It is named after the Duchess of Brabant, Marie-Henriette of Austria. Made entirely on the pillow, the pattern is constructed so that the leaves and flowers naturally join, and there is rarely a bar thrown across to connect them. As there is no réseau, the designs are more continuous.

Point plat appliqué (applied flat point): the term for a type of Brussels lace in which the design is appliquéd onto a machine-made net, instead of using a handmade réseau (ground).

Bibliography

Always in Vogue, Edna Woolman Chase & Ilka Chase, Victor Gollancz, 1954.

American Fashion Menswear, Robert E Bryan, Assouline, 2009.

Brides, Inc.: American Weddings and the Business of Tradition, Vicki Howard, University of Pennsylvania, 2006.

The Constance Spry Cookery Book, Constance Spry & Rosemary Hume, Dent, 1956.

Consuelo & Alva: Love, Power and Suffrage in the Gilded Age, Amanda Mackenzie Stuart, HarperCollins, 2005.

Costume & Fashion: A Concise History, James Laver, Thames & Hudson, 1969.

Country House Camera, Christopher Simon Sykes, Weidenfeld & Nicolson, 1980.

Dior by Dior, Christian Dior, Weidenfeld & Nicolson, 1957.

Dressed in Fiction, Clair Hughes, Berg, 2006.

Elizabeth Arden and Helena Rubinstein: Their Lives, their Times, their Rivalry, Lindy Woodhead, Virago Press, 2003.

Elizabeth Taylor: The Last Star, Kitty Kelly, Book Club Associates, 1981.

Fabrications and the Female Body, Jane Gaines & Charlotte Herzog (ed), Routledge, 1990.

Faithfull, Marianne Faithfull, Michael Joseph, 1994.

Fashion, Christopher Breward, Oxford University Press, 2003.

The Fashion Conspiracy: A Remarkable Journey Through the Empires of Fashion, Nicholas Coleridge, Heinemann, 1998.

Forget Not: The Autobiography of Margaret, Duchess of Argyll, WH Allen, 1975.

French Provincial Cooking, Elizabeth David, Penguin, 1960.

The Glamour of Bellville Sassoon, David Sassoon and Sinty Stemp, ACC Editions, 2009.

The Great Gatsby, F Scott Fitzgerald, 1926.

Hippie Hippie Shake, Richard Neville, Bloomsbury, 1995.

A History of Men's Fashion, Farid Chenoune, Flammarion, 1993.

I Do: A Hundred Years of Wedding Fashion, Caroline Cox, Scriptum Editions, 2002.

In the Mink, Anne Scott-James, Michael Joseph, 1952.

Jackie Oh!, Kitty Kelly, Ballantine Books, 1985.

Loose Change, Sarah Davidson, William Collins Sons & Co., 1977.

Love in a Cold Climate, Nancy Mitford, 1949.

Martha Stewart Weddings, Elizabeth Hawes, Random House, 1987.

The Mitfords: Letters between Six Sisters, Charlotte Mosley (ed), Fourth Estate, 2007.

A Moment in Time, HE Bates, Michael Joseph, 1964.

No Time to Die, Liz Tilberis, Weidenfeld & Nicolson, 1998.

Seduction, Caroline Cox, Mitchell Beazley, 2006.

The Silver and the Gold, Norman Hartnell, Evans Brothers, 1955.

Them & Us: The American Invasion of British High Society, Charles Jennings, Sutton Publishing, 2007.

Tiaras Past and Present, Geoffrey Munn, V & A Publications, 2002.

To Marry an English Lord: The Victorian and Edwardian Experience, Gail MacColl & Carol McD Wallace, Sidgwick & Jackson, 1989

Watson's Advanced Textile Design, Z Grosicki, Newnes-Butterworth, 1977.

Watson's Textile Design and Colour: Elementary Weaves and Figured Fabrics, Z Grosicki, Newnes-Butterworth, 1975.

Wedding Cakes & Cultural History, Simon R Charsley, Routledge, 1992.

Wedding Dress: 1740-1970, Madeleine Ginsburg, Victoria & Albert Museum, 1981.

The Wedding Dress: A Sourcebook, Philip Delamore, Pavilion Books, 2005.

The Wedding Dress, Maria McBride-Mellinger, Little, Brown and Company, 1993.

Wedding Dress Style, Catherine Woram, Quintet Publishing, 1993.

The White Dress, Harriet Worsley, Laurence King Publishing, 2009.

Index

Figures in italics indicate captions.

Acknowledgements

Author's Acknowledgements

Many thanks to Lisa Dyer, Lucy Coley, Jenny Meredith, Alice Payne and all at Carlton Books. Thanks also to Pam Hemmings, Dr Philippa Woodcock, Linda Wood, Paul & Glenys Richmond, Glenys Hollingsworth, Liz, Anne, Stella, Jenny and Heather. Special thanks to Allan Hutchings, always calm and efficient when successfully averting potential technical meltdown.

Publisher's Acknowledgements

The publisher would like to thank Cleo and Mark Butterfield at C20 Vintage Fashion (www.c20vintagefashion.co.uk) and Fur Coat No Knickers for dress hire; Kate and Kerry at Kerry Taylor Auctions (www.kerrytaylorauctions.com), Hannah O'Byrne at the Vintage Wedding Dress Company for images; David Sassoon at Bellville Sassoon and Anne-Fleur Labbé at Balmain. Special thanks also go to Olivia Smart and Bruce at Bruce Oldfield.

Picture Credits

The publishers would like to thank the following sources for their kind permission to reproduce the pictures in this book.

Key: t=Top, b=Bottom, c=Centre, l=Left and r=Right

The Advertising Archives (Image Courtesy of): 13l, 39l **Alamy:** /Bob Masters Classic Car Images: 199cr, /Bon Appetit: 199bl, /Oleksiy Maksymenko: 203tr **Alice Temperley:** 3, 190t, 190bl, 190br **Balmain, Paris:** 92tr, 92bl, 92br, 93tl, 93bl, 93r, 117t, 128tr, 128br, 129tl, 129bl, 129r, 162tl, 162b, 164t, 165l, 170t, 170b, 174b **Bellview Sassoon (Image Courtesy of):** 114l, 114r, 131l, 131r, 182tl, /©David Olins: 115 **The Bridgeman Art Library:** /©DACS/Giraudon/Private Collection/The Wedding Reception, c.1900 (oil on canvas), Beraud, Jean (1849-1935): 195cr (colour illustration), /©Museum of the City of New York, USA/ Evening gown, designed by Charles Frederick Worth (1825-95) 1914: 18, /©Museum of the City of New York, USA/Reception room at the Ritz-Carlton Hotel, 1915 or 1916 (silver gelatin print), Byron Company (fl.1890-1942): 195b, /Private Collection/Archives Charmet/A 'Fete Parisienne' Wedding Party in New York, fashion plate with designs by Premet, Jenny, Lanvin, Worth and Paquin, 1916 (colour litho), Dartey, (fl.1916): 24tr, /Victoria & Albert Museum, London, UK/Wedding dress worn by Margaret, Duchess of Argyll, 1933, Hartnell, Norman (1901-79): 46 **Bruce Oldfield:** 6-7, 176, 188, 189 **Corbis:** 17, /Bettmann: 28t, 31t, 33, 84, 85t, 123l, 126b, 173t, 173b, 205cr, /Fabian Cevallos: 165r, /©Condé Nast Archive: 26, 37t, 39r, 40, 48, 53r, 56, 58t, 60, 67, 70, 72, 77, 78t, 148b, 171, /Robert Eric/Sygma: 183, /Emmanuel Fradin/Reuters: 180, /Hulton-Deutsch Collection: 38tr, 62-63, 75, 132b, /JAPACK/amanaimages: 209bl, /Brooks Kraft/Sygma: 87, /David Lees: 172, /Laurence Mouton/PhotoAlto: 203bl, /Genevieve Naylor: 65, 66, 92tl, 97, /Ruben Perez: 168, /Andy Rain/epa: 74, /Christopher Simon Sykes/Arcaid: 199cb, /Orban Thierry/Sygma: 181b, /Underwood & Underwood: 201tr, /Pierre Vauthey: 146, 149bl, 164b, 166, 167l, 167r, 169l, 169r, /WWD/Condé Nast: 184, 185l, 186l, 186r, 187 **Etsy.com/Timeless Vixen Vintage:** 73 (all images) **Getty:** 86, 145br, 149cr, 191l, 191r, /FilmMagic: 179, /Ernst Haas: 89l, /Hulton Archive: 16b, 50, 51t, 51b, 76, 102br, 110, 120, 134l, 203br, /Last Resort: 199tr, /Lichfield Archive: 152-153, /Popperfoto: 12t, 13r, 47, 53l, 122c, 122b, 155r, /SSPL: 195cr (Phonograph), /Time & Life Pictures: 28b, 78b, 96, 132t, /Roger Viollet: 10, 42b, /WireImage: 175b istockphoto. com: /Natalya Bidyukova : 201cr (Dahlia), /Jennifer Byron: 203cr, /Evgeny Ivanov: 196(Frame), /Daniel Mitchell: 197tr (Cocktail), /Greg Nicholas: 197br (Classic Car), /Tania Oloy: 197cr (Art Deco Girl), /Andres Peiro Palmer: 202

(Rose), /Alexander Perl : 197tr (Orchid), /proxyminder: 196tl & 197cr (Orchid), /spxChrome: 206 (Peacock feather) **Kerry Taylor Auctions:** 8l, 20l, 31b, 89r, 106, 107l, 108l, 138l **Liberty Art Fabrics:** 20tr, 20cr, 20br **London College of Fashion:** /©The Woolmark Company Pty Ltd 2010/VADS www.vads.ac.uk: 103t, 116, 117b, 126t, 128l **Magnum Photos:** /Ferdinando Scianna: 163 **Mary Evans Picture Library:** 16t, 34, 36, 37b, 58b, 59t, 201bl, /Alinari Archives: 38tl, /Classic Stock/H. Armstrong Roberts: 79r, /©Illustrated London News Ltd: 22, 29, 64r, /Imagno/Christian Skrein: 205cb, /National Magazines: 49, 57, 59b, 94l, 95, 102t, 102bl, 103b, /Philip Talmage: 24tl, /Adrian Woodhouse: 58c **©The Museum at FIT:** 19r **©Norman Parkinson Archive:** 80, 83, 100, 109, 113, 124, 127, 130, 150, 159, 224 **Phillipa Lepley:** 185r **Picture Desk:** /Art Archive/Victoria and Albert Museum London/V&A Images: 35, /The Kobal Collection/MGM: 52, /The Kobal Collection/Paramount: 197cr **Press Association Images:** PA Archive: 157, 175t **Rex Features:** /Ernest Allen/Daily Mail: 121, /Chris Barham/Daily Mail: 122t, /Everett Collection: 195tl, 207tl, 209br, /Everett Collection/Paramount: 209cr, /James Gray/Daily Mail: 148t, /ITV: 201br, /Sipa Press: 85b, 178, 181t, /Snap: 195tr, 199br **Scala, Florence:** /Image copyright The Metropolitan Museum of Art/Art Resource: 1, 19l, 71 **Superstock:** /Desiree Mueller: 25l **Thinkstock:** 207cr, /Hemera: 205tr, 207br, /istockphoto: 204 & 205cr (Daisy), 205c (Hippie Girl), 207tr, 209tr **Topfoto.co.uk:** 45l, 45r, 55, 79l, /FotoWare FotoStation: 123r, /The Granger Collection: 32, 154, /PA Photos: 155l, /Roger Viollet: 107r, /Woodmansterne: 156 **Victoria & Albert Museum/V&A Images:** 9r, 12b, 21, 25r, 54, 64l, 94r, 111, 137r, 138r, 160, 161, 182tr, /©John French: 104 **The Vintage Wedding Company:** /www.thevintageweddingdresscompany.com/ (Appointment booking line – 020 8242 4380): 192, 212-213 (All images) **Zandra Rhodes Enterprises:** /Clive Arrowsmith, 149tl, /Photo: Robyn Beeche, make-up Regis, model Cathee Daymon: 174t, /Photo: Robyn Beeche, make-up Richard Sharah, 134r

Every effort has been made to acknowledge correctly and contact the source and/or copyright holder of each picture and Carlton Books Limited apologises for any unintentional errors or omissions, which will be, corrected in future editions of this book.